D1556577

CER

The Iron Age in Wessex: Recent Work

Edited by

A.P. Fitzpatrick and Elaine L. Morris

HAMPSHIRE COUNTY LIBRARY

The Hampshire COLLECTION

WITHDRAWN!

CLASS NO. R930·1094227
TITLE NO. 1 874350 1 6

C003051406

DIV.:82(10/91).
Account

The Iron Age in Wessex: Recent Work

Edited by

A.P. Fitzpatrick and Elaine L. Morris

Association Française D'Etude de L'Age du Fer
Trust for Wessex Archaeology Ltd

Published 1994 by the Trust for Wessex Archaeology Ltd,
Portway House, Old Sarum Park, Salisbury, England, SP4 6EB

on behalf of the Association Française D'Etude de L'Age du Fer

Copyright © 1994 Trust for Wessex Archaeology Ltd and the individual authors
All rights reserved

British Library Cataloguing in Publication Data
A catalogue record for this book is available from the British Library

ISBN 1-874350-11-6

Produced by Wessex Archaeology
Printed by Henry Ling (Dorset Press) Ltd, Dorchester, England

Cover illustration: Miniature later Iron Age shield from a hoard near Salisbury, Wiltshire. Length 77mm. The hoard, or deposit, appears to have incorporated large quantities of Bronze Age metalwork as well as Iron Age ones. The miniature shields provided for the first time the correct interpretation of a series of fragments from life size finds, several of which are from Wessex, and which appear to be from a distinctively British type of shield. *Photograph by Courtesy of the Trustees of the British Museum.*

English ⌗ Heritage

The Trust for Wessex Archaeology Ltd is a Registered Charity No. 287786

Contents

List of Illustrations

List of Contributors

Bedwin, Owen   Essex County Council, Planning Department, County Hall, Duke Street, Chelmsford, Essex CM1 1LF

Brown, Graham   Royal Commission on the Historic Monuments of England, Rougemont House, Rougemont Close, Salisbury, Wiltshire SP1 1LY

Butterworth, C.A.   Wessex Archaeology, Portway House, Old Sarum Park, Salisbury, Wiltshire SP4 6EB

Collis, John   Department of Prehistory and Archaeology, University of Sheffield, Sheffield, West Yorkshire S10 2TN

Corney, Mark   Royal Commission on the Historic Monuments of England, Rougemont House, Rougemont Close, Salisbury, Wiltshire SP1 1LY

Cox, Peter W.   AC Archaeology, Manor Farm Stables, Chicklade, Hindon, near Salisbury, Wiltshire SP3 5SU

Cunliffe, Barry   Institute of Archaeology, University of Oxford, 36 Beaumont Street, Oxford, Oxfordshire OX1 2PG

Davies, Susan M.   Wessex Archaeology, Portway House, Old Sarum Park, Salisbury, Wiltshire SP4 6EB

Ehrenreich, Robert M.   National Research Council, 2101 Constitution Avenue, NW Washington, DC 20418, U.S.A.

Fasham, Peter   Babtie, Shaw and Morton Public Service Division, Shire Hall, Shinfield Park, Reading, Berkshire RG2 9XG

Field, David   Royal Commission on the Historic Monuments of England, Rougemont House, Rougemont Close, Salisbury, Wiltshire SP1 1LY

Fitzpatrick, A.P.   Wessex Archaeology, Portway House, Old Sarum Park, Salisbury, Wiltshire SP4 6EB

Green, F.J.   Test Valley Archaeological Trust, Orchard House, Orchard Lane, Station Road, Romsey, Hampshire SO51 8DP

Haselgrove, Colin   Department of Archaeology, University of Durham, 46 Saddler Street, Durham DH1 3NU

Hearne, Carrie M.   Wessex Archaeology, Portway House, Old Sarum Park, Salisbury, Wiltshire SP4 6EB

Hill, J.D.   Churchill College, Cambridge CB3 0DS

Hughes, Michael   Planning Department, Hampshire County Council, The Castle, Winchester, Hampshire SO23 8UE

King, Anthony   King Alfred's College, Winchester, Hampshire SO22 4NR

Lawson, Andrew J.   Wessex Archaeology, Portway House, Old Sarum Park, Salisbury, Wiltshire SP4 6EB

Lobb, S.J.   Foyle Hill House, Foyle Hill, Shaftesbury, Dorset

McComish, David   Royal Commission on the Historic Monuments of England, Rougemont House, Rougemont Close, Salisbury, Wiltshire SP1 1LY

Maltby, Mark   Department of Conservation Sciences, Bournemouth University, Dorset House, Talbot Campus, Fern Barrow, Dorset BH12 5BB

Morris, Elaine L.   124 Midanbury Lane, Bitterne Park, Southampton, Hampshire SO2 4HD

Newman, Caron   Wessex Archaeology, Portway House, Old Sarum Park, Salisbury, Wiltshire SP4 6EB

Newman, Richard   Wessex Archaeology, Portway House, Old Sarum Park, Salisbury, Wiltshire SP4 6EB

Northover, J.P.   Department of Materials, University of Oxford, Parks Road, Oxford, Oxfordshire OX1 3PH

Peacock, David   Department of Archaeology, University of Southampton, Highfield, Southampton, Hampshire SO9 5NH

Reynolds, Peter   Butser Ancient Farm, Project Trust, Nexus House, Gravel Hill, Horndean, Hampshire PO8 0QE

Sharples, Niall   Historic Scotland, 20 Brandon Street, Edinburgh EH3 5RA

Soffe, Grahame   26 Bromsgrove Cottages, Faringdon, Oxfordshire SN7 7JQ

Wainwright, G.J.   English Heritage, Fortress House, 23 Savile Row, London W1X 1AB

Whinney, R.   Winchester Museums Service, Historic Resources Centre, 75 Hyde Street, Winchester, Hampshire SO23 7DW

Williams, David   Department of Archaeology, University of Southampton, Highfield, Southampton, Hampshire SO 9 5NH

Foreword

John Collis

Wessex is a land of mighty hillforts. Iron Age hill-top sites such as Maiden Castle and Hod Hill have dominated the later lowland landscapes of medieval and modern times, and found their place in folklore and literature, especially that of the Chalk downlands. They have inspired generations of archaeologists to study their origins and date, and their investigators almost form a roll-call of British Archaeology: General Pitt Rivers, J.P. Williams Freeman, O.G.S. Crawford, Professor Christopher Hawkes, Sir Mortimer Wheeler, and the Curwens, father and son. Between them they can almost claim to have laid the foundations of the discipline of archaeology: of modern excavation techniques; of field archaeology; and of air archaeology.

The present generation of archaeologists working on the Iron Age of Wessex may not be quite so grandiose in its claims; nonetheless they have been at the forefront, if not pioneers, in the development of settlement archaeology. The 1960s saw the beginning of large-scale excavation of rural settlements; Geoff Wainwright at Tollard Royal and Gussage All Saints, Dorset, or my own excavations at Owslebury, Hampshire; the birth of 'urban archaeology' under Martin Biddle at Winchester, Hampshire; and, above all for the Iron Age, the start of a quarter century of research by Barry Cunliffe into the hillfort of Danebury, Hampshire, and its surrounding landscape. With its wealth of data, Wessex has been the seedbed for new and theoretical approaches to the Iron Age: studies of settlement structure; of agricultural and industrial production; and of social and economic organisation. In his mould-breaking paper in 1964, Roy Hodson used the settlement of Little Woodbury near Salisbury as the type-site for his concept of an indigenous native Iron Age culture. Such has been the dominance of Wessex, that virtually every general discussion of the Iron Age in Britain inevitably leans heavily on it, and it is not without some justice that the museum in Andover has been called 'The Museum of the Iron Age'.

From the time of Pitt Rivers, hillforts have not been the only interest in Iron Age settlement archaeology. Smaller enclosed settlements are relatively easy to identify from their surrounding ditches, visible in some cases on the ground as standing earthworks, but especially from the air as soil- or cropmarks. Even now, after recent intensive agriculture, many field systems (the so-called 'Celtic fields') survive as lynchets. All these have been the subject of intensive study by Collin Bowen and his successors in the Royal Commission on Historical Monuments at Salisbury. Gerhard Bersu's excavation at Little Woodbury in 1938–9 rewrote the interpretation of Iron Age settlements in Britain, with the identification of large round houses, while the so-called 'pit-dwellings' were reinterpreted as underground silos for storing grain. The meaning of the enormous variety and shapes of these enclosures — 'Little Woodbury', 'banjo', 'spectacle', etc — still escapes us, while the question of the relationship between these undefended sites and the contemporary hillforts is still an academic battlefield in which any Iron Age warrior would feel at home! We know more about Iron Age settlements in Wessex than anywhere else in Europe; the data are rich, fascinating, and controversial.

This present volume attempts to bring together some of the most recent work, and make it more available to both scholars and the wider public. The occasion for its publication is the 18th Annual Conference of the Association Française de l'Etude de l'Age du Fer. The AFEAF is the major forum for discussion of the Iron Age in central and western Europe, and we have been honoured that this is the first of their conferences to be held wholly outside France. The proceedings will be published at a later date through Sheffield Academic Press. We also have the support of the Council of Europe through its Committee for Celtic Routes, whose aim is to promote, through tourism, a greater knowledge of the Iron Age origins of modern Europe.

As Chairman of the Organising Committee for the AFEAF Conference, I would like to thank all those who have made this present volume possible: to the two editors, and the many contributors; and to English Heritage and Hampshire County council who have provided financial aid.

John Collis,
Sheffield,
December 18th 1993.

Introduction: the Changing Iron Age of Wessex

A. P. Fitzpatrick and Elaine L. Morris

Meetings of the Association Française d'Etude de l'Age du Fer have frequently been complemented by exhibitions and their accompanying catalogues on the archaeology of the region hosting the meeting. In Wessex, however, museums such as Andover, Christchurch, Dorchester, and Salisbury have recently completed long-term displays which consider this topic. Butser Ancient Farm, the Cranborne Ancient Technology Centre, and the reconstructed Poole Harbour Log Boat also provide vivid images of the Iron Age for educational and research purposes. As the theme of the Wessex meeting is settlement archaeology, an introductory volume on recent work on the Iron Age — largely from the 1980s onwards — much of which has been concerned with settlements, is appropriate.

The Iron Age in Wessex is often thought of as a period which is well known and relatively easily understood. It is seen as having been inhabited by 'Celtic' peoples, most of whom were peasant farmers who lived as nuclear families in round houses and kept cows like Dexters and sheep similar to Soays. They grew crops such as wheat and barley, and legumes like beans. The martial pre-occupations of the upper echelons of society are reflected in the numerous hillforts. Life may have been short; but it also had a rationality. The logic of this structure was disturbed only by the onset of Roman influence (Haselgrove; Williams and Peacock this volume). Yet this dominant view has become an orthodoxy at exactly the time that developments have contrived its obsolescence. To understand this paradox it is necessary to examine some of the ideas which inform it and the ways in which the evidence has been interpreted.

With the exception of Barrett's work on later Bronze Age pottery in southern England, which redated a significant amount of material which had previously been thought to be Early Iron Age date (Barrett 1980), recent decades have seen few major changes in Iron Age chronology. In Wessex Cunliffe's clarification of the Early and Early/Middle Iron Age pottery linked to the radiocarbon sequence from Danebury has been important (Cunliffe 1984a), but in general 'when' is not perceived as a pressing question in Iron Age studies.

Neither has the *idea* of the Iron Age attracted much attention. Only recently has emphasis been placed on the Bronze Age–Iron Age transition (Sørensen and Thomas 1989), but the emphasis has been on the end of the Bronze Age, with few studies of adoption of iron working (Ehrenreich 1990). The idea of the Iron Age seems unproblematic.

Another influential factor in this dominant view has been the belief that what is essentially an interpretation of the chalklands of Wessex, Hodson's 'Woodbury Culture' (Hodson 1964), is valid for much of Britain, let alone Wessex, in whatever way that the region is defined. Consequently, the image of Wessex being typified by the appearance (but not the work; Reynolds (1979); this volume) of the Butser Ancient Farm has become the dominant image of the British Iron Age.

This image is often seen to be inhabited by 'Celtic' peoples, yet as they are usually portrayed, the 'Celts' are a *bricolage* of literary, linguistic, and archaeological evidence drawn from widely different times and places. There is rather less evidence for 'Celts', and particularly warriors, in Wessex than is often shown.

However, perhaps the key element in the dominant view has been the interpretation of hillforts, an interpretation which might be characterised as 'the king and his castle'. Yet almost everyone who has examined in detail the evidence for this view has pointed instead to the lack of it (Haselgrove this volume). Other than its scale there is little to distinguish, for example, Danebury from smaller farms, a point made by Wainwright and Davies (this volume) in relation to the nearby sites of Old Down Farm, a farmstead, and Balksbury, which has been called a 'hillfort'. As Sharples (this volume) also points out, the smaller settlements around Maiden Castle disappear when the occupation of the hillfort was at its peak.

As well as the questioning of the roles of any central place, the widespread recognition of culturally structured patterns of behaviour and deposition have been particularly important in challenging the dominant view. The recognition of these patterns has destroyed at a stroke the idea of Iron Age communities as rational beings operating to beliefs and value systems which can be easily understood or readily identified with through '"Celtic" ancestors'. What were once thought to be disused storage pits, providing simple samples to reconstruct diet and economy, can now be seen as having been filled according to a complex set of rules (Hill this volume). Clear structuring is also apparent in the materials goods are made from, what they were deposited with, and where (Fitzpatrick this volume). The entrances to houses, enclosures and hillforts all have a preferred orientation to the east or south-east. Above all, however, it is through the juxtaposition of the living and the dead on settlements which has set the Iron Age apart, as being different from the dominant view. Ultimately the limitation of relying on a single, timeless and traditional model of Celtic society is exposed. These ideas have not yet become a new orthodoxy nor, perhaps, would they wish to become one, but they clearly influence some works in this volume.

The comfortable image of the Iron Age of Wessex has not been supported by other recent developments. Materials analyses have been applied to a wide range of artefacts made from clay, copper alloy, glass, iron, and stone, and they have demonstrated a hitherto unsuspected complexity in the organisation of production and distribution (Ehrenreich; Haselgrove; Morris; and Northover this volume). Environmental archaeology has allowed a much better understanding of the methods and potential of Iron Age farming on the chalklands (Maltby this volume; Reynolds 1980; Jones 1986). At the same time these techniques have also begun to show how very different other parts of Wessex were such as the Dorset heathlands were (Hearne and Cox this volume). These allow the idea of a typical Iron Age of Wessex to be further challenged and allows a slightly different perspective than was possible for reviews undertaken barely a decade ago (Cunliffe 1984b; Champion and Champion 1981).

Much of the challenging new data have come from sites examined in response to development, often for housing or major infrastructure projects such as roads or pipelines. Initially this work was in the form of rescue excavations (Davies; Collis this volume) and subsequently in the form of excavations, often developer funded, which have been preceded by evaluations (Fasham; Fitzpatrick; Hughes; R. Newman this volume). In Wessex most of this work has been undertaken in the context of rural archaeology but deeply stratified urban archaeology has also contributed (Hughes; Whinney this volume). It is noteworthy just how much recent evidence has come from Hampshire, even though the pressure of development in Berkshire has been as intense. In some cases the widespread acceptance of archaeology as a material consideration in the planning system has allowed the preservation of sites to be achieved, leaving a tantalising glimpse into their potential (Butterworth; Lobb this volume). Nonetheless major research excavations and/or projects continue to be undertaken (Bedwn; Cunliffe; King and Soffe this volume) while other excavations have been intended to ensure the proper management of sites by seeking to understand their nature, extent and preservation (Cunliffe; Lobb this volume). The systematic field surveys of the Royal Commission on the Historical Monuments for England continue to make a major contribution, as increasingly do surveys of the aerial photographic evidence both by the Commission (Palmer 1984; McOmish 1989) and in development control (Hughes this volume).

Despite this systematic assessment, fieldwork can still yield major surprises. The recognition of such massive middens as at East Chisenbury (Brown, Field and McOmish this volume) and Potterne (Lawson this volume), or the deposits at La Sagesse (Green this volume) have introduced major elements into the way that the contemporary landscape and settlement development might be understood (Cunliffe 1990). Equally, while many burials were known from Wessex (Collis; Haselgrove; Hill this volume), the large cemetery at Westhampnett is of a rite and and type completely unknown before 1992 (Fitzpatrick this volume). At the same time the examination of relatively well known sites reminds us of the nuances of shifting settlement patterns (C. Newman this volume).

While fieldwork can bring surprises there are still notable lacunae in other areas of the Iron Age in Wessex. Other than those considered in this volume, artefact studies are often poorly served, in particular the evidence for '"Celtic" art', of which there are an important number of early pieces from Wessex (Megaw and Megaw 1991), is rarely considered.

Clearly, there is much new work to consider and assimilate, and to be set aside the works of earlier generations who are barely mentioned in this volume. There is not yet a new Iron Age of Wessex, but as this volume shows, there is a changing one.

Acknowledgements

The publication of this volume for the conference in April 1994 would not have been possible without the rapid response of the contributors who allowed it be compiled within six months. Equally its production would not have been possible without the support of Wessex Archaeology and we would like to thank Julie Gardiner, Rachel Griffin, Rosemarie Ives, Liz James, and Elaine Wakefield for their help. We are also grateful to Dr Philip de Jersey, Celtic Coin Index, Oxford University, and Dr Ian Stead, British Museum for their assistance in providing photographs.

Figure 0.1   Location of sites and surveys discussed in this volume

Part 1: Themes

1. Social Organisation in Iron Age Wessex

Colin Haselgrove

Despite the long tradition of research in Wessex, we know little for certain about the social organisation of its Iron Age inhabitants. Earlier studies focused largely on the chronological and cultural framework, while more recently the relative abundance of Iron Age settlement remains compared to the sparse funerary record has brought economic rather than social questions to the fore: agricultural production, central place redistribution and external trade. Where archaeologists have considered social organisation at all, it usually has been by extrapolating details from texts relating to other Celtic-speaking peoples. Clarke (1972), for instance, drew heavily on Caesar and the later Irish sagas in his well-known study of the Glastonbury lake-village. Following these sources, the heavily defended hillforts of Iron Age Wessex are generally seen as the seats of a dominant warrior elite, while the surrounding farmsteads housed a servile agricultural peasantry. Only in the Late Iron Age did major archaeological changes occur — the virtual abandonment of hillforts, the introduction of coinage, and the appearance of formal cemeteries — but these changes have generally been attributed to external stimuli such as invasion and continental trade rather than to internal social development (Haselgrove 1989).

In recent years, the relevance of this pan-Celtic model has been widely challenged (Hill 1993). If anything, the archaeological record implies that the social and political organisation of Celtic peoples varied significantly through time, and between regions. Moreover, modern large-scale excavation of hillforts and farmsteads alike has shown that the settlement material is far less straightforward than was previously realised. At Danebury, for example, many of the 2500 excavated pits yielded so-called 'special deposits', material deliberated placed in them as part of complex rituals conducted at the hillfort (Cunliffe 1993a). Far from representing ordinary domestic refuse and casual losses, many settlement assemblages appear to be highly selective, producing a distorted picture of the people who lived there. Thus, we can no longer speak confidently of rich or poor inhabitants, or even of permanently or seasonally occupied sites, without much more careful analysis of the processes involved in the formation of the particular archaeological record — which is only just beginning (Hill 1993a).

There can be little doubting the significance of Iron Age hillforts, given the labour invested in their construction, so understanding their role is clearly vital. As already indicated, the most popular model is to see them as the seat of local chiefs, together with their dependents and specialist producers attracted by their patronage, and surrounded by dependent farmsteads (Cunliffe 1993a). However, where systematic comparisons between hillforts and other settlements have been made, the expected differences do not in fact emerge; if anything, regional variations are more obvious, Dorset sites consistently producing more personal ornaments and other finds than their Hampshire counterparts (Sharples 1991a). Of course, not all of the elite need have resided in hillforts; some may have lived in the larger farmsteads such as Gussage All Saints and Little Woodbury. A more radical alternative is to see hillforts as communal structures, containing the social and religous focus of the community and providing for its surplus storage needs, but not as places of permanent elite residence at all (Cunliffe 1993a); they would only have been fully occupied at certain times of the year for communal gatherings, or in periods of danger. An extreme viewpoint is that hillforts were only occupied seasonally for agricultural use in summer by communities which lived for the rest of the year in lower-lying areas (Stopford 1987).

The existence, at all, of a separate elite class can also be questioned, since even the most extensively excavated hillforts yield remarkably little evidence of hierarchy. Unless visible signs of social ranking were deliberately suppressed, we are probably dealing with a relatively low level of social differentiation (Sharples 1991a), although the marked decrease in the number of occupied hillforts after 350 BC does seem to suggest some concentration of power during this period — whether in the hands of a particular class, or of whole communities. We should also note the virtual absence of developed hillforts from large areas of Wessex such as Cranborne Chase (Dorset–Wiltshire) and east Hampshire (Fig. 1). In these zones, another type of site, the banjo enclosure, is frequently found instead, often linked in pairs and sometimes forming part of a wider earthwork complex, as at Gussage Down or Hurstbourne Tarrant (Barrett *et al.* 1991; Corney 1989). Since there are no obvious ecological

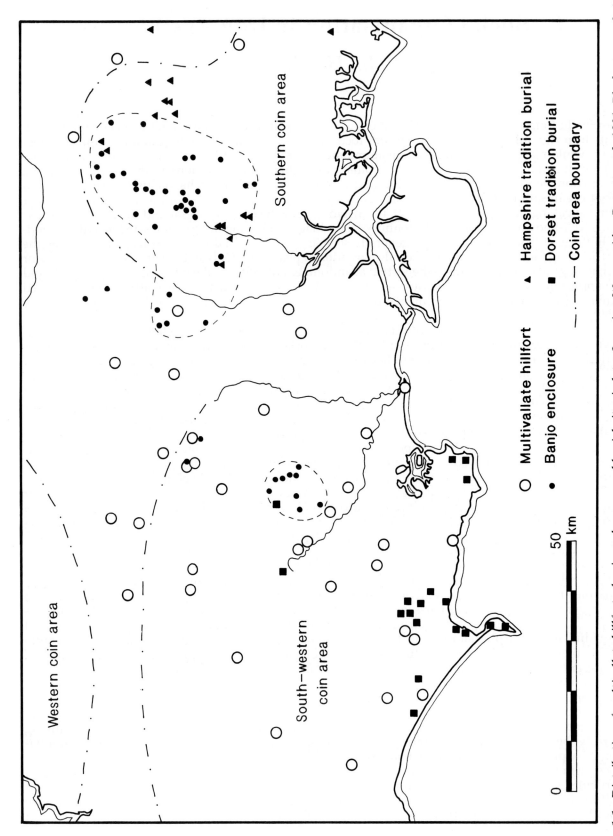

Figure 1.1 Distribution of multivallate hillforts, banjo enclosures, and burial sites in later Iron Age Wessex. After Barrett et al. 1991; Blackmore et al. 1979; Millett 1987, with addditions. Coin boundaries after Haselgrove 1987

Western coin area

Southern coin area

South–western coin area

▲ Hampshire tradition burial
■ Dorset tradition burial
–·– Coin area boundary

○ Multivallate hillfort
● Banjo enclosure

50   km

0

differences between the zones with and without hillforts, the contrast in settlement pattern suggests underlying social and cultural distinctions whose nature has yet to be elucidated.

Some of these divisions persisted into the Late Iron Age. The earliest indigenous coinage in Dorset is concentrated in Cranborne Chase, and spread from there, first into south Dorset and then throughout the rest of the county. Formal cemeteries, on the other hand, are virtually restricted to the hillfort zone in south Dorset (Blackmore *et al.* 1979), and the rite employed was inhumation. This contrasts with the non-hillfort zone in east Hampshire, where a tradition of rich, flat grave cremation eventually took root (Millett 1987), while the coin evidence hints at further sub-regional groupings around the Solent and in central Wiltshire (Haselgrove 1987), though these had virtually disappeared by the 1st century AD. Behind the self-governing *civitates* set up in the region by the Romans after the Conquest — the Atrebates, the Belgae, the Durotriges, and the Regnenses — there evidently existed a complex pattern of smaller units, linked in various ways into wider cultural or political groupings.

Since 1991, two important new studies of Iron Age societies in Wessex have appeared. Hill's work (1993a; in press) focuses primarily on Hampshire sites including Danebury, Winklebury, and the farmstead on Winnall Down (Fasham 1985). He suggests that markedly hierarchical societies only developed in Wessex in the 150 years before the Roman Conquest. Prior to this, the basic social matrix consisted of collectivities of independent and highly competitive household groups which are not neatly labelled as either tribes or chiefdoms. For Hill, the 'special deposits' found at many sites stem from periodic rituals held within the confines of the domestic settlement, involving feasting and the sacrifice of domestic animals, household objects and sometimes people. These rituals played a key role in the reproduction of Iron Age social relations, whereby individual households were tied together in larger communities, and the obligations between different sectors of society — men and women, adults and children, elders and juniors — were reaffirmed and renegotiated. On the smaller farmsteads, such rituals took place only once every few years, but at the hillforts which represented the main focus of the communities, they are noticably more frequent — perhaps two or three times per year (Hill in press). It was only the emergence of new cultural and economic forms in the Late Iron Age which brought about a clearer separation between ritual and everyday life, seen in the appearance of formal cemeteries and shrines, often located well away from the settlement.

Sharples' (1991a) study of Iron Age social development in the Maiden Castle area takes up many of the same themes as Hill. Sharples envisages a major upheaval in southern Dorset during the earlier 1st millennium BC, associated with the introduction of iron technology. The new metal undermined the position of the elite groups which had dominated late Bronze Age society due to their control of the long-distance trade networks through which prestige goods could be acquired. In these conditions of fragmentation, various groups came together to form larger communities, which competed with each other for the best agricultural land. This is evident both from the building of so many hillforts, and the facilities for food storage which they contain. In this situation, control of land which was capable of supporting a large community inevitably became one of the principal means of achieving status and power (Sharples 1991a). Between 500 and 200 BC, Maiden Castle gradually developed into the pre-eminent hillfort in southern Dorset; its nearest neighbours were absorbed into the expanded defences, while more distant hillforts were demilitarised and their inhabitants forced to live in undefended homesteads. During this expansion, the ramparts at Maiden Castle became more and more a symbol of the community's importance, with previously independent neighbours now having to participate in annual construction and maintenance work.

From about 200 BC onward, Dorset started to acquire a distinctive cultural identity, in part due to the development of a range of specialist industries on the peripheries of the main hillfort zone, notably a major pottery production complex in Poole Harbour. Sharples suggests that the major hillfort communities may have entered into a confederation against neighbouring peoples, thereby hoping to deflect internal stresses into inter-regional conflict, but also creating a semi-specialist class of warriors needed for the extended campaigns which ensued. Ultimately, these changes undermined the existing social order. Once developed, control of the new specialist industries and their associated exchange networks provided a source of power with which newcomers could successfully challenge the economic superiority of the hillfort elders, based on their control of agricultural production. The internal organisation of Maiden Castle broke down, and much of the population dispersed into the surrounding countryside, where new farms and field systems appear — this partitioning of the landscape may well reflect individual claims to land which was formerly in communal ownership (Sharples 1991a). The shift in emphasis back to individual status is also seen in burials and in the increased use of personal ornaments. Political authority, however, remained ill-defined compared to the rest of Wessex, where by the Late Iron Age power had evidently been centralised in the hands of a few individuals; when the Romans invaded, they had to fight their way piecemeal across Dorset, rather than dealing with single chiefs or rulers as seems to have occurred in the south-east.

2. Why We Should Not Take the Data from Iron Age Settlements for Granted: Recent Studies of Intra-Settlement Patterning

J.D. Hill

Deposits

Excavations on Iron Age sites in southern England (but not other parts of Britain) have always produced large quantities of pottery, animal bones, broken tools, and other objects. These have been interpreted as the rubbish from, and evidence for, the domestic, craft, and agricultural activities that took place on these settlements — the lower rungs of Hawkes (1954) 'Ladder of Inference'. They have been seen as directly reflecting the nature, scale, and location of Iron Age domestic organisation, subsistence, exchange, and society, a proposition strengthened by the large quantities of finds produced by excavations. Such assumptions are clearly seen in studies such as David Clarke's (1972) often quoted provisional model of Iron Age society (see also Halstead *et al.* 1978).

However, recent approaches have questioned such assumptions and closely examined the nature of archaeological deposits as the essential preliminary for interpreting any aspect of the period (Schiffer 1987; Hill 1993b). Haselgrove (1987) has investigated the depositional contexts of coin finds, while faunal specialists (e.g. Coy 1987; Serjeantson 1991; Wilson 1992; and especially Maltby 1985a; 1985b) have considered the taphonomy of animal bone assemblages. This approach investigates in detail the different factors that have contributed to the creation of animal bone assemblages. It shows that bone assemblages are never a direct reflection of the original composition of the livestock kept in the Iron Age.

This approach, drawing on ethnographic and experimental work, also has implications for all types of finds. It stresses the need to understand how material entered archaeologically recoverable contexts (ditch, pit, and post-hole fills, etc.), and what may have happened to that material before its incorporation as the essential preliminary for any interpretation of that material (Lambrick 1984 on pottery). Indeed, ethnoarchaeological and experimental studies (e.g. Hayden and Cannon 1983) suggest on a rural settlement how tiny a proportion of the rubbish can be expected to enter the archaeological record, and then how scattered and poorly preserved it should normally be. Simple calculations confirm how *small* and potentially unrepresentative, our apparently large Iron Age finds assemblages are (Hill 1989; 1993a; 1993b).

Traditionally the layout of Iron Age settlements and their finds have been interpreted in terms of chronological change, functional activity areas, and food and husbandry. These are the aspects which have fundamentally changed during the 1980s as increasingly the archaeological record has resisted the traditional functional interpretations and has been examined using developments in other parts of archaeology, namely in terms of symbolic and ritual behaviour.

In particular, the location and nature of finds deposition has been investigated in detail (compare interpretations of pits and finds in Cunliffe 1974 and 1991). Finds assemblages (both artefact and faunal) are mostly excavated from pits and ditches, and include material not easily recognised as garbage (Fig. 2.1), such as a range of human remains and and, more recently recognised, 'special animal deposits' — the product of feasting and sacrifice (e.g. Whimster 1981; Wilson 1981; Grant 1984a; Wait 1985).

Detailed study (Hill 1993b) of all classes of material found in pits and ditches has confirmed indications that the material from pits and ditches demonstrate complex and highly structured patterns (Grant 1984a; Cunliffe 1992). A minority of deposits are marked by individual layers dominated by a single category of finds (pot or bone, etc.) combined together according to rules which shaped the sequence of what was deposited, what could be combined together, or what had to be excluded all together. However, this minority of deposits actually accounts for perhaps 75–80% or more of all the pottery, animal bones and other finds recovered from Wessex Iron Age sites. These deposits were not made on a daily or even monthly basis, but more irregularly — perhaps only once a decade on many settlements — and should be seen as ritual. This turns Hawkes' Ladder on its head, as the material which was felt to securely tell us about the lower rungs of subsistence and economy in fact speak directly about the top!

This ritual tradition has its origins in the later Bronze Age ritual consumption of bronze and involved the deposition of human remains, animals, pottery, tools as offerings/sacrifices — symbols of an undifferentiated world of the domestic and agricultural. There is not space here to elaborate the full nature of this tradition, except to stress that all elements were treated in similar ways (Hill 1993a;

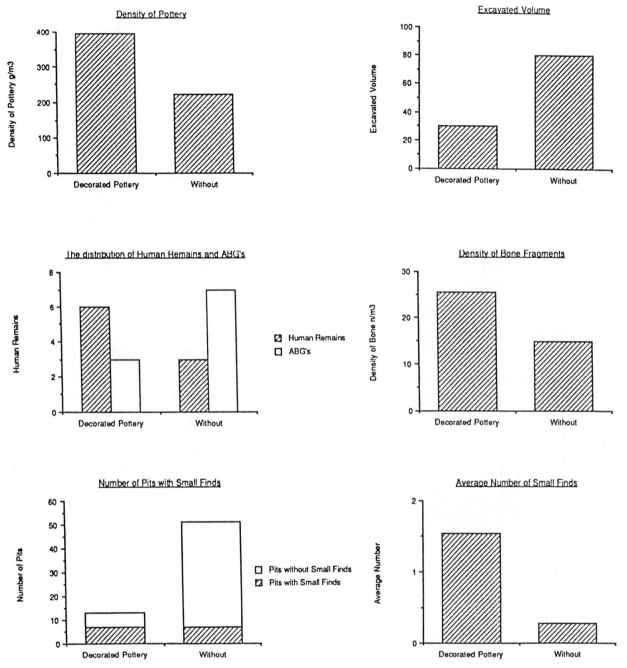

Figure 2.1 *An example of the results of structured deposition in Iron Age pit fills. The different characteristics of assemblages with decorated and undecorated pottery from Middle Iron Age Winnall Down. ABGs = Articulated or Associated Bone Groups, sometimes called 'Special Animal Deposits'*

1993b). As humans were deposited and treated in the same ways as the sacrifices/ritual consumption of animals, it is wrong to separate out the human parts of this tradition and consider it as mortuary practice distinct from the rest. Equally, these deposits were not simply confined to disused storage pits, as recent accounts have stressed (Cunliffe 1992; Bradley 1990; Hill in press), but are found in ditch fills, working hollows, post-holes, etc.

Space

Where these ritual deposits were made on and around settlements was not random (Parker Pearson in press). The boundary earthworks enclosing settlements and hillforts have become the increasing focus of attention (Fig. 2.2). Hingley (1990a) has argued that iron 'currency bars', or ingots, usually were deposited close to the boundary of the settlements/hillfort for symbolic/ritual reasons. This study is one of a number that have recognised settlement and hillfort boundaries as increasingly more than simply for stock control or defence — if for these functions at all (Hingley 1984a; 1990b; Bowden

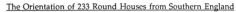

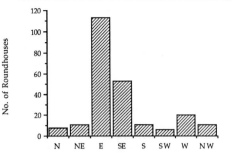

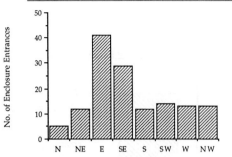

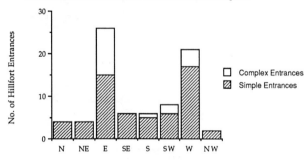

Figure 2.2 The orientation of round houses, non-hillfort enclosures, and hillforts showing the cosmologically inspired importance of doorways/ gateways facing in particular directions

and McOmish 1987; 1989; Parker Pearson in press). Indeed, the ditches that served to demarcate 'Little Woodbury'-type settlements may never have been complete open circuits, may have been deliberately backfilled soon after they were dug, and may have been the location for a range of ritual deposits (Bowden and McOmish 1987; Hill 1993a; 1993b). The ritual deposition of different types of material in these ditches was clearly structured, with human remains, small finds, and pottery preferentially deposited in the front halves as at Winnall Down and Gussage All Saints (Figs 2.3 and 2.4). These ditches served to mark a symbolic division of space which strongly correlated the inside and outside of the settlement with different values, associations and behaviours. As such, different types of material could only be deposited on the inside or on the outside of the boundary, even centuries after the actual boundary ditch had ceased to be a prominent feature, as for example at Middle Iron Age Winnall Down where this symbolic division of space was still felt.

With such a strong symbolic investment on the boundary, the locations where these boundaries were crossed were strongly marked. The ditch terminals either side of the settlement entrance were often the location for ritual deposits, with distinctions made between left:right, north:south (Hill 1993a). Settlement gateways were elaborate, and further emphasised by flanking or antennae ditches. These characteristics served to highlight the crossing of the settlement boundary and should also be considered when understanding the supposedly purely military nature of hillfort entrances (Bowden and McOmish 1987; Hill in press).

The entrances of settlements and hillforts were not positioned randomly either but usually faced east/south-east (Parker Pearson in press; Hill 1993a) (Fig. 2.2). Some hillforts also have paired entrances — easterly and westerly. An even stricter easterly orientation is found in Iron Age round houses (Boast and Evans 1985; Parker Pearson in press; Hill 1993a), which Oswald (1991) showed could not be determined by wind direction or other environmental factors. Rather, the correct direction from which to enter an Iron Age house or settlement was fundamentally linked to the cosmological principles embodied in the architecture and use of settlement space in this, as in many other 'non-complex' societies. In Iron Age Wessex, orientating house and settlement entrances in the general direction of the rising sun appears to have been particularly important. This preoccupation with easterly direction also led to a strong contrast between the north and south sides of houses and settlements in terms of the types of material deposited, settlement organisation and different activities (Parker Pearson in press; Fitzpatrick 1991a; this volume).

Society

These studies all challenged the common-sense assumptions that previously structured our interpretations. This recent work clearly shows that the layout of settlements and the organisation of deposits were symbolic, but not *just* symbolic. The irregular ritual deposits in different parts of the settlement served to physically engrave the cosmological concerns of ritual onto the spaces in and through which Iron Age peoples lived. This symbolism embodied in the organisation of settlements would have been ever present, and it is unlikely that Iron Age peoples would have themselves distinguished the practical from the symbolic. For them it was probably how things are — their rationality, their common-sense (Hill 1993a; see also work on pre-Roman Iron Age households in

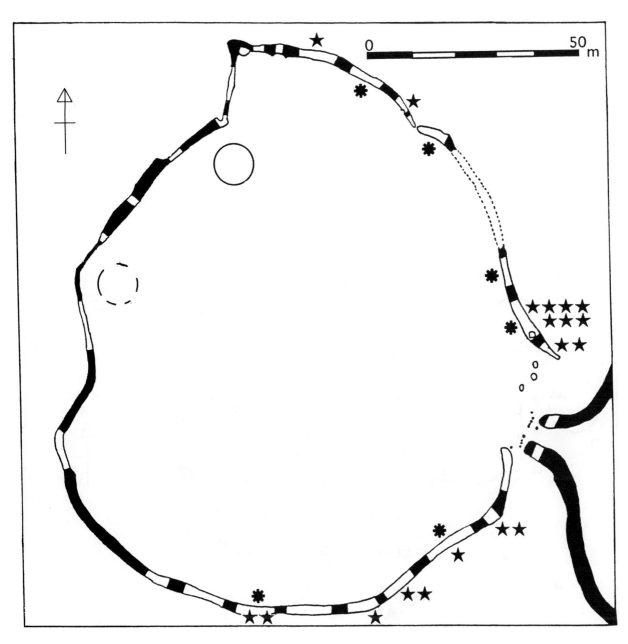

Key: Human Remains ✳   Small Finds ★

*Figure 2.3   The distribution of human remains and small finds from the enclosure ditch at Gussage
All Saints, phase 2, showing the preference for depositing such finds at the front of the enclosure, here
and at Winnall Down*

Holland; Therkorn 1987). This connects the ritual penetration of the everyday and the organisation of
household/settlement space to those fundamental relationships and practices through which society
was continually reproduced (Barrett 1989; Foster 1989; Austin and Thomas 1990). These particularly
include gender relations (Hingley 1990c; Hastdorf 1991)

The full implications of these studies have yet to be felt. Both the assumptions and the specific
interpretations of Clarke's provisional model of Iron Age settlement organisation have been found
wanting. We can not simply assume that the finds we recover are a direct record of the past. As such
every use of material recovered from settlements, from simply phasing through the reconstruction of
ceramic exchange and animal husbandry regimes to the nature of social organisation, requires a far
more critical understanding of how the evidence we are using actually entered the archaeological
record. It should demand that we do not take the data from any Iron Age settlement excavation across
northern Europe for granted.

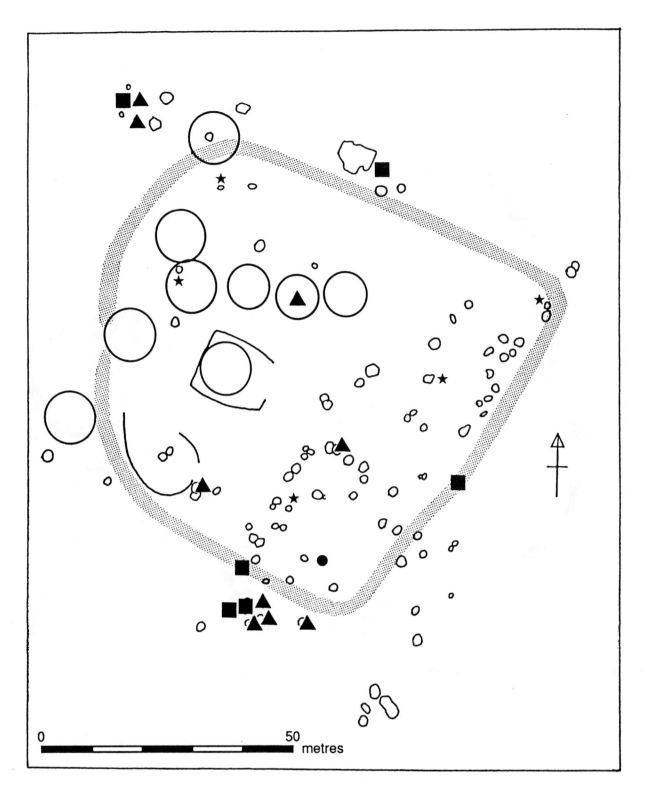

Key: Complete Adolescent/Adult Body   ■

        Partial Adolescent/Adult Body   ●

        Neo-natal/Infant Remains   ▲

        Individual Fragments of Human Bone ★

Figure 2.4   The distribution of human deposits during the unenclosed Middle Iron Age phase of occupation at Winnall Down. The importance of the former, now infilled, ditch in structuring the location of these deposits can be seen

3. Animal Exploitation in Iron Age Wessex

Mark Maltby

Introduction

A large number of Iron Age settlements in Wessex are situated on chalk. The alkaline nature of this subsoil allows for good preservation of animal bones. In addition, the common practice during this period of digging pits, gullies, ditches, quarries, and other holes into the chalk had aided the survival of bones which subsequently had been deliberately deposited or accidentally incorporated into these subsurface features.

The increased interest in settlement archaeology in Britain in the last 25 years, combined with the growing realisation that animal bones were worth collecting for the information they can provide about diet, animal husbandry, and human attitudes to animals, has resulted in the accumulation of a substantial body of data from a large number of sites in Wessex. The faunal samples include the largest assemblage as yet collected from a British prehistoric site, over 240,000 fragments from the extensive excavations of the interior of Danebury hillfort. Two major reports on this material have been produced (Grant 1984a; 1991). In addition, excavations of several other Wessex hillforts have produced smaller but nevertheless substantial samples. These include Winklebury in Hampshire, Maiden Castle (Armour-Chelu 1991) and Poundbury in Dorset and South Cadbury, Somerset.

There have also been a number of important assemblages obtained from other settlements. There is no space to include them all but some of the most important assemblages from Hampshire include those from the sites of Winnall Down/Easton Lane (Maltby 1985b; 1989), the banjo enclosure in Micheldever Wood (Coy 1987), and Owslebury near Winchester; Old Down Farm, Balksbury, and Portway near Andover; and Brighton Hill South, Cowdery's Down, Viables Farm, and other sites in the Basingstoke area. In Dorset, the samples from Gussage All Saints (Harcourt 1979) and Eldons Seat, Encombe are the best known but there are now several other Iron Age samples available for comparison, particularly from the Dorchester area. Several small Iron Age settlements in Wiltshire (e.g. Coy 1982a) have also produced material.

It is difficult in a short summary to do justice to the large amount of detailed research that has been carried out on this faunal material. This guide will address just three topics as follows:

- species representation
- the exploitation of domestic stock
- human attitudes to other animals

It is hoped that the discussion of these topics will highlight some of the questions and problems being raised by detailed faunal analyses (see Coy 1982b; Coy and Maltby 1987; Grant 1984b; 1984c; Maltby 1981; Maltby and Coy 1991; Wilson 1992).

Species Representation

All the samples obtained from Iron Age sites in Wessex are dominated by bones of domestic animals. In nearly all cases, sheep and/or cattle are the dominant species. Their relative abundance varies at different sites. Sheep bones have been usually the most commonly identified (sometimes contributing over 50% of the identified bones) and there is some evidence that sheep might have been kept in greater numbers on settlements situated on the higher downland, whereas cattle are better represented on settlements on lower ground. This could well reflect the distribution of suitable grazing land and water supplies. However, species abundance or, more accurately, the abundance of their bones, has also been shown to vary on these sites because of other factors such as sampling and retrieval techniques, disposal practices and bone preservation. Nevertheless, on the chalklands it seems likely that sheep were kept in the largest numbers, although cattle provided the most meat.

Pig bones are less well represented on Iron Age sites in Wessex than on sites in many parts of northern and central Europe. This probably reflects the comparative lack of substantial areas of suitable woodland for pannage in the Wessex chalklands by the Iron Age. In most samples pig bones are recovered much less frequently than cattle or sheep (nearly always forming less than 20% of the identified sample) and sometimes are also outnumbered by horse bones. They may not have been kept at every settlement. One exception is the settlement at Groundwell Farm, Wiltshire (Coy 1982a), where pig bones were ranked second to sheep/goat fragments. Perhaps significantly, this settlement was not situated on the Downs but on lower valley soils, in a vicinity where more woodland may have been available. Goat bones have been identified in most samples but they usually form only a tiny proportion of the sheep/goat assemblage. Horse bones have been found in all but the smallest samples. They are poorly represented at Danebury but on a few sites provide over 10% of the identified bones. Dogs are the only other domestic species commonly identified on most Iron Age sites.

Other species are rarely encountered. Cats have only been found in a few later Iron Age assem blages. Bones of wild mammals nearly always form less than 3% of the identified sample. Red deer, roe deer, and hare appear to have been occasionally exploited for meat. Fox, badger, weasel, stoat, and a number of small mammals have also been recovered from some sites. There is also a restricted range of bird species recorded on these sites. Domestic fowl do not seem to have been exploited until the latter part of the Iron Age and their bones have been found only in small numbers on a few sites. Over 30 other species have been recorded but none of them appear to have been more than an occasional addition to the diet and a number of species represented may not have been eaten at all. Fish bones have been rarely recovered, even on sites where sieving has taken place.

The Exploitation of Domestic Stock

Ageing, sexing, butchery, and metrical data have provided information about how the major domestic species may have been exploited. On most sites, there is evidence for a high proportion of first year sheep mortalities. Some of these represent neonatal mortalities indicating that lambs were probably reared nearby. There is also a substantial peak of animals that were culled between six and twelve months, before they had reached full body weight. Adult animals are also well-represented in most samples but the frequency of animals killed between 18 and 36 months — the prime age for culling for meat — is variable and quite low on some sites. Sheep were probably exploited for both milk and wool as well as meat but there is no strong evidence for specialisation in any single commodity. The sheep were of a small, slender horned type, yielding low carcass and fleece weights.

There are also high numbers of first year cattle mortalities at Danebury (Grant 1984a; b) and Gussage All Saints (Harcourt 1979), although this varies in different phases at both sites. Most of the other cattle represented were adult. Calf mortalities, although not uncommon, have not been found as frequently on other settlements, where adult cattle, presumably including animals used for dairy production and traction are found in the greatest numbers. The cattle were very small in stature and there is little evidence for improvement prior to the Roman invasion.

On most sites, the peak killing of pigs took place in their second or third years, when the animals were nearly fully grown. The vast majority of the horse bones recovered belonged to adult animals, often over ten years old. On several sites there is a bias towards males. Horses, most of which were the size of New Forest ponies, were used mainly as working animals, although many were subsequently eaten. Some dogs were also eaten but presumably were mainly valued for other attributes, particularly as herding animals.

Human Attitudes to Other Animals

Much of the detailed work on animal bones from Wessex Iron Age sites has been concerned with the analysis of intra-site variation in the assemblages. In some cases, variations resulting from differential preservation and disposal of waste after episodes of carcass processing have been demonstrated. However, the main focus of recent interest has been the study of associated groups of bones.

Virtually all Wessex Iron Age sites have produced evidence for the disposal of complete or partial carcasses of animals in pits or other features. Although some of these burials may have had no significance other than disposal of unwanted carcasses, detailed studies of their context and associations with human remains and other finds have shown that many of them had some special significance and represent deliberate depositions (Maltby 1985a; Hill 1993a). Such depositions form a higher proportion of the remains of horses, dogs, and perhaps wild mammals and birds than other species but examples of sheep, cattle, and pig depositions can also be cited (Grant 1984c; Wilson 1992). It may not be possible to determine the precise ritual significance of these depositions but they do serve to remind us that animals were not simply regarded as providers of meat, milk, and other products but served an important role in how the human populations viewed the world as well.

Future Work

Work on Wessex Iron Age faunal assemblages has established a basic picture of how animals were exploited. The value of detailed intra-site analyses of animal bones and other finds in investigating a range of activities has also been demonstrated. It remains to carry out much more detailed inter-site analyses. Regional and chronological changes in the exploitation of animals in Wessex are not clearly understood. Settlements, their inhabitants and their stock clearly could not function in isolation. The relationship between them needs closer scrutiny.

4. Butser Ancient Farm

Peter Reynolds

Butser Ancient Farm was set up in 1972 specifically as a programme for research and education. Its remit to study the agricultural and domestic economy of the period *c.* 400 BC to AD 400 has remained largely unaltered. The period embraces the Late Iron Age and early Roman period. The overall objective was and is to create practical working research programmes based directly upon the archaeological evidence as interpreted from excavations

During the last 20 years the Ancient Farm has occupied three locations. The first site on Little Butser, from which the farm draws its name, was a northerly spur of Butser Hill in Hampshire. The base geology of the site was Middle Chalk overlaid with a shallow friable rendzina soil just 100 mm deep. Given its geology and aspect, it offered a worst option scenario for the proposed research programme but in its defence it once supported a Bronze Age–Iron Age farmstead, the occupants of which cultivated the valley to the north and east. The primary advantage of a worst option lies in the immediate acceptability of the data. This site was in continuous operation from 1972–89.

In 1976 a second site was developed in the valley bottom on Hillhampton Down on the southern slopes of Butser Hill. This shared the same geology but with a deeper (300 mm) soil cover of friable rendzina, clay with flints and Chalk granules. It was operated as a research site in conjunction with Little Butser but its primary purpose was as an open air museum open to the public and available as an educational resource for schoolchildren. Given the independence of the Ancient Farm from any statutory funding, either national or local, it was necessary to develop a sustaining source of income.

On both these sites the infrastructure comprised research fields and stock areas, animal paddocks, and an enclosure within which were built constructs based upon specific archaeological data. The livestock maintained at the farm comprise five breeds of sheep (Moufflon, Soay, Manx Loughton, Hebridean, and Shetland), Old English Goats, Dexter cattle, and Old English Game Fowl. Occasionally Tamworth/European Wild Boar-cross pigs are also kept. The differing natures of both sites allowed direct comparisons to be drawn between the different bioclimatic zones. The major advantage of this second development was a redefinition of the binary purpose of the Ancient Farm as being a research and an educational establishment.

At the beginning of 1991 both these sites were vacated and a new site developed at Bascomb Copse near Chalton. The underlying geology is Upper Chalk with a loamy soil averaging 350 mm deep. This new location offers the typical option of the Chalk downlands of southern England as exploited in all periods of the past. This site has the same resources developed but with the added bonus of potential development. It also combines the twin focus of research and education in a single location. As with the previous sites the objective is to carry out a 1:1 scale empirical trials to elucidate the archaeological data.

From the inception of the Ancient Farm in 1972 it was realised that for this approach, full-scale empiricism, a basic methodology was critical. Without a strict system which applied to all aspects of the work, the results would be incompatible and not allow any form of ultimate integration. It has been envisaged even in the early 1970s that given a large enough database rigorously acquired over a long enough period, computer simulation could be employed. This would extend the data to embrace far greater regions than those to which the research was manifestly restricted, and to respond to questions not originally formed at the beginning of the programme.

The resultant methodology is essentially cyclical in form. The archaeological data, the evidence recovered by excavation, along with whatever documentary sources are available (and reliable) form the base or prime data upon which the archaeologist/ prehistorian mounts an hypothesis. The testing is in the form of a physical experiment which by definition requires replication. The conduct of the experiment must be consistent from start to finish. An experiment which is changed or modified during its course immediately invalidates the original question and the experiment itself. Given adequate replication, usually a minimum of five replicates, the data from the experiment can be compared to the original data upon which the hypothesis was raised. If there is agreement between the sets of data the hypothesis can be tentatively accepted as valid, but with the caveat that several different hypotheses raised on the same data can also be validated, a condition referred to as the multiplicity of hypothesis validation. If there is no agreement the hypothesis is not merely invalidated but actually proved to be wrong. The value of this methodology lies especially in the seemingly worst case situation. By building an experiment the prime data is subjected to extremely close scrutiny in order to execute the experiment, a process which emphasises aspects previously unconsidered or even unrecognised. Even after the committal of an experiment it can be readily seen that there are fundamental errors which are further focused upon during the course of the experiment. The resultant

Figure 4.1   The new Bascomb copse site of Butser Ancient Farm viewed from the south, 1992. Photographs by Elaine Wakefield

negative correlation allows greater insight into the original data and the ability to construct a second or even a third experiment leading to a validated but different hypothesis.

Necessarily, experiments vary in nature in direct response to the type of hypothesis. Broadly experiments/hypotheses fall into five categories. The first and perhaps most obvious category is that of structure, the creation of constructs based upon patterns of post-holes and stake-holes. The word reconstruction is to be eschewed since it is totally inaccurate. The vast majority of buildings evidenced from pre- and protohistory survive only in the form of negative evidence, the position where posts and stakes once stood. Reconstruction is properly applied to the putting together and restoration of buildings of which adequate remains survive. The second category of experiment involves process and function where trials are mounted to examine the effects of usage on archaeological features like pits or objects like ploughs or, alternatively, the effect upon tools in the execution of their hypothesised purpose. Within this category one must place technological resources like pottery kilns and furnaces in the sense that experiment can determine the limits of their performance as well as their efficiency. The third category of experiment is devoted to simulation trials. In this kind of experiment one seeks to discover how an archaeological feature reached its ultimate state as recovered by excavation. Perhaps the best example is the experimental earthwork or ditch and bank. Excavation discovers buried ditches which reveal deposition layers within them brought about by natural erosion processes. The layers are normally irregular and asymmetrically deposited. In order to gain an understanding of both the irregularity and asymmetry the only course of action likely to yield a valuable result is to construct a 'new' version which can be studied against climate and time. The Ancient Farm is currently constructing a major research programme of simulation trials involving octagonal earthworks on different rock and soil types.

The fourth category of trial, described as probability trials, is in a real sense the logical extension of the first three categories. In such a trial one seeks to establish within closely defined parameters probable outcomes or results. Inevitably such results have to be viewed as probability statements very much defined by the constants built into the experimental procedure. The best example of a probability trial is the growing of prehistoric type cereals in order to establish potential yield factors of these cereals within the probable technology available within a specific time period. Within such trials the variables of weather and soil type can be regarded as semi-constants provided they are recorded in detail. More significant in terms of probability are the presumed constants of treatments, sowing rates, and management. Also within this category of experiment fall deductive hypotheses and their testing. The use of this type of trial relies upon data supported validated hypotheses which could not be unless a prior unsubstantiated process or activity had taken place. For example in Britain there is no evidence of threshing or threshing locations yet cereals had to be threshed before they could be processed into food or prepared for storage. In effect it is a function which had to have taken place for without it there would be nothing — *sine qua nihil*

The fifth and final category of experiment is best described as technological innovation. Within this category fall the initial application of machines or trials which seek to improve or enhance archaeological practice. Particularly in this the case with prospection machines like fluxgate gradiometers and soil magnetic susceptibility meters, ground radar, and even X–rays borrowed from other disciplines. The examination and testing of these devices to assess their potential value are, in fact, experiments. Similarly monitored field trials can be used to facilitate the understanding of recovered archaeological data. For example a long series of trials have been conducted by the writer to determine artefact movement within the modern and the prehistoric ploughzone in order to assess the value of the soil as an archaeological layer deserving the same detailed analysis as those layers arguable undisturbed by subsequent activity.

All these categories of experiment have been pioneered and extensively practised at the Ancient Farm. The one important factor which has been deliberately excluded from the nature of experiment is the human. As far as possible the experiments are scientific trials with variables being measured against constants with emphasis being placed on replication and predictability of subsequent trials. Data whenever possible are expressed numerically. No importance has been attached to 'time taken to achieve' since the variable of human motivation and skill are impossible to evaluate or calculate. Similarly 'living in the past' forms no part of the scientific work of the Ancient Farm. Such activities are signally instructive to the participants and may or not be character forming. There is undoubted value and profit to gain from some forms of re-enactment in the field of education and interpretation but there is little of scientific worth likely to extend our knowledge. In a very real way the mental impedimenta which unavoidably burdens modern man precludes any real understanding of his historic counterparts let alone his prehistoric ancestors.

The objective from the beginning of the Ancient Farm has been to work within the constraints of the above methodology concentrating upon the problematic archaeological or prime data. Each of the three sites have been managed in such a way as to seek to integrate all the different experiments so that not only can the individual experiments be studies *per se* but also foreseen relationships between the experiments can be evaluated and unforeseen relationships might be identified.

The primary focus of the research has been upon the agricultural economy of the later Iron Age. From 1972 growing trials have been carried out with the typical cereals of the period, emmer (*Triticum dicoccum*) and spelt (*T. spelta*) on a range of soil types in different bioclimatic zones. Other cereals have been incorporated into the trials including club wheat (*Traestis-compactum*) old bread wheat (*Tr. aestivum*), einkorn (*Tr. monococcum*), and barley (*Hordeum vulgare*). For treatment variability the legumes celtic bean (*Vicia faba minor*), peas (*Pisum sativian*) and vetch (*Vicia sativa*) have also been cultivated. Field aspect, soil type, manuring and non-manuring, crop rotation, and fallow rotation are all incorporated as variable treatments. An important element of these cropping trials has been the study of arable weeds in terms of their presence and absence and their value as irritants or benefits. Cultivation experiments utilising different types of cattle drawn ard have been conducted examining both the efficiency of the ard as a tool on the one hand, on the other the effects of use on the ard itself. Associated observations within the cultivation programme include the monitoring of lynchet formation on field boundaries and dishing within field areas. Trials with the magnetic susceptibility meter across manured and non-manured zones within field areas along with lipid analysis of treated soils suggest a positive method of determining manuring activity. The cropping trials have also afforded opportunities to carry out pollen rain catchment along with the development of a new pollen rain trap.

The second aspect to the cropping programme has been an intensive programme of grain storage in underground silos. A large range of variables have been examined over a period of 20 years yielding significant results. Grain can be stored very successfully in simple pits in Chalk, Limestone and sand rocks both short and long term. Short term storage of *c.* 6 months the grain has a germ- inability in excess of 90%. Germinability, though not edibility, deteriorates the longer the storage period. Critically a pit has an in- determinate life span. No sign of souring was observed during 15 years of trials. The impli- cations of these storage experiments demand a re-evaluation of their currently accepted economy and use.

A parallel research focus has been upon the houses and structures of the Late Iron Age. A large number of different round houses has been built on each of the three sites, each house being a specific construct based upon the best available excavated data. It has always been a particular aim to project and test a structure within the constraints of the archaeological evidence. A generalised or composite structure has never been built at the Ancient Farm. Two significant constructs have yielded the greatest reward to date. The Pimperne house construction allowed a real distinction to be drawn between constructional and structural evidence and on its dismantlement in 1990 it was found that a building of 13 m diameter could adequately exist beyond the life of its structural post-holes, implying that dating evidence found within the post-pipe did not necessarily indicate a time after its destruction. An even larger construct based upon excavation at Longbridge Deverell Cow Down, 15.4 m in diameter, built in 1992–3, has demonstrated that a free span of some 13 m is relatively simple to achieve.

Figure 4.2   The partly-built Longbridge Deverill Cow Down house, 1992.

Since the early 1980s a major research pro- gramme into experimental earthworks has been carried out involving the construction of simple V–section ditches 20 m long, 1.5 m deep, and 1.5 m across with dump banks, with built-in variables of berms and no berms, turf retaining walls, and turf cores based on an octagonal plan. The plan is dictated by different weather patterns experienced from the major points of the compass. The research design entails the study of erosion and revegetation through time against recorded climate. The programme at present has four major earthworks on Upper, Middle and Lower Chalk and aeolian drift. The proto-experimental earthwork built at the Hillhampton Down site in 1976 and excavation in 1981 shared startling rapidity of vegetable colonisation and stabilisation as well as a totally unexpected skew of the deposition layers.

In addition to these core research programmes, subsidiary programmes have researched into metallurgy and kiln technology. Further programmes are run in conjunction with other institutions both here and abroad. Several of these have involved the testing of prospection devices and their research applications with special reference to magnetic susceptibility

In conclusion the Ancient Farm is an open air research laboratory designed to carry out experiments to enhance our understanding of the archaeological data both on the site and elsewhere. While it has its own menu of long term research programmes it is also available as a facility for other researchers both national and international. In this sense it is neither site nor period specific. The future path of the Ancient Farm is to enhance the immediate facility the one hand, on the other to expand its own remit to encompass a wider period span including Roman and post-Roman programmes. It is presently a unique resource.

5. The Organisation of Salt Production and Distribution in Iron Age Wessex

Elaine L. Morris

The archaeological evidence for the winning of salt from seawater is as elusive as ever. The number of new locations where salt production took place along the south coast of England during the Iron Age is constantly increasing, but our actual understanding about the processes of production and the mechanisms of dispersal are still limited. In contrast, however, what we have learned in the past 15–20 years is about the level of intensification of salt production and the extent of the distribution of salt in ceramic containers. What use was made of this commodity is a primary question for future research.

Intensification of Production

The discovery of new production locations along the Dorset coast, principally those at Wytch Farm on the south side of Poole Harbour (Cleal 1991; Cox and Hearne 1991) and Rope Lake Hole on the south side of the Isle of Purbeck (Hawkes 1987; Woodward 1987), has allowed a development in the discussion about the nature of salt production — not a discussion about the technology of production but one about the locations, dating, and frequency of production sites (Cox and Hearne 1991, 229). That discussion examined the dramatic evidence for increased production with the sudden appearance of several production sites of later Iron Age date on the previously uninhabited southern shores of Poole Harbour. This period witnessed the intensification of salt production which had been present in Dorset from the Early–Middle Iron Age onwards (Farrar 1975; Poole 1987), and also from the pre-saucepan phase of the Middle Iron Age in Hampshire/Sussex (Bradley 1992).

Therefore, it is now possible to see a model of the production of salt on the south coast of Wessex as having an early phase based on seasonal, small-scale enterprises (Bradley 1975), not dissimilar to the household production level for making pottery mainly for home use with a small amount destined for others (Peacock 1982, 13–7), intensifying during the later Iron Age with more producers spending more time making salt for a wider network of consumers similar to the household industry level of pottery-making (Peacock 1982, 17–25). This eventually led to the end of salt production on such a loosely-based, part-time system utilising simple ceramic moulds in the early Roman period to one which was more able to respond to greater consumer demands with the growth of Roman towns and markets (Bradley 1992). The use of full-time workers, with permanent facilities located at inland brine springs sources where the salt is already present in concentrated solution, and an investment in metal cauldrons for heating the salt are postulated as the signs of a true industry developed during the Romano-British period.

Transportation and Distribution

New excavations have also revealed the extent of the transportation of salt to inland settlements. This pattern is a biased one because it is totally dependent upon the utilisation of the distinctive briquetage containers to dry and transport the salt inland to settlements of all types. The use of these containers as transportation vessels appears to occur almost exclusively in Hampshire. If salt was extracted from the briquetage containers at the production sites and placed into bags for travel inland, then it would not be possible to observe this archaeologically. However, if the salt had been decanted into pottery vessels, then it may be possible to identify the mineral through chemical analysis if the pottery had not been made with saltwater, or if the pottery had been made on the same site and could be shown to been made specifically for the transportation of salt.

Iron Age sites in Hampshire where fragments of briquetage containers have been found far from the coast include Winnall Down (Morris 1985), Micheldever Wood (Morris 1987a), and Trafalgar House (Morris 1982) in the Winchester area; Winklebury (Smith 1977, 88), Rucstalls Hill (Oliver and Applin 1979, 60 and 66), and Brighton Hill South and Beggarwood Lane (Rees in press a) in the Basingstoke area; and Danebury (Poole 1984; 1991a) and Area 6—Charlton (Morris in prep.) in the area around Andover. Surprisingly, however, there are a number of sites in Hampshire where fragments of these distinctive containers have not been found, such as Old Down Farm (Davies 1981), Lains Farm (Bellamy 1991), and Easton Lane (Fasham *et al.* 1989), despite the expectation of finding such sherds amongst the ceramic material.

Examination of museum collections is currently taking place in order to: (1) identify all the settlement sites in Hampshire where briquetage containers have been found, (2) quantify the amount of this material, and (3) determine whether the salt was being transported from Kimmeridge or Poole Harbour in Dorset, or Hengistbury Head, Southampton Water, and the Solent, or Portsmouth–Langstone–Chichester Harbours on the Hampshire/Sussex border (Bradley 1975; 1992). It has been assumed that the briquetage containers found at Danebury are from the Hampshire production sites based on general temper range present (Poole 1984, 429–30) but this still has not been confirmed through petrological analysis of the ceramic container fabrics found at that site, or on any of the other settlements in Hampshire.

The relative amount of briquetage material recovered from several of the known consumer sites has been quantified and compared in a ratio to the pottery recovered to determine whether similar or different amounts of salt had been used at various types of sites (Table 5.1). It appears that there is no difference in the amount of salt used between hillforts and settlements within broad phases of occupation but that the amount does appear to have increased from the earlier to later Iron Age, as discussed above.

Outside Hampshire, only rare examples of briquetage from Dorset production sites have been identified away from the source. Only one site, the hillfort at Maiden Castle, produced fragments of

Table 5.1   Salt index: the ratio of salt container material to pottery by weight for five sites in Hampshire

Site	Type	Phase	Qty salt containers (g)	Qty pottery (g)	Salt index
Danebury	hillfort	cp. 1–3/EIA	423	89,328	0.005
		cp. 4–6/MIA	995	186,690	0.005
		cp, 7–8/LIA	3382	370,239	0.009
Beggarwood Lane	settlement	MIA	23	4000	0.006
Brighton Hill South	settlement	EIA	0	4719	0.000
		MIA–LIA	232.5	13,682.5	0.017
		LIA–early Roman	49.5	86,1113.0	<0.001
Winklebury	hillfort	EIA/MIA	0	25,873	0.000
Winnall Down	settlement	EIA	0	25,873	0.000
		MIA	426.5	69,885	0.006
		early Roman	314	86,570	0.004

Data from Poole 1984; Lock pers. comm.; Rees in press; Smith 1977; Hawkes 1985; Morris 1985

several different fabric types (Poole 1991b), and rare pieces of briquetage have been recovered in the town of Dorchester, but never in exclusively pre-Roman contexts (Cleal 1993; Woodward 1993). No sherds of briquetage have been identified from the numerous Iron Age settlement sites in Wiltshire or Sussex.

The close link between pottery production and salt production, however, may contain the key to understanding the transportation of salt inland if pots were used as transporters. The frequency and eventual dominance of Poole Harbour pottery in Late Iron Age assemblages excavated in Dorset, south Somerset and west Wiltshire (Morris this volume) demonstrate that there was a lively trade in ceramics at that time — such a trading system must have included salt. Otherwise, there may well be a difference in the use of salt amongst these areas, or the absence of its use, which could prove the key to our understanding of the distribution of briquetage.

Conclusion

Future studies into the organisation of salt production and distribution must address the issues of this variation in the dispersal of salt to consumers and what the consumers were using the salt for, particularly since there is a clear increase in the production and trade of this commodity during the Iron Age in Wessex. It is important to balance the diachronic study of salt procurement and the mechanisms of its trade with an investigation into the use of this commodity, and in so doing be able to say something about the system within which the material moved.

6. Ironworking in Iron Age Wessex

Robert M. Ehrenreich

Introduction of Iron into Britain

Iron smelting and smithing were probably first introduced into south-western Britain in roughly 700 BC along traditional trade routes with north-west France (Ehrenreich 1985). This hypothesis is based on the fact that south-western Britain contained most of the early iron smelting furnaces (Cleere 1981) and three of the earliest iron manufacturing sites, including the Early Iron Age promontory fort of Trevelgue that contained quantities of slag indicative of large-scale smelting (Cleere 1981; Salter and Ehrenreich 1984). The sites discussed are shown in Figure 1.

The bronze–iron transition in Britain was probably fuelled by the realignment of European trade routes between the seventh and fourth centuries BC (Ehrenreich 1990). The reduction in cross-Channel trade during this period would have decreased the quantity of bronze imported and restricted the basis by which Late Bronze Age elite sustained authority. Bronze output from the Devon–Cornwall region may have been increased to compensate for the loss of imports, but the quantity produced would have been insufficient to sustain the entire island (Northover 1984). Also, the socio-economic upheaval caused by the collapse of the trade routes would have adversely affected trade within Britain, further exacerbating the bronze shortage. Thus, the transition in Britain from a bronze-base to an iron-base technology was probably influenced by a dwindling bronze supply. This shortage was the result of external factors beyond the control of British society, however.

Iron Manufacturing in Iron Age Wessex

Although iron ore is common throughout Britain (Tylecote 1986), Iron Age iron production appears to have been dominated by craft specialists (Ehrenreich 1991). Only four Iron Age settlement sites in Wessex show evidence of smelting. Occasional iron production to satisfy domestic needs may have occurred on the Early Iron Age sites of All Cannings Cross and Swallowcliffe Down and the Middle–Late Iron Age phase at Little Woodbury (Cleere 1981; Tylecote 1986). Excavation of the Late Iron Age phase of Gussage All Saints revealed definite smelting remains, but these may be indicative of a specialised metallurgical establishment that produced bronze and iron horse-trappings for export. If so, then the iron smelted would have been for use on the site for artefact production and not for trade as raw stock (Spratling 1979).

The dearth of iron production sites in Wessex implies that its inhabitants must have been reliant on others for metal. Trace element analysis suggests that the Devon–Cornwall region was one of the

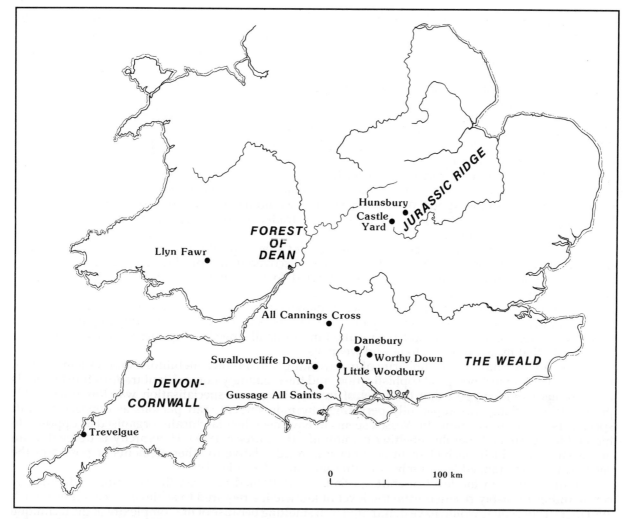

Figure 6.1   Location of the regions and sites discussed

main iron sources during the Early Iron Age (Ehrenreich 1985). Iron with high-cobalt, high-nickel concentrations was most prevalent in Wessex during this period. The only currently known British source for this metal is the Great Perran lode near Trevelgue (Groves 1952). Although no link between this ore and Trevelgue has been established, the sourcing of this iron and the presence in this region of the earliest, British iron-production centers would support the hypothesis that Devon–Cornwall was providing most of the iron during this period.

The relative quantity of highcobalt, highnickel iron in Wessex decreased during the Middle and Late Iron Age, implying that nearby iron production centers probably supplanted the distant Devon–Cornwall sites (Ehrenreich 1985). Large-scale iron production during the Middle–Late Iron Age appears to have been restricted to the island's three richest ore sources: the Weald (12 sites), the Forest of Dean (seven sites), and the Jurassic Ridge (three sites). The iron produced was traded in standardised forms, known as currency bars, throughout Britain and perhaps even to the Continent (*BG* 5.12.2; *Geog.* 4.5.2). The two most common currency bar forms were a sword-shaped type, which is high in phosphorus and probably came from sources along the Jurassic Ridge (Ehrenreich 1985), and a spit-shaped type, which is low in phosphorus and clustered around the Forest of Dean (Cleere 1981; Ehrenreich 1985). The available evidence suggests that the iron smelting segment of the metals society was highly specialized throughout the Middle–Late Iron Age in Britain (Ehrenreich 1991).

The scarcity of sites discovered along the Jurassic Ridge might imply that largescale iron manufacturing did not occur there. Four factors dispute this conjecture. First, the high-phosphorus sword-shaped currency bars were found concentrated along the Jurassic Ridge (Allen 1967). Second, a large portion of the Middle–Late Iron Age artefacts in Wessex were made from naturally high-phosphorus metal (e.g. 60% for the Middle Iron Age; Ehrenreich 1985). Third, the Hunsbury, Northamptonshire, hillfort shows every indication of having been a centralised, iron production centre for sword-shaped currency bars. The site actually sits on a high-phosphorus iron ore source and contained a full complement of blacksmith's tools and a blank for a currency bar (Ehrenreich 1985; 1991). Fourth, metal-lurgical remains recovered from Castle Yard, Northamptonshire, suggest that a more advanced level of smelting technology may have existed for this region than for the rest of Britain (Knight 1984).

Thus, the extensive, associated evidence indicates that the Jurassic Ridge was a significant iron manufacturing area.

Ironworking in Iron Age Wessex

Smithing expertise was at a very basic level during the British Iron Age. Ironworkers were generally incapable of altering the properties of their tools and weapons. The deliberate use of steel was extremely limited and the application of advanced heat-treatments was even rarer, as shown by the presence of only three known quenched artefacts from the Worthy Down settlement and Danebury (Ehrenreich 1985). The naturally phosphorus-rich iron from the Jurassic Ridge seems to have been deliberately exploited during the Late Iron Age to enhance the properties of artefacts, however. Since high phosphorus contents increase the hardness of iron (Kaloyeros and Ehrenreich 1991), the preferential use of this metal would have been a non-labour-intensive method for improving the properties of tools and weapons. Wessex blacksmiths would have recognised Northamptonshire iron by the distinctive currency bar shape by which it was traded. Currency bars and scrap metal were the predominant raw stock used.

Smithing was performed on both small settlement sites and hillforts to satisfy the needs of the inhabitants (Ehrenreich 1991). No site has yet been discovered that produced a surplus of standard iron tools or weapons for export. Each site tended to make their own implements as required (Ehrenreich 1991). This may have been due to an insufficient demand for new artefacts. Whereas bronze objects must be completely recast when damaged, broken ironwork can usually be repaired by welding. Thus, new iron artefacts may only have been required when an existing implement could no longer be recycled. This would have resulted in too small a need to support a dedicated smithing community that mass-produced tools and weapons.

The broad distribution and similarity of ironworking remains on both hillforts and settlement sites, the general lack of technological sophistication, and the seemingly non-existent trade of finished tools or weapons would suggest that the level of ironworking craft specialisation was low during this period. Ironworking was apparently performed by independent craft persons as opposed to craft specialists. Thus, ironworking in Wessex seems to have been heterarchically organised as opposed to hierarchically aligned like the smelting community (Ehrenreich 1991). Heterarchy is defined as an organisation in which 'each element is either unranked relative to other elements or possesses the *potential* for being ranked in a number of different ways' (Crumley 1987).

The differences in the level of craft specialisation attained between the smelting and smithing communities probably resulted from the level of knowledge required to achieve success (Ehrenreich 1991). Craft specialists would have dominated iron smelting because of the complexity of the technique and the uncertainty of viable iron production. Iron forging would have been more generally performed because methods for enhancing the properties of iron tools were basically unknown. Anyone who could forge iron into a desired shape was essentially a successful blacksmith. Thus, the iron manufacturing and ironworking communities were distinct entities with very different levels of craft specialisation.

The presence of the few quenched artefacts indicates that some smiths in Wessex were attempting to develop new methods to improve their iron artefacts, however (Ehrenreich 1991). The limited number of these artefacts suggests that any techniques developed remained proprietary and not generally distributed. This secrecy was normal, as shown by the 16th century publication by Biringuccio (1942). This volume contains numerous 'secrets' for the production of superior tools. Although many of these processes may seem absurd today, some are metallurgically sound (Martin and Foley 1979). Thus, the Wessex ironworking community should not be seen as simplistic, but as dynamic and complex with many different ironworkers all attempting new techniques and not confined to a set hierarchy (Ehrenreich 1991).

7. Bronze, Silver, and Gold in Iron Age Wessex

J.P. Northover

Ten years ago a survey of this same subject (Northover 1984) was necessarily speculative because only a very small amount of Iron Age non-ferrous metalwork had ever been studied metallurgically. Although typology was undoubtedly important, discussion was still weighted towards art history, while the debris from such an important foundry site as Gussage All Saints was published only piecemeal (Wainwright 1979; Foster 1980; Howard 1983) and the metal used there never characterised. Since then much has changed; metallurgical studies are now an integral part of the post-excavation process and, on occasion, part of the excavation itself, while other research projects now have similar support. The result of this effort is that it is now possible to present a much more coherent picture of non-ferrous metalworking in Iron Age Wessex.

The term Iron Age follows conventional continental usage, that is an early or first Iron Age corresponding to Hallstatt C and D and a later or second Iron Age corresponding to the La Tène period. It must not be forgotten that in southern Britain, the pre-Roman Iron Age lasts another century beyond that on the opposite shores of the Channel, and the way in which Roman technology encroached upon and eventually came to supersede indigenous methods is an important issue in the archaeology of the first century AD.

The Beginnings

Careful evaluation of all references to early iron objects in Britain has shown that there are no realistic occurrences before the Hallstatt C. During this period surviving iron objects are few, and often of very high quality as in the Llyn Fawr deposit (Savory 1976, 123–5, nos 291–4; O'Connor 1980, 420–1, no. 218), from a little way outside our region. Bronze was still the dominant metal for utilitarian purposes but there were some changes in the way it was used compared with the preceding Ewart Park period of the Atlantic Late Bronze Age. The use of lead as an alloying addition to bronze was generally reduced although it was retained as an aid to casting some of the more complex shapes such as cauldron fittings. At the same time, the quality of finish improved quite radically for everyday objects and the elaboration of the most prestigious, such as the cauldrons, increased by as much as an order of magnitude in terms of labour costs.

Connections with Atlantic Europe were maintained, evidenced, for example, by the small scatter of Armorican socketed axes in southern Britain. At the same time, Wessex had its own non-functional type of axe frequently found in hoards. This is the faceted socketed axe of Blandford type; but in contrast to the lead-rich alloys of the Armorican axes, the Blandford axes are made from a very high tin alloy, giving them a silvery appearance. At the same time connections, however direct or indirect, with what was becoming the western Hallstatt core area in southern Germany and the Alps are much more prominent than before. In Wessex itself, a number of recent hoard finds (O'Connor 1980, 230–68, otherwise mostly unpublished, and in one case *sub judice*) is beginning to tell us something about the postion of bronze and even a little about the technology. The concentration of large finds is very much in the chalk uplands, with several important finds in and around Salisbury Plain. Also, for the first time, we have scrap hoards including casting debris; the two examples so far known are both from hilltop sites.

The following, Hallstatt D, period is much more shadowy, although growing less so as more objects are seen to belong there. For example, it is no longer possible (Cunliffe 1991, 419–25) to dismiss Hallstatt D fibulae as recent imports. Also, although mostly from outside our region, the last vestiges of the Atlantic cauldron tradition can be placed here alongside imported vessels; previously there seemed a positive reluctance to do so and the cauldrons had been dated as late as Late La Tène (Raferty 1984, 227–34). Similarly, there has been a suspicion of early dates for many iron socketed axes and attempts to divorce them from their bronze precursors; surely some belong here. The metalwork of the Hallstatt period as a whole in southern Britain was partially surveyed by O'Connor in 1980 (230–68). Even though we can recognise diagnostically British bronze types in this period, such as the ornamented dagger sheaths from the Thames, we have no notion of the type of site on which any of them might have been made.

The Resources

For the Hallstatt C–D period, bronze analysis has established little in the way of characteristically British groupings. Typically the metal is a low lead, low impurity, medium to high tin bronze, presumably a mixture of existing scrap and new metal, while clearly some direct imports have survivied. Perhaps the best clue to the continued exploitation in the south of British metal resources lies in the high tin contents of the Blandford faceted socketed axes mentioned above, but alternative sources are possible even here.

We are on rather firmer ground when we consider the metal of the La Tène period in Wessex and surrounding areas. A series of post-excavation studies, notably at Hengistbury Head (Northover 1987; Salter and Northover 1992), Mount Batten, Devon (Northover 1988a), Maiden Castle (Northover 1991a) and Danebury (Northover 1991b), have shown La Tène bronze compositions in Wessex to be dominated by a single type with cobalt as its most distinctive inpurity. This bronze is lead-free and leaded bronze, in fact, does not become important again until the end of the first century BC. The evidence of distribution, falling off to the north and east, and parallels with Bronze Age metal types suggest very strongly a source in south-west England, possibly around Dartmoor, convenient also for sources of tin. This metal was also used elsewhere in southern and eastern England and in south Wales and it may well have been exported (Northover 1988b). Some confirmation may be supplied by lead isotope analysis but this has yet to be applied to Iron Age bronze. Cobalt, unfortunately, is not always included in comparative analyses from France and elsewhere on the continent.

Exact parallels for this composition can be found in cauldrons from La Tène itself, which also match British examples in form and in the composition and technology of the iron. Such exports, if substantiated, provide good support for the notion of a long-distance metal trade from Britain. More intriguing connections are suggested by the use of this metal in the earliest British potin coinage (van Arsdell 1989; Northover 1992) given its probable appearance in the Massiliote prototypes of this coinage. This, though, is one of its latest datable appearances, its earliest being among the earliest La Tène metalwork in Wessex. There is no good evidence of its use after the mid-first century BC. We must assume that the political and economic upheavals and reorientations of that period totally disrupted the trade. Prior to that there must always have been some import of bronze from continental Europe and this traffic seems to intensify during the first century BC. One striking example of this is the antimony-and-nickel-rich bronze appearing in the later potin coinage — evidence of immigrations in the second quarter of the century?

Other copper sources were undoubtedly exploited in the La Tène period in Britain, most notably a copper source in the Welsh Marches producing copper with a substantial zinc impurity (Musson *et al.* 1992) but this does not reach Wessex. However, the possibility that raw copper could be made with 3–4% zinc means that we must exercise some caution when trying to understand how brass (a copper–zinc alloy) reached Britain in the late pre-Roman Iron Age. The earliest brass in Britain may be some Trinovantian coins (Northover 1992), possibly recycling Roman originals. Brass fibulae were certainly imported and, a little later, made in Britain (Bayley 1990) and brass gradually entered circulation as scrap, often getting mixed with bronze. So far there is no definitive evidence for the manufacture of brass in Wessex or surrounding areas prior to the arrival of the Romans.

Products, Technology, and Workshops

Metal production was clearly at a rather low ebb at the end of the Hallstatt period and production does not seem to have risen significantly until well on in the La Tène. By the second century BC the range of types produced, and their number, were increasing rapidly. Although copper alloys were now never as important quantitatively as iron, nevertheless their production was a significant economic activity, even more so when they entered the coinage. This is not the place, nor is there room, for a survey of the full range of products of La Tène bronzesmiths in Wessex; what is important here is to categorise them by the technology by which they were produced.

Whereas Hallstatt C bronze was predominantly cast using Late Bronze Age piece moulds technology, there was an increased emphasis on wrought or part-wrought products in Hallstatt D, notably vessels, sheaths and pins. Probably the greatest weight of metal in the La Tène period went into cast products, notably horse harness and vehicle fittings as produced at Gussage All Saints (Foster 1980). The key technical development which can be associated with the spread of La Tène styles was the general use of lost-wax casting (there is no evidence to say what late Hallstatt types were actually cast in Britain, and how). It is surprising that this change came so late but a high degree of competence with the piece-mound alternative may have offered some competition.

Sheet bronzework was first established in southern Britain no later than the last quarter of the second millennium BC. It was generally confined to the most prestigious objects such as cauldrons and shields, possibly reflecting high level control of a new technology and support of the substantial labour costs involved. This remained substantially the position for a long time, although smaller sheet ornaments do appear in Carp's Tongue contexts. The Hallstatt period added a small number of sheet products to include dagger sheaths and appliqués, but the real expansion came in La Tène times when, in addition to free-standing objects such as metal vessels and sword scabbards, sheet bronze was very extensively used to clad other material such as wood and iron, for example in the later Iron Age decorated buckets like that from Marlborough, Wiltshire (Vidal 1976). We must also remember the number of composite articles that was made such as bronze and iron cauldrons, or iron linch pins with bronze heads.

Excavation has revealed something of the workshop context in which bronzeworking was carried on. Production of bronze castings certainly took place at small village or settlement sites of which Gussage All Saints is the model. Putting a date to the complex of metallurgical activities at Hengistbury Head is problematic but it seems that bronze casting may well have been the earliest activity there, early the the first century BC (Salter and Northover 1992); later still is a significant deposit of foundry debris in the immediate pre-Roman occupation of Silchester, Hampshire. Taken together with the evidence from Maiden Castle and early La Tène crucibles from Danebury, we can chart the evolution of both moulds and crucibles throughout the period. While the moulds exhibit gradual improvements in the feeding and gating of castings, the crucibles show a pattern of advance and regression in technical efficiency.

In contrast, the evidences for the production and use of sheet bronze are particularly concentrated on hillfort sites. Sheet fragments as a proportion of total bronze finds are very much higher at Danebury and Maiden Castle than at undefended settlement sites. Maiden Castle, indeed, contained a workshop area where sheet metal objects, probably cauldrons, were being either made, repaired or scrapped (Northover 1991a). The association with hillforts possibly relates to a need to control some types of production but the lack of quality hillfort excavations restricts the material available for research. The same can be said of metalworking at oppida; the limited evidence from the recent excavations at Silchester suggests a range of metallurgical activity appropriate to an urban setting. The special case of Hengistbury Head will be discussed further in the next section as much of the activity is connected with precious metals. However, despite this growing body of metallurgical evidence we do not know where, or if, sword scabbards were made in Wessex and although there are local variants of fibulae we do not know where those were made either.

It is impossible to leave a discussion of La Tène bronzework without considering one of its most important attributes, its decorative quality (Northover and Salter 1991). The founders' skill with lost-wax casting allowed much detail to be formed in the mould but, equally, sheet bronze and flat products such as mirrors showed how engraving, chasing and repoussé could be used to create figurative and abstract pictures and add texture to both two- and three-dimensional surfaces. Colour could be added through opaque glass inlays and through artificial patination, although investigation of Iron Age abilities in this direction has scarcely begun. Although there are tin-plated Hallstatt fibulae in France and a La Tène I fibula inlaid with tin from Flag Fen, Cambridgeshire, tin plating as a decorative element does not emerge until the late first century BC and reaches its zenith on mid-first century AD fibulae. It really does seem to be a product of contacts with Romanised Gaul and its more general application is probably post-Conquest although used by craftsmen still working in the native tradition. Gilding occurs in first century BC contexts (Stead 1991) but has not been detected in Wessex, while bronze itself was used as a plating formed by hot dipping (Northover and Salter 1991).

Gold, Silver, and the Coinage

Gold objects disappear from the archaeological record in Wessex and in the rest of southern Britain during Hallstatt C, if not by the end of Ewart Park. Simple ribbon torques with embellished terminals linger on in Scotland and Ireland until some ill-defined point in the Iron Age along with the very occasional import. For Wessex and neighbouring regions, the next appearance of gold is in the form of the imported Gallo-Belgic coinage, from the end of the third century BC onwards. This coinage, deriving from the area of the Ambiani in northern France, was probably based on a natural gold with up to 20–25% silver and very little copper. As the Gallo-Belgic series developed it became progressively debased, always with the same standard silver–copper alloy chosen, presumably because it minimised colour change while lowering the melting temperature. When the first British gold coins derived from this series were issued, the same debasement obtained, necessarily so because the Gallo-Belgic coinage was almost certainly the source of the bullion used until the Roman Conquest of Gaul and the suppression of the Gallic gold coinage (Haselgrove 1987; van Arsdell 1989; Cowell 1992; Northover 1992).

After a hiatus when the finite supply of gold meant that most tribes' coinage became quite debased, sinking to 30% gold or less, those with the stronger economies re-established a gold standard, this time with a red gold with 40–45% gold and 40–45% copper. In Wessex, the Atrebates did this successfully as did the neighbouring Dobunni but the Durotriges, who had already struggled to maintain a gold coinage, abandoned the metal and moved to silver and then struck copper and, much later, cast bronze. These analyses suggest, not unsurprisingly, that at least one source of silver for the Durotriges was that of the Coriosolites. In contrast, the secondary silver denominations issued by the Atrebates were most probably recycled Roman republican denarii and quinarii.

While most tribes with access to gold bullion issued a gold coinage, the Iceni in Norfolk diverted a substantial portion of their metallic wealth into the series of torques seen in the Snettisham treasure and other East Anglian hoards (Stead 1991; Northover 1992). This story impinges on Wessex in the form of late Iron Age gold and silver objects at Hengistbury Head (Salter and Northover 1992). The button terminal torque, although parallelled at Snettisham, could be an import since its square-section wire seems to be a continental trait. The associated gold bracelet also seems alien and should be considered an import but the decorated torc terminal is typical Snettisham. Unfortunately it is so corroded that analysis cannot help us give it a context in the Snettisham production. At Hengistbury it may have been about to be recycled into the coinage at a stage when the Durotriges used white gold staters. Other silver waste at Hengistbury is most probably of Roman date and could be involved with the scrapping and re-refining of recalled Celtic silver coins in the immediate post-Conquest era, a process possibly carried out at Silchester as well.

The metallurgical analysis and technical study of Iron Age metals is a particularly fruitful enterprise but much remains to be done to make a coherent picture. The results also help illuminate the scattered classical writings connecting southern England and Iron Age metallurgy and makes them seem a little less fantastic.

8. Coinage and Currency in Iron Age Wessex

Colin Haselgrove

On analogy with other pre-industrial societies, a range of objects in Iron Age Wessex probably served functions which we nowadays associate with currencies, acting as a means of payment or as a standard of value for particular kinds of transaction, without this role being readily apparent to us as archaeologists. These include perishable commodities such as salt cakes, textiles and livestock, as well as artefacts like brooches, glass beads, or shale armlets. However, the only objects which stand out — because they have no immediate utilitarian function — are the iron bars which appear on several Wessex sites during the third and second centuries BC. These iron bars were made in various standard sizes and weights, sword-shaped and spit-shaped forms being the most common, and they were evidently of value as they were frequently buried together in groups. Many of these are found beneath settlement boundaries, or in natural settings such as rocks and caves, and probably represent ritual offerings, rather than abandoned hoards (Hingley 1990a).

Although coinage began to be used extensively in south-east England during the later second century BC (Haselgrove 1993), neither the imported Gallo-Belgic gold from northern France nor the early cast bronze coinage of Kent seems to have penetrated into Wessex in any significant quantity. Similarly, the cluster of Ptolemaic bronze coins found in the Winchester area had no discernible influence on local developments, whether or not they are contemporary imports (Biddle 1975). Imported Gallo-Belgic gold of the early first century BC is only slightly more common, finds including a small hoard of early Gallo-Belgic C staters (Fig. 1, 1) from Hurstbourne Tarrant in north Hampshire and a few isolated Gallo-Belgic D quarter-staters (Fig. 1, 2). However, the presence of these types in Wessex is significant as they provided the model for the earliest indigenous coinage of the region. Some of the base metal coins from Brittany and Normandy found in Wessex also probably entered Britain around this time (Fig. 1, 3), although the main influx of Armorican imports (Fig. 1, 4) dates to the Gallic war (57–51 BC) and afterwards.

Before long, the advantages of gold coinage over traditional valuables as a medium for wealth storage and payment led to its being imitated locally. One of the earliest indigenous gold coinages, known as British A2 (Fig. 1, 5), circulated on the eastern side of Wessex, but the first indisputably local issue was British B (Fig. 1, 6), which has a distribution centred on Hampshire and Wiltshire, extending into both Dorset and Somerset. These British series retained the crude head-horse designs of Gallo-Belgic C and were struck to a similar weight standard (over 6.0 g), but the fineness is much lower — only 47% gold for British A2 and 38% for British B as opposed to 70% for the prototype. British A2 was probably made by adding silver and copper to melted-down imported staters, while British B was derived from it by adding yet more silver (Cowell 1992). A date between 80–60 BC is likely for these developments; a hoard recently found near Whitchurch in north Hampshire contained over 100 worn British B staters associated with imported Gallo-Belgic E staters, which can themselves be confidently dated no later than the 50s BC, in fresh condition (Burnett and Cowell 1988).

At about this time, some kind of local coin-issuing group was developing in the Solent area, which subsequently disappears from the record. Types confined to the area include even cruder and baser stater imitations (British C, D; Fig. 1, 7) and a series of thin silver issues, which are unlike any other coins found in Britain (Mack 321; Fig. 1, 8). The tradition appears to derive from Picardy or Normandy, where a number of analogous thin silver issues were in circulation (Allen 1965). Also probably local to this district is an unusual struck bronze type, with a stylised cock on the reverse (Evans G9; Fig. 1, 9). Due to its strong Belgic affinities, the type has long been thought to be imported, but there have now been several finds on the Hampshire–Sussex border. Like the thin silver, the idea of struck bronze coinage never took hold in central southern England, and its circulation was short-lived.

From the 50s BC, Wessex was increasingly dominated by two major coin-issuing groups, one in the east, the other in the south-west. The first of these originated in the Cranborne Chase area, where a series of very debased gold staters and quarter-staters (derived respectively from British A and Gallo-Belgic D) made its appearance at about the time of Caesar's conquest of Gaul (Fig. 1, 10 and 11). The earliest South-Western issues still contain up to 14% gold, but were followed by progressively lighter and more degraded types, initially in fairly good silver (75–80%) (Fig. 1, 12), but ending with coins which are essentially of bronze (Fig. 1, 13). The later staters have a much wider distribution, taking in all of Dorset and parts of neighbouring counties. The series eventually ended with a series of barbarous coins cast from a ternary alloy of copper, lead, and tin (Northover 1992), which seem to be more or less confined to the area around Hengistbury Head (Fig. 1, 14). This adherence to such debased standards may in some way reflect the region's strong cultural links with Brittany and Normandy, where the local coinages were similarly debased, rather than simply shortage of precious metal.

The other main coin-issuing group, which covered most of Berkshire, Hampshire, Surrey, and Sussex, is quite different in character. It is headed by an extensive gold coinage depicting a triple-tailed horse copied from a prominent mid first century BC Belgic type (British Q; Fig. 1, 15), together with a series of rarer silver issues (Fig. 1, 16), best known from recent finds on Hayling Island (Briggs et al. in press) and from just outside Danebury (van Arsdell 1991). The silver was one source of inspiration — the coinage of the Cotswold region is the other — for a localised coin grouping which developed in north central Wiltshire in the later first century BC (Robinson 1977) (Fig. 1, 17).

Within a generation of Caesar's Conquest of Gaul, the Southern rulers had started striking a sophisticated gold and silver coinage, including fractions, which bears the issuer's name and sometimes additional details (Fig. 1, 23–6). The introduction of silver fractions, in particular, must indicate that coinage was now being used in a much wider range of transactions — though it probably never became a general medium of exchange — and its issuers had evidently come to grasp the potential of coin types and legends as vehicles for their own prestige and propaganda. The first to name himself was Commios (Fig. 1, 18) — usually identified with the Gaulish Atrebatic ruler and former ally of Caesar, who escaped to Britain in 50 BC — and he was followed by three other rulers who all use the patronymic 'Commios filius' on their coinage: Tincommios, Eppillus, and Verica. Whether all three were actually brothers can be doubted, although there was certainly some overlap in power, with Tincommius controlling a mint in the south and Eppillus one at Calleva (Silchester), as his coins proclaim (Fig. 1, 19), while Verica eventually succeeded them both (Bean 1991). Early in the first century AD, Eppillus seems to have taken over control of Kent, and transferred his mint there (Fig. 1, 20).

The early types of Tincommius and Eppillus followed traditional designs, but they both subsequently began to strike highly Romanised issues, copying Roman coin types and so well executed that the die-cutters may have been trained in the Roman world (Fig. 1, 21 and 22). All three 'Sons of Commios' were probably among those British rulers who negotiated treaties with the emperor Augustus, becoming in effect Roman client kings, and both Eppillus and Verica occasionally use the latin title REX on their coins (Fig. 1, 19 and 25). Such is the fineness of their silver coinage (over 96%) that Roman coinage imported into Britain, perhaps in the form of imperial subsidies must be regarded as the most likely source of the metal (Northover 1992).

Verica's reign apparently lasted for nearly four decades (Fig. 1, 23–6). However, during the latter part of it, he seems to have lost control of the Calleva mint to a usurper from north of the Thames named Epaticcus, who proceeded to issue his own Southern style gold and silver coinage. This would be fairly rare today but for a series of late hoards and treasure deposits, notably the massive find beneath the Roman temple at Wanborough, Surrey. Epaticcus' coins proclaim him as the brother of Cunobelinus (Fig. 1, 27), the principal ruler in eastern England at this time, and he was briefly succeeded by Cunobelinus's son, Caratacus, who later led British resistance to the invading Romans (Fig. 1, 28). Presumably it was one or other of them who caused Verica's expulsion from his kingdom (Dio Hist. 60.19.1), thus providing Claudius with the pretext he needed for the Roman invasion of Britain in AD 43. With the Conquest, Iron Age coin production came to an abrupt end in Wessex, although a fair amount of the existing silver coinage, especially the debased South-Western types, evidently remained in circulation for up to a generation before it was finally supplanted by official Roman issues.

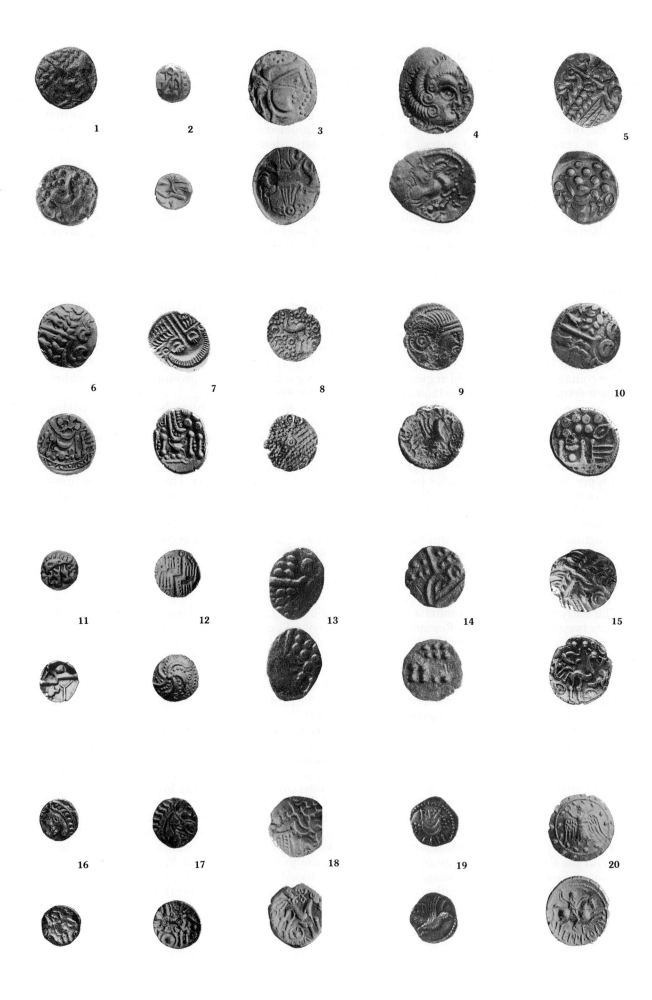

1

2

3

4

5

6

7

8

9

10

11

12

13

14

15

16

17

18

19

20

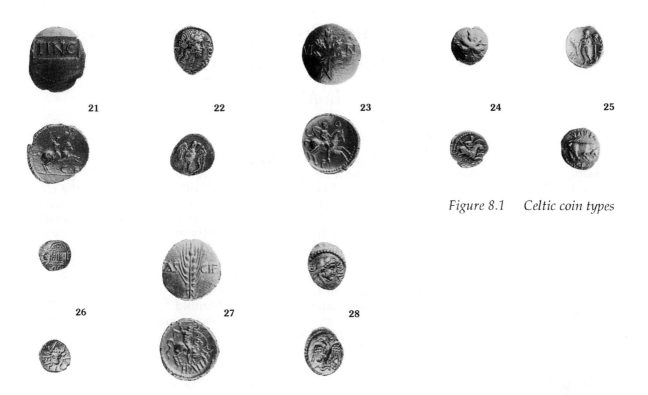

Figure 8.1   Celtic coin types

	Type	Weight (g)	Provenance	Present location	CCI
1	Gallo-Belgic C	4.23	Danebury, Hampshire	MIA	72.0363
2	Gallo-Belgic D	1.40	–	BM	69.0475
3	Baiocasses lyre (billon)	6.75	–	BM	68.0839
4	Coriosolitae cl. II (billon)	6.33	–	–	92.0503
5	British A2	6.37	–	NMW	67.0349
6	British B	6.09	Chute, Wiltshire	BM	68.0792
7	British D	5.08	Compton Down, West Sussex	–	92.0689
8	Hants thin silver	0.48	Hayling Island, Hampshire	–	91.0418
9	Evans G9	2.90	'South-east coast'	–	92.0685
10	early SW (VA 1235)	5.14	Near Chichester	–	92.1091
11	early SW (VA 1242)	–	–	–	–
12	SW starfish	–	–	–	–
13	SW bronze (VA 1290)	–	Ilchester, Somerset	–	84.0232
14	SW cast (VA 1323)	2.04	Holdenhurst, Hampshire	RHM	79.0054
15	British QA	–	–	NMW	86.0078
16	British LZ8	–	–	NMW	86.0079
17	Imit. Dobunnic	1.10	Mildenhall, Wiltshire	BM	69.0049
18	Commius	5.25	Hastings, East Sussex	HM	61.0150
19	Eppillus Rex Calle	–	?Wanborough, Wiltshire	–	86.0146
20	Eppillus Com. F.	5.43	–	BM	69.0226
21	Tincommius C.F.	5.30	Titchfield Down, Hampshire	BM	69.0154
22	Tincommius	–	–	NMW	86.0074
23	Verica Co. F.	5.36	–	BM	69.0276
24	Verica F. Rex	1.03	–	BM	69.0305
25	Verica Rex Commi F.	1.04	Near Chichester	–	93.0272
26	Verica C.F.	0.29	Chichester	CM	72.0058
27	Epaticcus Tasci F.	5.30	Bentworth, Hampshire	BM	69.0323
28	Caratacus	1.23	West Wycombe, Buckinghamshire	–	89.0015

MIA = Museum of the Iron Age, Andover; BM = British Museum; NMW = National Museum of Wales, Cardiff; RHM = Red House Museum, Christchurch; HM = Hastings Museum; CM = Chichester Museum

9. The Organisation of Pottery Production and Distribution in Iron Age Wessex

Elaine L. Morris

In the absence of known production centres and a well-established market system, the production and distribution of Iron Age pottery in Wessex must be approached through the nature of the pottery recovered from settlements. The identification of both the temper and other inclusions in the clay matrix and the geological provenance of those inclusions is a primary aid towards elucidating the zone where specific wares were produced (Peacock 1968; 1969). The amount of pottery produced, generally deduced from the proportion of that ware within an assemblage, and the frequency of the ware on settlements located away from the source zone (Hodder and Orton 1976; Plog 1977) can provide an indication of the intensity of production. This measure may be compared to the modes of production modelled from ethnographic studies (Peacock 1982, 8–11). These two methods can then be combined with a model which assists in the identification of local and non-local pottery in an assemblage by defining the resource exploitation range of raw materials by potters (Arnold 1981; 1985, 32–60). This combination of approaches can be used to identify changes in the procurement and utilisation of pottery from a variety of sources, both local and non-local examples, from the earlier to the later Iron Age.

The Model

The requirements for pottery manufacture are good weather, suitable clays and temper, fuel, and water. The first is seasonal and dependent upon latitude and rainfall; the last two are also requirements for ordinary living and therefore do not constitute the main requirements for pottery production alone. Only suitable clays, and tempering additives if required, represent the primary variables which determine whether pottery making can or cannot take place in an area.

Arnold (1981; 1985, 32–60, figs 2.5, 2.6) has investigated the distances which modern potters in sedentary communites are willing to travel on foot to obtain clays and temper for making their pots. He discovered that amongst the 111 examples where information is available 84% of potters were willing to travel up to 7 km to obtain sutable clays and 97% were willing to travel up to 10 km to obtain tempering additives if those clays did not have the required characteristics for the pots being made. These distances for procuring clays and temper has been designated the maximum ranges of exploitation (Arnold 1985, 50). In fact, most of the potters were obtaining their material from within less than 5 km of their home bases. Arnold points out that this information should be significant to archaeologists since they can examine the clay resources in an area up to 7 km from a settlement where pots have been found and determine, using petrological or other forms of analysis, whether those vessels were likely to have been made from local clays or not. If temper was used, then the local area of resource exploitation should be enlarged to c. 10 km. If comparing two settlement site assemblages, it would be necessary to ensure that the sites were not likely to have shared the same resources, ie. that the sites were at least 20 km apart.

Therefore, if the pottery from a settlement is made from clays and inclusions which are known to exist in the local area, then the vessels could have been produced locally. This would be an example of local production for local consumption, which could be compared to household production (Peacock 1982, 13–7). However, if the vessels were made from clays and inclusions which were not found in this immediately local zone, but were made from resources located at some distance such as 20, 30, 40, or more kilometres away, then we would have identified likely examples of pottery acquired through exchange or trade. This would indicate pottery production for exchange, not simply for local use, had occurred which could be compared to a household industry (Peacock 1982, 17–25). If all of the pottery found at settlements in an area had been produced from a concentrated source or zone located some distance from those settlements, such as from 20–50 km, and the pottery was still handmade and without the use of kilns, then it is quite clear that the household industry level of production had been attained whereby potting was a major source of family income, as opposed to farming (Peacock 1982, 80–9). The large variation in the intensity of production, whether a potter spends a small amount of time producing pots for exchange or trade or the majority of their time is spent in this manner, may necessitate the discussion of an intermediary mode of production between this low technology level of production where human effort is the main differentiating factor and that of technological investment observed with the workshop industry system incorporting re-useable kiln structures, turntables, and permanent workshop structures (Peacock 1982, 25–43).

This is a model of pottery production based solely on resource exploitation and assemblage variation; it does not consider the nature of consumer requirements, population size and density, and transportation systems. The development of such a simple model within which to begin to examine the nature of later prehistoric pottery production is long overdue. It provides the first stage of a long-term research programme into artefact production systems generally (Morris in press).

With this model, it is possible to examine certain aspects about the changing nature of Iron Age pottery production and distribution in Wessex. There is no uniform study of this area but selected areas, wares and sites have been examined in detail, and will provide the basis for this overview.

Early Iron Age (seventh/sixth–fifth century BC)

Several Early Iron Age assemblages from sites in Dorset have been examined using petrological analysis to determine the nature of inclusions found in the pottery fabrics and the sources for the wares. Most of this research has indicated that at this time, pottery production in the western part of Wessex was undoubtedly based on local production for local consumption within a 10 km resolution of resource detail and distribution. For example, at the Rope Lake Hole settlement on the south coast of the Isle of Purbeck, all of the earliest pottery was made from fabrics which were derived from sources located within a 10 km radius to the north (Davies 1987). The range of fabrics included coarsewares tempered with shell, Limestone, or flint, and also a small amount of sandy fabrics made from the Tertiary sands and clays of the Eocene deposits around Wareham–Poole Harbour. The latter source eventually was exploited more fully and developed into a major Late Iron Age industry (see below). Even the finewares were produced from local resources. A similar pattern was the case for the Early Iron Age phases at the settlement sites of Gussage All Saints (Gale 1979) and Hog Cliff Hill, Dorset (Ellison and Williams 1987), and at the hillfort of Maiden Castle (Brown 1991), but with a specific difference. The fabrics in these three assemblages consisted of a variety of clays and tempering additives from a number of local sources, one rare non-local fabric (Gale 1979, group five <0.1%), and also a small quantity of the Wareham–Poole Harbour sandy fabrics, which proved to be outside the local 10 km distance. This suggests that some pottery production for exchange beyond local consumption was taking place at this time.

A slightly different pattern has emerged for the unusual site at Potterne in Wiltshire (Gingell and Lawson 1984; 1985). The majority of the pottery from the midden-like deposit belongs to the Late Bronze Age period, but the upper most levels could have been created during the early part of this Early Iron Age phase. Petrological analysis (Morris 1991a) has demonstrated that at approximately 20% of the coarse and fineware pottery from the final phase of deposition was produced from oolitic Limestone-tempered fabrics; the closest deposits for this very diagnostic inclusion type are located 15 km or more to the north-east. In addition, the remaining pottery consists of only one range of fabric types, fine and coarser local quartz sand-bearing wares. Previously, a whole range of tempering additives, all from local sources, had been utilised. Currently there are no other Early Iron Age sites in Wiltshire for which detailed fabric analysis has been conducted on the pottery.

So here we can see the development of differences between the pottery production systems even for such a small area as two modern counties within western Wessex. The main problem, however, with understanding these developments and differences is the paucity of examples where provenancing work has been conducted on sizeable collections.

Detailed research has been conducted on pottery from Early Iron Age sites in Hampshire. Three sites with pottery of this date from the Andover area of north Hampshire have been examined with comparable results: the hillfort at Danebury (Morris forthcoming a); and the settlements at Old Down Farm (Wandibba 1981; Davies 1982, table 8: fabrics 1–4, ?5, 16, 17) and Lains Farm (Morris 1991b). All three have Early Iron Age assemblages composed of from 40–65% non-local pottery, with the remaining 35–60% probably made from local resources. The range of temper or inclusions in the wares, however, is broad again as for the Dorset sites with oolitic Limestone, fossil shell, flint, chaff, silt, and coarse and fine sand fabrics present. The vessels in the non-local fabrics are made from resources found at least 15 km distance, with most from over 25 km away from this area. In the southern part of Hampshire, excavation of the riverside midden at La Sagesse Convent in Romsey (Green this volume) has produced a sizeable collection of pottery dated to the end of the seventh/early sixth century BC. All of these vessels were probably produced from local resources in the immediate area with the exception of one possible non-local example. So this time we have variation within a single modern county with regard to the nature of pottery production and procurement for this period.

A single assemblage of late seventh century BC date from Berkshire has been examined in some detail, ie. Dunston Park (Mepham and Morris forthcoming). Here, too, as for southern Hampshire, there is a possibility that a small quantity of non-local pottery had been obtained by the inhabitants of this single dwelling farmstead but otherwise the vast majority of vessels could have been made within the local area. In West Sussex during the eighth–seventh century BC, the production of fine pottery for exchange had occurred with a distribution up to 20 km (Hamilton 1980, 203; 1984, 58), alongside local coarseware use. Analysis of all the later prehistoric pottery in Sussex has been conducted recently by Hamilton as a doctoral thesis and this information will soon be available.

One major study is currently examining the full range of red-finished or 'haematite-coated' wares (Middleton 1987), including the furrowed bowls and the scratched-cordoned wares of central southern England (Cunliffe 1984a, 253-4), and also red-finished vessels generally from Dorset to Kent (A. Middleton, pers. comm.). Clear differences have been recognised amongst the types of surface treatments and the sources of these very distinctive fineware vessels which will provide useful data for the study of pottery production during this period.

Middle Iron Age (third–first century BC)

This phase witnessed a gradual change in the production and distribution of pottery in Wessex, and also in the use of selected temper types in several areas which make simple petrological analysis by thin section microscopy an unsuitable technique for revealing resource provenancing except on a broad scale. As for the Early Iron Age however, many sites have been published with no investigation into the nature of pottery production and the procurement of vessels recovered.

In Dorset, Middle Iron Age assemblages such as those from Gussage All Saints, Hengistbury Head, and Maiden Castle contain a significant proportion of Wareham–Poole Harbour products (Gale 1979; Cunliffe and Brown 1987; Brown 1991). Sites in north Hampshire have assemblages dated to this phase which clearly show a change in that the presence of the non-local wares is still as significant as that for the Early Iron Age but that the more common occurrence of saucepan pots heralds an increase in frequency of flint-tempered wares. These, while unprovenanced to source other than the chalklands of central southern England, demonstrate a strong development in both the refinement of temper processing and an apparent uniformity in vessel shape and size. Neither of these general observations has been tested statistically, but such research is potentially rich in information especially if it were to be linked to an investigation into the clay matrices used to produce these very distinctive flint-tempered wares.

It is important to determine whether the sources for these very characteristic Middle Iron Age flint-tempered wares found in Hampshire, Berkshire, and Sussex are locally produced for local use or manufactured for exchange, as has been assumed (Cunliffe and Brown 1987, 305-9), since current interpretations have suggested that the variations found between between areas within Wessex are likely to be part of a process of regionalisation (Sharples 1991b, 260-3). It would be interesting to determine whether the production of these wares had taken place near major hillforts or as in the case of the Wareham–Poole Harbour wares well away from any hillfort and in a marginal agricultural zone (Peacock 1982, 86) but rich in other raw materials (Cox and Hearne this volume). This is a key phase of the Iron Age for understanding the development of social and economic organisation but one which has had only limited investigation through artefact analysis.

Late Iron Age (first century BC to mid-first century AD)

As mentioned above, it is highly probable that potting was developing from a household industry for limited exchange into one for wide regional exchange or into the beginnings of a workshop industry mode of production around Wareham–Poole Harbour in Dorset. It is most likely that there were several potters working possibly in a nucleated workshops format but without a serious investment in kiln structures or turntables and wheels (Peacock 1982), which is suggested by the subtle variation in the fabrics amongst the handmade vessels of this period (Lancley and Morris 1991). It is not until the latest pre-Roman Iron Age that we can first see these production locations with the remnants of possible rudimentary kilns at the East of Corfe River site (Cox and Hearne 1991). The primary data which gives us information about the scale of this production system is in the dominance of the pottery at all types of sites, not only in Dorset but also in Somerset (Alcock 1980; Ellison 1982; Morris 1987b) and west Wiltshire (Wainwright 1968). This level of product saturation has been interpreted as part of the full expression of regionalisation (Sharples 1991b), in this case of the Durotrigian tribal group, and it developed into a major Romano-British industry while still maintaining handmade technology. The appearance and distribution of amphora is discussed in detail elsewhere in this volume (Williams and Peacock).

One of the surprises at this time, however, is how little impact there was from the large and varied types of imported vessels from France, found for example at Hengistbury Head (Brown 1987), on the local indigenous Dorset pottery industry. One of the few attributes which had been adopted is the rough panel with burnished lattice-decoration, a north-western France technique found on graphite coated bowls and jars (Brown 1987, 213, Ill. 153). Many of the other possible innovations, such as wheelthrown technology, rouletted and rilled designs, graphite coating, cordoned decoration, and pedestal bases, were not adopted. This strongly suggests that there was a selection process singling out specific cultural traits for incorporation into the regional identity, not a whole hearted adoption of foreign attributes. This is in complete contrast to other areas, such as Berkshire, where rilling, cordons on squat jars and bowls, and wheelthrown technology were readily adopted.

In both Hampshire and Berkshire, a handmade production system for flint-tempered coarseware pottery appears to have developed from a minor local tradition and arisen around the pre-Roman focus at Silchester (*Calleva Atrebatum*), while various grog-tempered and sandy finer wares were introduced to make wheelthrown cordoned jars and bowls and other rilled vessels, as well as dishes or platters (Manning 1974; Timby 1985). These products are frequently found at settlements in the immediate region within 10 km of Silchester, in association with amphorae and British-made butt beakers (Lobb and Morris in press; Lobb this volume). However, it is not yet possible to determine where the vessels were being made or how they were distributed. Similarly in West Sussex, a clear case for the introduction and permanent adoption of a wheelthrown pottery technology has been presented (Bedwin and Holgate 1985; Hamilton 1985), which is in contrast to East Sussex which fostered a continuation of the Iron Age handmade potting tradition throught the Roman period (Green 1980), a situation which is reminiscent of that in Dorset. Here the handmade Durotrigian Late Iron Age pottery industry developed only in range of products available and in its huge national distribution for the next four centuries of Roman occupation.

This short contribution about pottery has concentrated solely on investigations into the organisation of production and distribution. It has not considered pottery function and use (see Lambrick 1984; Skibo 1992), form and style, or deposition. These topics all merit full discussions in conjuction with other artefact classes such as textile manufacturing equipment, quern production, distribution and use, and both bronze and iron metalworking and deposition.

10. Roman Amphorae in Iron Age Wessex

David Williams and David Peacock

The Wessex region provides evidence for the earliest importation of Mediterranean amphorae by the tribes of Late Iron Age Britain. These large double-handed pottery vessels were made primarily for transportation by sea of such significant agricultural products as wine, olive-oil, olives, salted fish, and the fish-sauces *garum, liquamen, muria,* and *alec* (Fig. 1).

The two common varieties of Dressel 1, the important late Republican amphora, are both present on a number of late Iron Age sites in Wessex. The earlier Dr 1A with its characteristic short triangular rim, dates from shortly before the middle of the second century BC until round about the middle of the first century BC. The larger Dr 1B, with its thick, near vertical, collar rim, seems to have been produced a little earlier than once thought, for a recent find from Burriac, Catalonia, bears a *titulus pictus* which mentions the two Roman consuls who served in 90 BC (Miró 1986). This may take the start of production back to the last years of the second century BC, while it continued to have been made until the last decade of the first century BC. It is clear then that there was a certain degree of overlap in the production of both varieties. *Tituli picti* found on these vessels make it clear that wine was overwhelmingly the main content carried. In recent years there has been some evidence for the production of Dr 1 amphorae in southern France (Laubenheimer 1985) and also northern Spain (Simon Keay, pers. comm.). However, the vast majority of these vessels were made in Italy, more especially in the regions of Campania, Etruria and Latium (Tchernia 1986). Petrological and visual examination of Dr 1 fabrics from all the major find-sites in Wessex points to an Italian origin.

The majority of Dr 1 finds in Wessex generally amount to only a handful of estimated vessels at each find-site (Fitzpatrick 1985) (Fig. 2). The exception is Hengistbury Head in Dorset, a peninsula which forms the southern edge of Christchurch Harbour (Cunliffe, this volume). The site seems to have been an entrepot engaged in a late Iron Age import-export trade with the continent. Indeed, the Hengist- bury Head/Poole Harbour area of Dorset appears to have been the main focal point for the internal distribution of Dressel 1 amphorae into the Wessex region. The nearby Isle of Wight may also have played some part in this trade, since an increasing number of Dr 1 finds have been made there in recent years.

A minimum of 30 vessels of the earlier Dr 1A form have been recovered from Hengistbury Head. This is quite a modest figure when compared to some of the Late Iron Age French sites, where finds of these vessels can run into the thousands (Tchernia 1983). Nevertheless, they represent the largest number of Dr 1A amphorae from a single British site. A few Dr 1A rims have been found north of the Thames, but the distribution of this form seems to be essentially southern British. The small numbers suggests importation from tribes across the Channel in France, where the reported finds of Dr 1

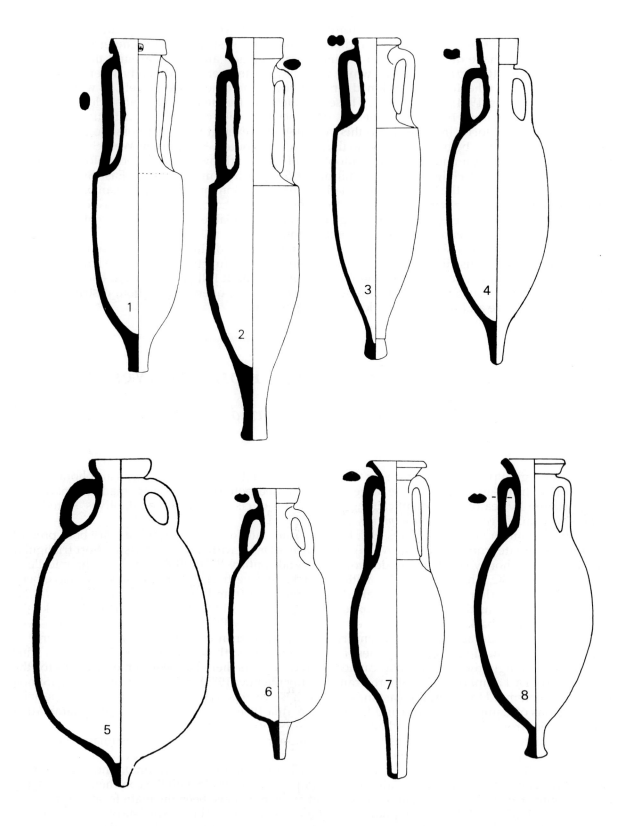

Figure 10.1 *Types of amphora mentioned in the text: 1 = Dressel 1A; 2 = Dr 1B; 3 = Dr 2–4;*
4 = Dr1–Pascual 1; 5 = Early Dr 20 (Oberaden 83); 6 = Haltern 70; 7 = Beltrán I; 8 = Dr 7–11.
Scale approximately 1:10

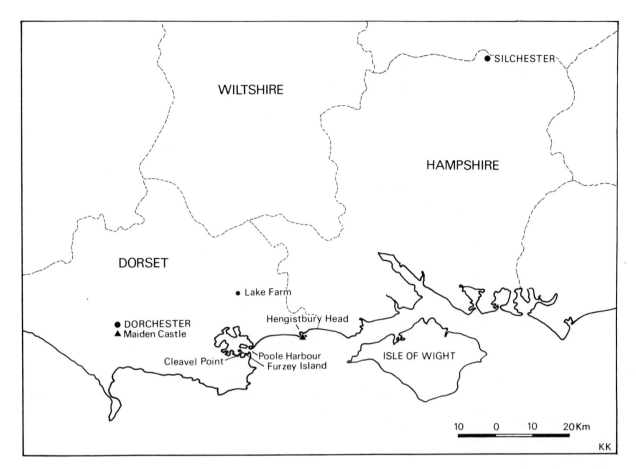

Figure 10.2   Archaeological sites mentioned in the text

amphorae have increased significantly in recent years (Galliou 1984). However, another possibility is that some may have come direct from the Mediterranean by way of the Atlantic coast, as there seems to be evidence of an early Roman wreck of this period off the Hampshire coast (Peacock 1984).

In contrast, while Dr 1B occurs on a growing number of sites in the south, the largest numbers are still to be found north of the Thames and are probably mostly post-Caesarian in date (Peacock 1984; Fitzpatrick 1985). In Wessex, Hengistbury Head has again produced the most finds from a single site, but the estimated number of vessels is only six (Williams 1987a). The lengthened period of overlap with Dr 1A now recognised, opens the possibility that they may have arrived at Hengistbury at the same time.

The direct successor to the Italian Dr 1B amphora was the Dr 2–4, although for some years there again appears to have been a certain amount of overlap in production of both types in Italy. The form of the Dr 2–4 was significantly different to that of the 1B, being modelled instead on the eastern Aegean Koan type, with a small beaded-rim and long bifid handles. When this new amphora was introduced in Italy in about the middle of the first century BC, the opportunity was also taken to slim down the thickness of the body of the vessel, allowing it to carry more wine per body weight than the more bulky Dr 1B, thereby making for a more economical form (Peacock and Williams 1986, 51–3).

In the Wessex region, Italian Dr 2–4 amphorae appear at Silchester in Period 1 deposits dated to *c.* 50–15 BC, and increase in numbers in Period 2, dated just prior to the Roman Conquest. During the latter period, a few sherds of the Catalan amphora form Dr 1–Pascual 1 are also found at the site. However, further south, Dr 2–4 are not found so frequently in pre-Roman contexts. At Hengistbury Head, for example, recent excavations by Barry Cunliffe recovered three times the number of sherds of Dr 1–Pascual 1 than for Dr 2–4 (43:15) (Williams 1987a).

These finds, together with others in the region, suggest that during the last years of the first century BC and early years of the first century AD, more wine was being imported to the southern Wessex area from Catalonia in north-eastern Spain than from Italy. The wine from the latter region had an excellent reputation in Roman times and was only slightly less prized than the better Italian vintages (Pascual 1962; 1977). The amphorae which carried this Catalan wine, called Dr 1–Pascual 1, were modelled on the Italian Dr 1B form, as part of the name implies. Finds of this type of amphora on north-western European sites are generally dated to the Augustan period or slightly later (Peacock and Williams 1986, Class 6). The finds of Dr 1–Pascual 1 in Wessex occur in two distinctive fabrics, both of which contain granitic material: a hard, dark red to reddish-brown fabric with glistening flakes of mica, and a softer, creamy white fabric (Williams 1981). This form was also produced in France on a smaller scale (Laubenheimer 1985), but both the granitic fabrics described above are characteristic of a Catalan origin. The majority of Dr 1–Pascual 1 finds have come from two sites, Hengistbury Head, and more particularly Cleavel Point, Ower, on the shores of Poole Harbour (Williams 1987a; 1987b; 1991). The overall distribution appears to be broadly biased towards central southern England (to the Wessex find-sites listed in Williams 1981 can be added Dorchester, Maiden Castle, and Silchester). Significantly, these Catalan amphorae seem to be arriving in Wessex at a time when Italian wine in Dr 2–4 amphorae was being primarily directed towards the south-eastern parts of Britain (Peacock 1971; Sealey 1985; Williams 1986). The greater numbers of Dr 2–4 at Silchester may possibly relate to the proximity of the River Thames, which might have provided an easy route for contact with the eastern part of the country.

A small number of amphorae from the Roman southern Spanish province of *Baetica* are also present on late Iron Age sites in Wessex. These are represented by sherds from the large globular olive-oil container Oberaden 83/Dr 20, the cylindrical shaped Haltern 70, which may have held *defrutum*, and the longer, ovoid-shaped varieties of fish-sauce amphorae which are probably made up for the most part of Dr 7–11 and Beltran I.

Due to the similarities of fabric between Dr 20 and its first century BC precursor, the Oberaden 83, it is impossible to tell to which form small bodysherds of this fabric belong. However, the majority of this pre-Roman material probably comes from the more developed and slightly later Dr 20, although a number of the earlier Oberaden 83 vessels are certainly present in Wessex. Three separate Oberaden 83 rims have been found at Silchester, and another possible rim at Lake Farm, Wimborne, while a small section of spike from Furzey Island, Poole Harbour, may also belong to this form (Williams 1991). Other Oberaden 83 rims are known from outside the Wessex area at Prae Wood and Gatesbury Track in Hertfordshire (Peacock 1984). All this suggests that Baetican olive-oil may have arrived in Wessex as early as the last decades of the first century BC (Williams and Peacock 1983). One of the main uses for olive-oil would have been for cooking, and its appearance in pre-Roman contexts implies more than a passing acquaintance with the Roman way of life.

Acknowledgements
Many of the amphora identifications mentioned in the text were undertaken as part of the English Heritage Ceramic and Lithic Petrology Programme. Thanks are due to Mike Fulford (Silchester) and Maggie Darling (Lake Farm) for allowing us to mention amphorae finds ahead of publication.

Part II: Settlements and Surveys

11. The Impact of Development on the Iron Age in Hampshire

Michael Hughes

Hampshire is rich in the remains of the pre-Roman Iron Age from impressive hillforts to Late Iron Age oppida and from 'banjo' enclosures to field systems. Whilst some of these are recognisable as earth works, most can only be detected through excavation, field survey, geophysical prospection and from aerial photography.

Because of their national importance, around 70 Iron Age sites in the county are legally protected under the *Ancient Monuments and Archaeological Areas Act*, 1979. English Heritage, on behalf of the Department for the National Heritage, also are undertaking a countrywide survey of archaeological sites and monuments in order to create a significant increase in the number of scheduled ancient monuments. However, the vast majority of Iron Age sites in Hampshire, which are in many cases as important as those legally protected, have no statutory protection and are threatened by development. Because of the uncertainty facing their future preservation, Hampshire County Council has acquired three hillforts, including Danebury, where Professor Barry Cunliffe has recently completed a 20-year excavation programme, Abbotstone Down, and Buckland Rings, as well as leasing Beacon Hill, near Newbury.

Most of Hampshire's Iron Age sites lie in the countryside, although evidence of Iron Age occupation has been revealed as the result of post-war development programmes in both Southampton (Cottrell 1986; Smith 1984) and Winchester (Qualmann *et al.* in press). In the rural areas, the biggest threat to their survival comes mainly from farming and forestry practices. Development schemes such as the spread of urban centres since the last war, the construction of new roads, pipelines, and other public utilities, and mineral extraction have also threatened archaeological sites. In recent years there has been an increase in planning applications to build new golf courses in the countryside, often close to urban centres.

Figure 11.1   Banjo enclosure, presumably of Iron Age date, near Northington, Hampshire

Figure 11.2   Banjo enclosure, presumably of Iron Age date, near Preston Candover, Hampshire

As a response to the serious rate of attrition of the archaeological heritage, the Government recently issued its policy on archaeological remains and how they should be preserved or recorded. Planning Policy Guidance No. 16 *Archaeology and Planning* issued in November 1990, gives advice on how archaeology is to be dealt with under the development plan and development control systems. This significant step to place archaeology more centre stage in the planning process has led to a number of important, yet legally unprotected, sites to be physically preserved or where this has not been possible or feasible, the controlled excavation of their remains.

Consequently in Hampshire, the County Archaeologist and his staff give advice and make recommendations to developers and local planning authorities on mitigation strategies for archaeological sites which may be affected by development proposals. In order to make professional decisions on the impact of a particular development on an important Iron Age site, for example, the County Archaeologist will seek information on the site from the County Sites and Monuments Record, which holds data on all known archaeological sites in Hampshire. This data base has a statutory locus in planning legislation and is given further status in the Planning Policy Guidance No. 16.

Through field survey and the interpretation of air photographs, the map of Iron Age Hampshire is rapidly changing, already an increase in the number of 'banjo' enclosures (Figs 11.1 and 11.2) has been recorded together with the identification of a number of very complex Iron Age and probably multi-period sites to the north and east of Winchester (Barrett *et al.* 1991, fig. 6.6). The sketch-plotting of Late Bronze Age or Iron Age field systems from air photographs has also extended their known distribution to all areas of the Hampshire chalklands.

Important contributions to Iron Age studies in Hampshire and Wessex in recent years that have come from the impact of development have resulted from the series of excavations in advance of various major road construction programmes such as sections of the M3 and the A303 trunk road to the west of Andover. However, as all these rescue excavations took place prior to the issue of the Government's advice and the recent changes in Government inter-departmental policies and funding, English Heritage (and in its previous guise as the Ancient Monuments Division of the Department of the Environment) has grant-aided the entire programme.

Of all the excavation programmes, the work on the M3, firstly under the auspices of the M3 Archaeological Committee and latterly the Trust for Wessex Archaeology, has made the most impact on our understanding of Iron Age rural settlement and associated farmimg practices in Hampshire as well as elsewhere in southern England (Fasham 1985; 1987; Fasham *et. al.* 1989; Fasham this voulme). The recovery and analysis of environmental data from the excavations has also made an important contribution to Iron Age research.

The rescue investigations on the M27 revealed evidence for an unenclosed Iron Age settlement, whilst work in advance of the road construction of the A303 uncovered part of an already known Iron Age settlement as well as providing more useful evidence on the origins and functions of linear earthworks and their relationship to nearby prehistoric fields (Bellamy 1991).

Other Iron Age sites excavated over the past two decades as the result of other forms of development and that have yielded some additional information on Iron Age Hampshire, are those on the growing urban fringes of Basingstoke (see Butterworth, and R. Newman this volume) and Andover (see Davies, and Davies and Wainwright this volume), and those discovered as the result of pipeline construction (Neal 1980) and mineral extraction.

However, since archaeology has been a material consideration in the planning process, more sites including those of the Iron Age have been physically preserved. Two Iron Age enclosures, for example, recognised from air photographs and validated by field survey and geophysical prospection, have been preserved as open spaces within two seperate housing developments on the southern edges of Basingstoke.

It is hoped during the 1990s that through the enhancement of the Sites and Monuments Record from the results of published excavations, field survey, air photographs and evaluations undertaken in advance of the determination of planning applications, that our knowledge of Iron Age Hampshire, and indeed all other periods, will be enriched.

12. Recording the Prehistoric Landscape of Wessex

Mark Corney

The Royal Commission on the Historical Monuments of England (RCHME) was established in 1908 to record the national wealth of upstanding architectural and archaeological monuments. Since this date, the terms and scope of reference have been updated by periodic revisions to the Royal Warrant which governs the activities of RCHME. The latest version, issued in April 1992, states that RCHME are '...to provide for the survey and recording of ancient and historical monuments and constructions connected with, or illustrative of, the contemporary culture, civilisation and conditions of life of the people of England from the earliest times (including ancient and historical monuments and constructions in, or under, the sea bed within the United Kingdom territorial sea adjacent to England) by compiling, maintaining and curating the National Monuments Record of England as the basic national record of the archaeological and historical environment; by identifying, surveying, interpreting and recording all buildings, sites and ancient monuments of archaeological, architectural and historical interest in England...'.

The Field Section of RCHME specialises in detailed topographic survey of upstanding earthwork monuments and their landscapes. This is normally in the form of a hachured plan, (see Fig. 12.1), produced using a combination of a Total Stations survey package and taped measurements. The favoured scale for detail survey of major monuments such as hillforts is 1:1000. Ground survey is frequently complemented by air photographic transcription to enable the broader landscape to be analysed. An example of direct interest is the landscape survey of the broader environs of the hillfort at Danebury (Palmer 1984). In recent years RCHME has also made increased use of geophysical prospection to clarify points of detail. In addition to the surveys produced by the Field Section, RCHME now holds the former Ordnance Survey Archaeology Division records which include surveys of most major earthwork monuments. These were produced at a scale of 1:2500 and used for the depiction of archaeological monuments on all Ordnance Survey maps in the 1:2500–1:50,000 scale range. These plans show the basic form of the monuments (although finer detail was often omitted due to cartographic constraints) and are a valuable basic record upon which more detailed investigations may be founded.

Publication of field investigations has always been a high priority of RCHME. In the past this has taken the form of an inventory, based on the county administrative unit and subdivided by parish.

Figure 12.1   Detail of the hachured survey of Stockton Earthworks, Wiltshire, showing a probable univallate enclosure overlain by settlement remains of Late Iron Age and Romano-British date. Crown Copyright

These volumes include both archaeological and architectural monuments of note. In the last decade this approach has been modified and thematic volumes are now the norm.

RCHME has a long tradition of field survey within Wessex, commencing in the county of Dorset in the mid 1940s. The county was covered in a series of five volumes published between 1952 and 1975 (a full list of RCHME publications relating to Wessex appears in Appendix 12.1). The volumes included a high proportion of surviving probable Iron Age sites and landscapes amounting to 32 hillforts, 82 other settlements and enclosures, 83 field systems, and 62 linear features. Many of these were surveyed in detail and remain an important archive and resource for further study.

The shift in emphasis from inventory publication to thematic investigation is well illustrated by a volume published in 1991 which reassessed the field archaeology of Cranborne Chase and the major linear earthwork of Bokerley Dyke (Bowen 1991). Located in north-east Dorset, close to the boundary with Hampshire and Wiltshire, this study is a major contribution to later prehistoric landscape studies in Wessex. It combines ground and aerial survey with a critical reappraisal of material excavated by General Pitt-Rivers in the late nineteenth century and demonstrates the potential of non-destructive field archaeology within the region. In addition to detailed plans and text, the field evidence (including all features recorded by air photography) is presented on a map produced at a scale of 1:25,000, allowing the later prehistoric landscape to be viewed in relation to topography, drainage and modern features. The use of large area mapping was first employed by RCHME in Wessex to produce a survey of the broader environs of the hillfort of Danebury, Hampshire. Derived entirely form air photographic sources, the resulting publication formed the third volume in the Danebury excavation report series (Palmer 1984) and presented a series of detailed transcriptions of settlement and related features, ranked according to size and morphology, with a short commentary on each theme. The accompanying map in that volume presents the later prehistoric landscape over an area of 4502 km around Danebury hillfort.

More recently, southern Wiltshire has been the subject of a major landscape project with a strong later prehistoric emphasis. Detailed ground survey has greatly enhanced our knowledge of a number of important sites of Iron Age and Romano-British date. At Yarnbury, a major multivallate hillfort on the southern fringe of Salisbury Plain, ground survey identified the remains of a minimum of 120 circular structures and associated pits within the hillfort defences. To the west of Salisbury, on Grovely Ridge, an important series of late Iron age settlements have been investigated in some detail (Corney 1989). One, Stockton Earthworks, a settlement covering 27 hectares, can now be seen to have begun as a univallate hillfort (Fig. 12.1) which is overlain by late Iron Age and Romano-British occupation. Preparation of a volume on southern Wiltshire is well advanced and publication is anticipated during 1996 (RCHME forthcoming). Fieldwork on the adjacent area of Salisbury Plain is still in progress and promises to be a major contribution to prehistoric landscape studies.

In addition to RCHME generated projects, the Field Section also undertakes request work for external organisations. These surveys can be for management purposes, record enhancement or as part of a specific research project. A recent example of the latter was the total resurvey of the multivallate hillfort of Maiden Castle, Dorset, in advance of the 1985-6 investigations (Sharples 1991b). Other areas investigated within Wessex in recent years include the prehistoric and Romano-British relict landscape within Micheldever Wood, Hampshire. This lead to the identification of a further 'banjo' enclosure and elements of field systems unrecognised during earlier surveys (Fasham 1983). The Micheldever Wood survey illustrates the archaeological potential of woodland areas in Wessex and has lead to the creation of an archaeological trail as a public amenity. The survey of the wood was a joint venture between The Forestry Commission, Hampshire County Council, and RCHME.

Other specific request surveys recently undertaken include the hillforts of Cissbury Ring, East Sussex, Badbury Rings, Dorset, Caesar's Camp, Berkshire, and South Cadbury, Somerset. There can be little doubt that non-destructive field survey has a major role to play in the recording and interpretation of later prehistoric landscapes in Wessex. RCHME is the lead national body for such investigations and future work in Wessex will include a detailed study of the Avebury region.

The above text can only provide a brief introduction to RCHME's activities in Wessex. Further information on recent work can be obtained from the Salisbury Office at, RCHME, Rougemont House, Rougemont Close, Salisbury, Wiltshire, SP1 1LY. Unpublished surveys and their supporting archive can be consulted at RCHME, The National Monuments Record Centre, Swindon, Wiltshire (due to open in June 1994).

Appendix 12.1

RCHM(E) publications pertaining to the Iron Age archaeology of Wessex. (Arranged in chronological order of publication)

RCHM(E), 1952, *An Inventory of the Historical Monuments in Dorset. Volume I — West*, HMSO.

RCHM(E), 1970a, *An Inventory of the Historical Monuments in the County of Dorset. Volume II — South-East*, (Parts 1, 2 and 3), HMSO.

RCHM(E), 1970b, *An Inventory of the Historical Monuments in the County of Dorset. Volume III — Central Dorset*, (Parts 1 and 2, HMSO.

RCHM(E), 1972, *An Inventory of the Historical Monuments in the County Of Dorset. Volume IV — North Dorset*, HMSO.

RCHM(E), 1975, *An Inventory of the Historical Monuments in the County Of Dorset. Volume V — East Dorset*, HMSO.

Palmer, R., 1984, *Danebury, an Iron Age hillfort in Hampshire. An aerial photographic interpretation of its environs*, RCHM(E) Supplementary Series 6, HMSO.

Bowen, C., 1990 *The Archaeology of Bokerley Dyke*, RCHM(E).

Corney, M., 1990 'The Marleycombe Hill Area', in Rahtz, P., 'Bower Chalke 1959: excavations at Great Ditch Banks and Middle Chase Ditch', *Wiltshire Archaeological Magazine* 83, 1–49.

RCHM(E), forthcoming, *A Wessex Landscape I: The Field Archaeology of South Wiltshire*.

13. The Danebury Environs Project

Barry Cunliffe

At the beginning of the Danebury project a programme of fieldwork was initiated to study the 'Danebury Region' — defined as an area of Chalk downland some 20 by 25 km stretching from west of the river Bourne to east of the Test and from the tertiary rocks of the Dean Hill anticline in the south to the high clay-covered Chalk downs north of Andover (Fig. 13.1). The initial stage of this survey, bringing together the entire array of air photographic evidence then available, was published as Volume 3 of the Danebury reports by the Royal Commission on Historic Monuments (England) (Palmer 1984). The volume provided the essential background upon which the Danebury Environs Project was designed.

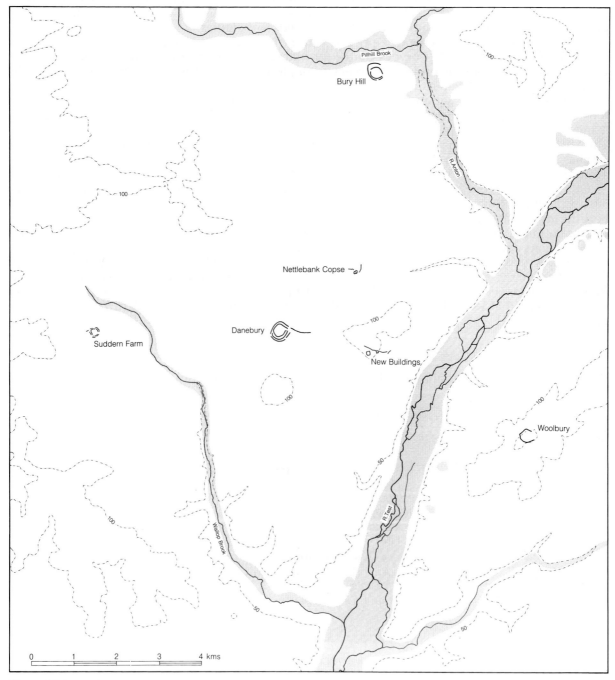

Figure 13.1   The Danebury Environs Project, sites examined to 1993

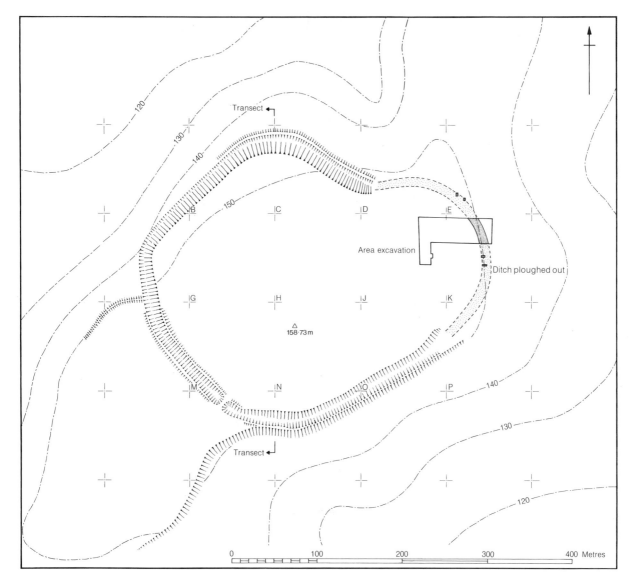

Figure 13.2   Woolbury hillfort

The Danebury Environs Project began in 1989 and is scheduled to last for seven years, the last fieldwork season taking place in 1995. The principal aim of the project is to study the changing social and economic systems within the Danebury region in the period from the end of the Bronze Age to the beginning of the Roman occupation and to consider the most appropriate strategies for selecting certain elements of the historic landscape for long-term preservation. Each season a single site is chosen for examination according to a precisely designed research strategy.

In 1989 excavation focused on the hillfort of Woolbury, 6 km south-east of Danebury, to test the nature and duration of the occupation of Danebury's nearest neighbour and to examine the relationship of the developing hillfort to a series of linear boundaries defining areas of coaxial fields. As a result of the work it was possible to demonstrate that the ordered partition of the landscape in this region took place in the Mid–Late Bronze Age. The hillfort (Fig. 13.2), which occupied a focal point in the organised landscape, was not built until the fifth century BC. Unlike Danebury it failed to develop as a major central place although a low level of use continued associated with the farming of the adjacent arable.

In 1990 the hillfort of Bury Hill, 7 km north of Danebury, was sampled, again with the intention of defining its status in relation to Danebury. Here the earliest phase of hillfort building (Bury Hill 1) probably pre-dated the construction of Danebury but there was no evidence of internal occupation until the site was totally redefended (Bury Hill 2) in *c.* 100 BC at the very end of the main Danebury sequence (Fig. 13.3). The evidence of contemporary use suggests that the economic base differed noticeably from that of Danebury and surprisingly large quantities of horse gear may indicate specialist, high-status, activity. Taken together the evidence from the three hillforts, and that from

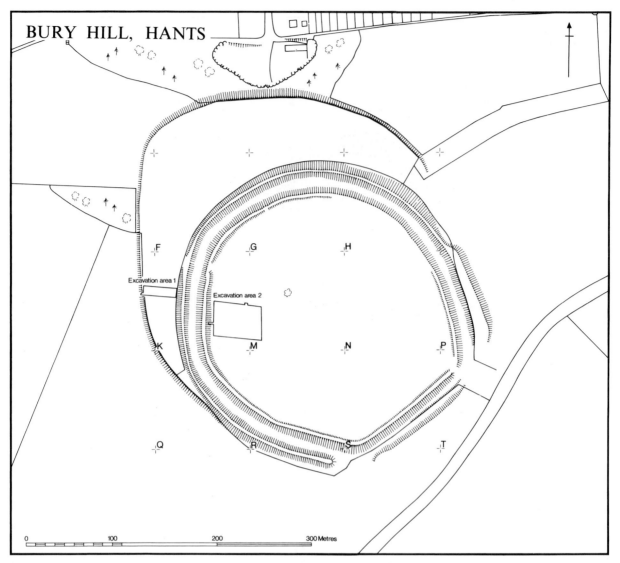

BURY HILL, HANTS

Excavation area 1

Excavation area 2

F   G   H
K   M   N   P
Q   R   S   T

0   100   200   300 Metres

Figure 13.3   Bury Hill hillfort

others in the region, is enabling a coherent picture to be constructed showing, for the first time, something of the complexity of the situation at this level in the settlement hierarchy.

In 1991 attention turned to a large double-ditched enclosure at Suddern Farm 4 km west of Danebury. Enclosures of this kind, though rare, occur throughout Wessex, raising questions of their status and function in relation to the larger hillforts and the smaller farmsteads. Suddern Farm proved to be long-lived, acquiring its massive enclosure ditches (Fig. 13.4) only in the middle of the first century BC by which time the neighbouring hillforts had been largely abandoned. Pottery suggests that the site was of high status.

In 1992 a complex of rectangular enclosures, associated with the linear earthwork running from Danebury, was examined at New Buildings (Fig. 13.5). The earliest enclosure, served by a road and linked by it to an area of coaxial fields, proved to be of Mid–Late Bronze Age date. Only later was the linear ditch system laid out to incorporate the enclosure. Occupation continued into the sixth century after which the site was totally abandoned.

Finally in 1993 a banjo enclosure at Nettlebank Copse was examined – the first such enclosure to be totally excavated (Fig. 13.6). Two distinct phases were defined: a farmstead, enclosed by a palisade, dating to the fifth–fourth century BC and the later banjo which was in use throughout the first century BC and into the first century AD. The functions of the two sites differed markedly but details must await the assessment of the finds.

Two more excavations are planned to complete the programme. The data recovered under the control of strict sampling procedures is being processed in a manner which allows direct quantified comparisons to be made between sites. When complete, the Danebury Environs Project will provide a detailed insight into the development of an area of the first millennium Wessex landscape.

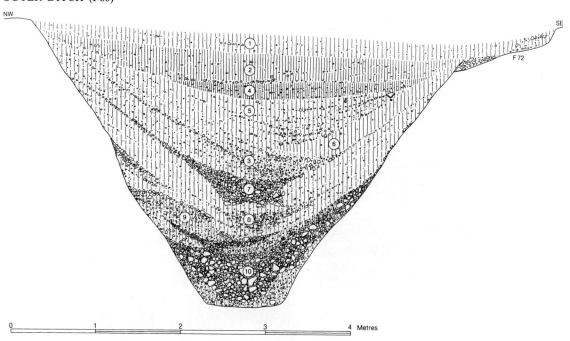

SUDDERN FARM 1991
OUTER DITCH (F66)

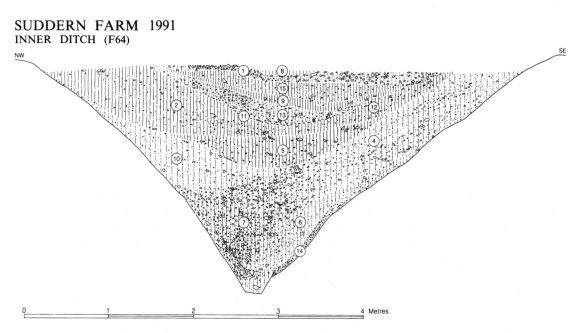

SUDDERN FARM 1991
INNER DITCH (F64)

Figure 13.4   Suddern Farm, sections across the enclosure ditches

Figure 13.5   New Buildings, linear ditch and pit alignment looking west with Danebury in the background, 1992

Figure 13.6   Nettlebank Copse under excavation in 1993

14. Potterne

Andrew J. Lawson

The rich later prehistoric site of Potterne lies on the north-west facing shoulder of an Upper Greensand spur at 95 m OD. The site owes its rediscovery in 1982 to its location partly beneath the modern cemetery in Brownleaze Lane on the edge of the village, the centre of which is some 3 km south of Devizes in Wiltshire. Pottery, now conventionally recognised as Early Iron Age in date, was first collected from the area in 1894 when the fields, then called Blackberry, served as allotments. This collection housed in Devizes Museum was enlarged by further finds gathered on at least six further occasions since the cemetery was established in the 1920s. Attention was focused on the site when, in July 1982, a gravedigger reported the discovery of a Late Bronze Age gold torc of a previously unparalleled type (Taylor 1984). Subsequently, a trench 8 m by 1. 5 m was opened by Chris Gingell in an attempt to establish the context of the bracelet. Here, as in the sides of newly-dug graves, stratigraphy as deep as 2.08 m was recorded. The observed layers were prodigious in well-preserved pottery and animal bone in a hard, mineralised state.

Because planning permission had been sought for the extension of the cemetery, further seasons of excavation were planned to evaluate the site. In 1983 two 5 m square trenches were placed 50 m east of the original sondage at the planned limit of the cemetery extension. These trenches encountered the same rich form of deposit apparently overlying postholes and other structural features. An extension of one trench demonstrated that the archaeological deposits ran beneath a well-formed lynchet (initiated by Romano-British farming) south of the cemetery (Gingell and Lawson 1984).

In the following year an area 20 m by 10 m, including the 1983 trenches, was excavated, whilst a series of test pits beyond the cemetery evaluated the nature of the deposits further afield. Simultaneously, a gridded auger survey was conducted to establish the extent of the deposit which was shown to cover at least 3.5 hectares and to have altered the original profile of the hillside (Fig. 14.1). Subsequent observations to the north and metal detector finds near Rangebourne Mill (Turnbull 1983) suggest that contemporary prehistoric activity was not restricted to the area investigated by excavation and augering.

During the 1983 season it proved difficult to observe stratigraphy in the homogeneous dark deposit, yet changes through depth were observed in the finds. Similarly, articulated vertebrae and later, spreads of sherds, were to imply that wholesale mixing of the deposit had not occurred. Consequently, the 1984 excavations employed a rigid method of excavation in 1m squares with spits at regular 0.10 m intervals, thus creating an artificial control against which changes in lithology or finds could be gauged. At the same time different methods of excavation (wet sieving 2.6%, trowelling 10%, picking) were used to establish the most efficient method. At the base of the principal trench an array of post-holes was discovered (Gingell and Lawson, 1985). However, the positions of some packing stones and of hearths suggest that some postholes may have been cut from a higher level but the nature of the matrix and similar fill of the postholes made it impossible to gauge from what level they were dug. Nonetheless, a clearly zoned diagonal spatial pattern emerged. At the south end of the trench a terrace surmounted by a fence-line, probably replaced on more than one occasion and propped up with struts resting against a line of large Greensand blocks, defined an area of post-built structures and firing activities. The central zone was devoid of features and perhaps served as a road whose use and run-off had caused erosion of the bedrock whilst the northern zone also contained post-built structures (Fig. 14.2).

Six radiocarbon analyses have been undertaken which show a consistent pattern in calibrated dates:

- the average mean for the lowest level is in the sixteenth century BC;
- the average mean for the mid-level lies in the ninth century BC; and,
- the average mean for the upper level is in the eighth century BC.

These are supported by a single archaeomagnetic date.

Micromorphological examination of the deposit matrix has shown that this is almost exclusively layered graminae ash residue, often with amorphous coprolitic matter and coarse phytoliths with varying amounts of charcoal, calcite ash, and clay. Towards the top of the deposit there is evidence of agricultural reworking and the addition of some local soil. The presence of coprolitic material suggest that cess was responsible for the rapid mineralisation of the objects within the accumulating deposit. Hence, it has been possible to compare mineralised weed seeds and cereals with carbonised examples. Barley and wheat appear to be of equal importance. Spelt wheat was present throughout in the same proportion as emmer, bread wheat being a minor component. Waste in the form of chaff and weeds of cultivated land were also represented. To date 134,000 animal bones have been recovered, largely representing domesticates, with cattle predominating in the earliest levels and sheep in the latest. Deer were represented by bones and antler, the latter worked for artefacts.

Approximately 100,000 sherds (1 tonne) of pottery were recovered. In the stratigraphically earliest assemblage ovoid, barrel-shaped, hook-rim and straight-sided jars in flint and fossil shell fabrics conventionally dated between the eleventh and ninth centuries BC, predominate. Through time sandy fabrics become more common as do furrowed vessels and carinated bowls and later, biconical and long-necked types. Red-finished surfaces, incised decoration and white infill appear in the median deposits while the latest deposits include narrow-mouthed, round-bodied jars and the increasing use of incised motifs usually dated to the eighth or seventh centuries BC (Morris 1991a).

Other artefacts recovered from the site include 163 bronze fragments; pieces of lead; iron objects (most of which are probably not prehistoric); non-ferrous metalworking debris; worked flint; 88 shale objects including bracelets, beads, pendants and vessels; worked stone; amber and glass beads; 247 worked bone and antler objects; and other miscellaneous finds.

Computer analysis of the ceramic assemblage demonstrates that the deposit at Potterne accumulated without substantial break or disturbance, only the uppermost part being reworked by Romano-British and later ploughing. Physical analysis of the deposit suggests that it comprises burnt straw and dung with redeposited artefacts. Although less than 1% of the site has been investigated it can be suggested that initial settlement evidence was buried by dumped material. This in turn was later resettled as the location of activities intermittently shifted from one part of the site to another.

By modern standards it would seem unacceptable practice to live or behave as licensed totters on what may have appeared rather like a corporation rubbish tip. The unprecedented nature of the Potterne site means that it and similar sites have not been used to characterise social organisation in the landscape of the early first millennium BC. The communal activities which lead to prodigious quantities of artefacts being procured, discarded, collected, and dumped find no similar expression in British prehistory. Throughout the first millennium the evidence of communal activity is clear in the construction of defended, often hilltop, sites. Before the need for ostentatious hillforts, energy appears to have been expended and social cohesion achieved in a different form, the resultant evidence

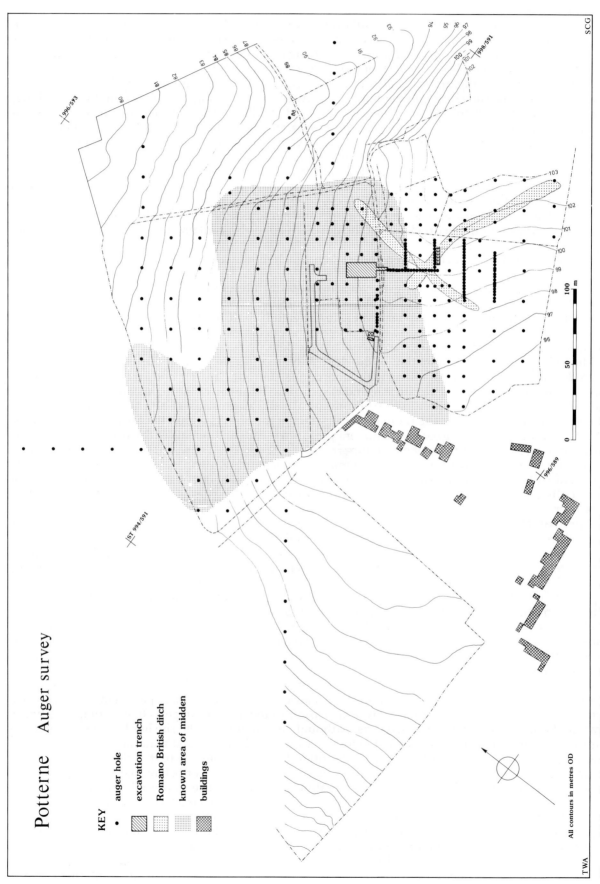

Figure 14.1   Potterne, Wiltshire, the extent of archaeological deposits suggested from augering

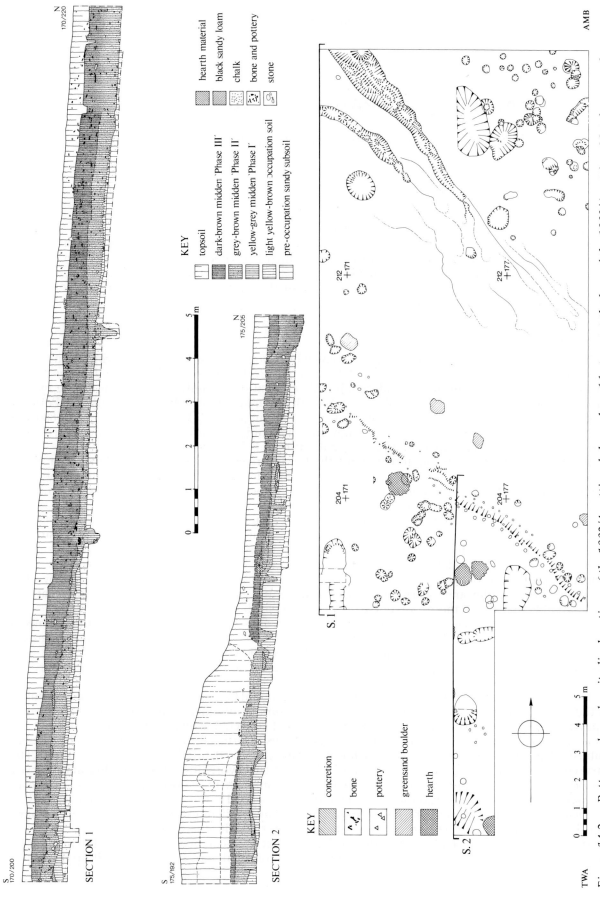

Figure 14.2   Potterne, above: longitudinal sections of the 1983/4 cutting; below: plan of features at the base of the 1983/4 cutting. Not drawn to the same scale

being more difficult to locate in the modern landscape. Yet a variety of sites (All Cannings Cross, East Chisenbury, Bishops Cannings, etc.) can be shown to exhibit similar characteristics. It appears that at such sites the refuse of stabling and human activities was not spread on neighbouring agricultural land. Whether mundane stabling and domestic refuse disposal, successive settlement (as at Choisy-au-Bac, Oise; Talon 1987), ceremonial feasting or sacrifice as in the continental *Brandopferplätzen* was the cause of such sites may become apparent as additional sites are examined in the future.

15. East Chisenbury Midden Complex

Graham Brown, David Field, and David McOmish

Introduction

The midden complex at East Chisenbury was discovered by the Royal Commission on the Historical Monuments of England and the Salisbury Plain Training Area Conservation Group. The midden lies within the Salisbury Plain Military Training Area which is owned by the Ministry of Defence and covers 93,000 acres. This is the largest surviving piece of natural Chalk downland in western Europe and represents 41% of Britain's remaining area of Chalk downland, and as such it contains some of its finest surviving archaeological landscapes.

Survey

Fieldwork revealed that the complex was dominated by a mound of truly enormous proportions which was part of a comprehensive sequence of landscape development which included an enclosure partially stratified beneath the mound. Small scale excavations recently undertaken on the mound have shown the site to have cultural affinities with the midden complexes excavated at Potterne (Gingell and Lawson 1985) and All Cannings Cross (Cunnington 1923), with a date range of 800–600 BC. East Chisenbury stands on its own though, since the midden survives as a prominent earthwork and as such it is the first of its kind recorded in a southern British context (Fig 15.1).

East Chisenbury sits at the western end of a chalk spur projecting into the valley of the River Avon; a location which commands extensive views in all directions and forms a focal point in the local topography. The chalk spur is defined to the north by a steep but now dry, valley. To the south, the ground falls gently away from the site.

The mound is clearly defined as a circular spread of material covering an area of between 4–5 ha. The natural break of slope is a further 100 m to the north of this and ground modelling profiles suggest that the midden did extend to the edge of this natural division. A multi-phase field system has encroached upon the midden structure, particularly at its present northern extreme, where a large lynchet of prehistoric date has truncated the deposit. In addition, medieval ridge and furrow overlies the prehistoric complex and, bearing in mind that the entire area was under plough until recently, it is remarkable that any of this group of earthworks survive above ground.

An auger survey across the surveyed area at East Chisenbury indicated that the mound attained a depth which is, in places, in excess of 2 m. This implies that even after the varied and extensive agricultural episodes on the spur top, approximately 65,000 cubic metres of undisturbed material survive. This is a staggering quantity and one can only guess at the volume of the mound before the onset of the various destructive agencies.

In a sense this recent work is a rediscovery. Finds of material together with other documents housed in the British Museum collections make it clear that a number of individuals stationed at the nearby Upavon Aerodrome during the Second World War had collected artefacts from the vicinity of the mound, whose presence went unrecognised. Indeed, Leslie Grinsell in his archaeological gazetteer published in the *Victoria County History* for Wiltshire (1957, 69) briefly detailed these finds. The surviving earthwork component was not noted by later surveyors, including the Ordnance Survey whose task it was to record surviving archaeological monuments in the British Isles. This is made all the more puzzling since it is clear the midden mound is associated to the east with a massive embanked enclosure, *c*. 4 hectares in area, which was first mentioned by the distinguished antiquarian Sir Richard Colt-Hoare during the earlier part of the nineteenth century (Colt-Hoare 1810).

With hindsight it is no real surprise that such a long list of researchers failed to see the mound. Its excessive monumentality and extent make it barely distinguishable from a natural hilltop feature — it looks like a natural undisturbed hilltop (Fig. 15.2).

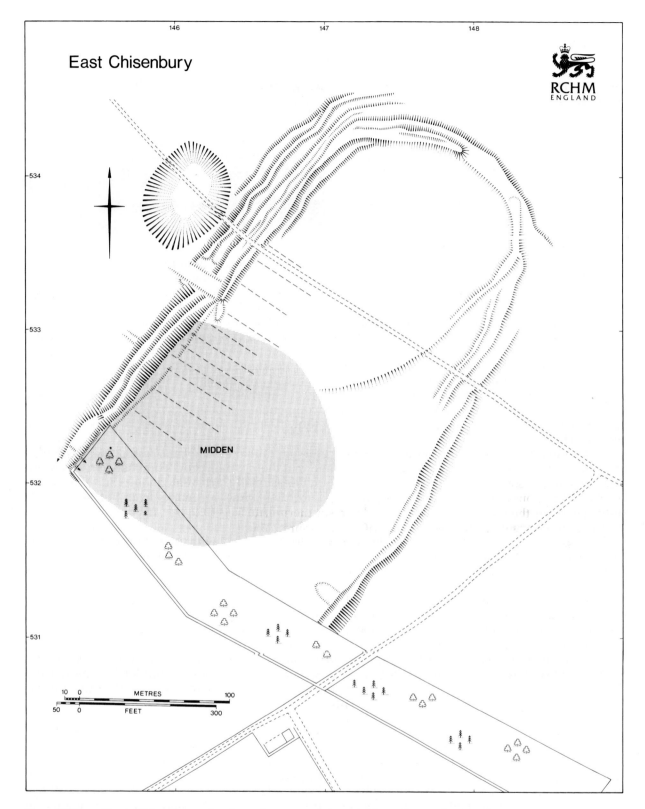

Figure 15.1   East Chisenbury, hachured survey of the midden. Crown Copyright

Excavations

The following summary of the excavations on the mound are based on an examination of only *c.* 0.05%
of the total mound area, so sweeping conclusions should be treated with caution. Funding was absent,
and initially unrequested; the costs of excavation met by the individual excavators involved. Since
excavation revealed the potential of the site, a number of specialists have expressed an interest in
carrying out research relating to East Chisenbury, primarily on environmental and geomorphological

Figure 15.2   East Chisenbury, Wiltshire, the midden viewed from the north

analysis. The results of this work are at present unknown and will, through financial necessity, remain so for the time being.

The initial results of the excavation are still being assessed but a brief summary of the main findings can be made. Primarily, it was noted that the mound was composed of a complex and diverse interweave of non-homogeneous deposits. These varied greatly in terms of colour, texture, and thickness and contained an enormous and as yet unquantified artefactual assemblage. It is clear that it is dominated by a large ceramic component with early All Cannings Cross affinities. A high proportion of the pottery recovered consists of decorated fine and coarsewares both employing a wide range of coloured, applied slips. Brown, black and red predominate, with 'haematite' additives present in smaller numbers. The most distinctive forms identified are short necked furrowed bowls. It is apparent that a wide range of decorative motifs have been used, the most commonly observed of which are finger tip or finger pinched impressions noted around the vessel rim or shoulder. Other linear tooled and incised geometric patterns are also employed. It is especially noteworthy that undecorated sherds are rare. The large size, and unabraded condition of the sherds suggests that this pottery has been spared the worst ravages of the post-depositional process and that an explanation should be sought for the excellent survival. In addition, sherd size and fabric analysis will be a useful adjunct to the chronological subdivisions at present known. Other components of the artefactual assemblage include spindle whorls, worked bone and stone, worked flint, part of a shale bracelet, a glass bead, and metalwork.

The midden contains a large, and also well preserved, faunal assemblage. Initial analysis of this suggests that sheep are present in large numbers and that there is a disproportionately large percentage of neonatal or foetal lambs within this category. Occasionally, articulated joints survive though individual segments are more commonly found, some displaying cut marks from butchery. Large numbers of coprolites were recovered which are at present unclassified, but are thought to include dog, pig, and human specimens.

Interestingly, a fragment of human skull was also uncovered with its exterior surface facing upwards. This had apparently been deliberately placed within the midden and grouped around it were a number of sherds of pottery from the same vessel and a fragment of sarsen stone. It was clear that this was a carefully placed deposit.

At the base of the midden deposit two metal objects were found. These were significant since their stratigraphic position allowed the initiation of the midden build-up to be closely dated. These include the broken blade end of a socketed axe of local Sompting type (Coombs 1979), and a tanged chisel of a type which is found almost exclusively in Llyn Fawr contexts in the British Isles.

Remains of a pre-midden settlement were also found. Two hearths and a series of post- and stake-holes were cut into the natural ground surface and separated from the midden by a partial and undeveloped turf-line. It is possible though that the midden began accumulating at the same time as this settlement was being used or occupied.

Discussion

The deposit and cultural material summarised here and defined as a midden is clearly more complex than the term intimates. Why does so much settlement debris survive at East Chisenbury and, importantly, by what processes was it formed? The enormous scale of the deposits stand in contrast to those from other contemporary sites. Thus the site at East Chisenbury stands out as being unusual and different, and clearly the result of practices which had meaning beyond the purely functional.

The highly demarcated nature of the midden deposit clearly shows that there is a structural element to it. The excavations began on the assumption that the midden would resemble those excavated elsewhere and present a reasonably homogeneous deposit. This was misguided, since within the recorded stratigraphy there are a series of features including apparently prepared and compacted chalk floors or platforms which were noticeably clean of any artefactual material. The complexity of the deposit make it very difficult without full analysis to make any judgement about the formation of the midden. Nonetheless, it is tempting to see each layer, each horizon as an event layer or episode. The survival of the mound is a complex interaction of anthropogenic activities allied to geomorphological processes. It is possible to postulate for instance that the deposition of cultural material, which includes both organic and inorganic matter, would have been accompanied by soil deliberately deposited with this material. We must also consider the chronological and spatial nature of deposition. Whether or not there were areas which were used more often than others remains unclear.

East Chisenbury is a site which defies categorisation in the present state of knowledge. It is clear that certain activities were repeatedly carried out here over a period of time which led to the build up of the mound. Much of the cultural residue surviving concerns the preparation, storage and consumption of food, and at East Chisenbury we are witnessing these activities on a massive scale. The large artefactual assemblage is the by-product of feasting. This is not waste material since there are undoubtedly ritual aspects to this behaviour (Barrett 1989); it is within this context that the midden complex at East Chisenbury should be placed.

16. Early Iron Age Stream Deposits at La Sagesse, Romsey, Hampshire

F.J. Green

An ancient water channel containing a high density of well preserved animal bone and ceramic evidence of Early Iron Age date was located in a former stream bed on the La Sagesse Convent site in Romsey. The excavation was confined to the foundation trenches for a proposed new presbytery. The site was sampled for molluscan evidence. No charred or waterlogged plant evidence was located, though human remains were recovered.

The excavation was located adjacent to a canalised or artificial water course just over 100 m south of Romsey Abbey (Fig. 16.1). The site is located on the western edge of the 'ey', or island, between the existing braided channels of the River Test, around which the modern settlement of Romsey has developed. The site had been subjected to deliberate terracing in the post-medieval period as part of the Abbey mill complex. The terracing had removed all post-Roman archaeological deposits and was cut by surviving foundations for former mill buildings that had been demolished in the late nineteenth century.

Removal of the top soil on this site revealed immediately a poorly cemented tufaceous deposit containing abundant ceramic and animal bone evidence. Such tufaceous deposits filling former stream beds have been widely recorded in the Romsey area from the early work in the nineteenth century by Charles Lyell onwards. Figure 16.2 demonstrates that the poorly cemented tufaceous deposit clearly filled a palaeo-channel, contexts 5–31. The artefacts were all contained within the various tufaceous deposits. Many of the artefacts were found to straddle the interfaces between layers, and much of the material was found contained within small silty lenses, which may represent natural drag lines within the stream bed. All the finds were themselves coated in a thick calcareous concretion. Whilst the deposits were excavated archaeologically, these types of deposits do present peculiar difficulties for those engaged in their excavation (Needham 1991, 58).

The only clear structural evidence from this site consisted of three posts or large driven stakes. One of these was clearly associated with later Roman activity, the others were contemporary to the artefact assemblage and the depositional processes. This evidence has been interpreted as forming part of a plank walk way that may well have connected the various small islands in this part of the flood plain of the River Test. Only further work might establish the veracity of this suggestion.

Apart from ceramics and human and animal bone, the archaeological finds also included fired clay loomweights (Rees forthcoming) and fictile material associated with iron smelting. A thermoluminescent date is awaited on a possible tuyère recovered from the lower levels of the stream channel.

The pottery has been subject to detailed analysis by Elaine Morris (Morris forthcoming b). The pottery group is considered unique, not least because of the very large mean sherd size (19.4 g). The analysis of the ceramic fabrics indicates that the pottery could have been made locally from clays originating in the Hampshire basin deposits within 3–6 km of the site, mostly from the Bracklesham Beds, and 11 distinct fabrics have been identified. The ceramics were divided into fine and coarse wares based on subtle variations in tempering and fabric. The quality of the material from this site has allowed the opportunity to examine in some detail the definition of early iron age pottery vessel forms. One new class of vessel form, 'the miniature' was recorded with a capacity of less than 100 cc. Other forms included medium to large capacity bowls of bi-partite and tri-partite form, some with both internal and external burnishing and others only internally burnished. The vessels display different types of shoulder and carination and forms with 'nostril' lugs also occur.

Only one large geometric decorated fineware jar of situlate form, which is externally burnished, was recovered from this site. Whereas a wide range of medium to large capacity closed forms were recorded, consisting of coarse ware jars decorated with finger tip, finger nail or multiple slash motives on exterior rim edges. A typical range of small shouldered carinated round bodied bowls decorated with furrows or incised or stabbed, geometric designs was also recovered.

The vessels were predominantly manufactured using coil techniques. A number of the vessels showed 'fire-clouding' and spalling. A great variety of decorative designs and motifs have been recorded from this collection. The range of designs are strikingly individual; no two vessels have identical techniques employed, and both undecorated fine and coarse wares exist. Some 17 vessels in this assemblage were identified as having a red finish involving the application of oxide by one of a number of means and including the use of burnishing, particularly for bowls and some jars.

The detailed analysis of the ceramics from this site also indicates that the material is essentially *in situ* with little evidence of vertical or lateral movement.

It is clear that this assemblage belongs to the Early Iron Age, seventh to the early sixth centuries BC. The range of forms and some of the fabrics are similar to other sites in the Hampshire and Dorset area, but the assemblage is also part of the decorated phase of the wider Late Bronze Age tradition of Wessex and the Thames Valley regions of southern England.

As with the ceramic evidence the preservation of the animal bones was excellent, with most bones well preserved and a very low rate of unidentified fragments along with a low (less than 10%) rate for loose teeth (Bourdillon forthcoming). Some of the bones had been lightly gnawed by dogs. This suggests that the bones were deposited relatively quickly and were not subject to heavy chewing because they had been left around for a long time.

The bones included evidence of red deer, roe deer, and the exploitation of wild pig. However, bones of domestic cattle dominated the assemblage, horse being well represented, with less sheep/goat evidence than has been found on many Iron Age sites in Wessex and rather more pig. The pattern of butchery and the mixed nature of the bone assemblages suggests domestic food waste. The assemblage did produce evidence of articulated remains, a cattle front leg, parts of two or three dogs, and

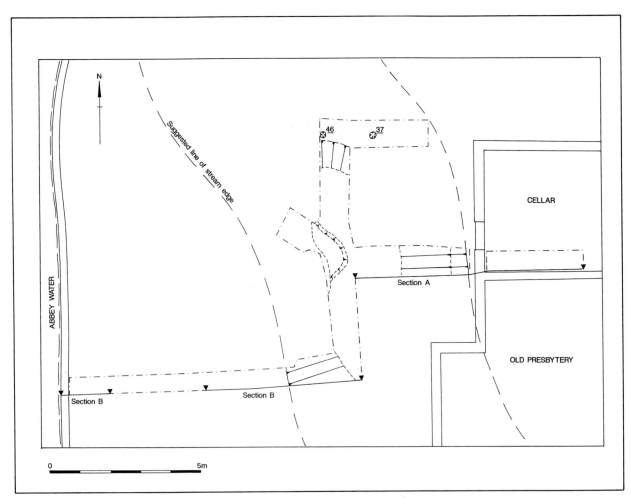

Figure 16.1   La Sagesse Convent, Romsey, Hampshire, plan of excavated features

considerable remains of a cormorant skeleton. A range of butchery evidence has been recorded indicative of food waste. The bones were generally discarded without being opened to extract their marrow.

The balance of species represented, for example cattle compared with horse, is comparable to evidence from other local Iron Age sites, with some evidence for sheep and very slight evidence for goat. Most significantly is the ratio between pig: sheep/goat which is lower than sites such as Danebury. This may reflect the location of the site in the valley floor rather than up on the chalk downland and the evidence is much more directly comparable to that from the Late Bronze Age riverside site of Runnymede Bridge (Done 1980).

Overall the animal bone evidence is suggestive of domestic food waste with some exploitation of wild species, possibly resulting from the site's valley floor location. Further bone assemblages from these types of site context are clearly required before any significant patterns of animal exploitation can be established.

Environmental data was largely confined to the taking of a column, with six samples, for Mollusca, augmented by a single spot sample (Allen forthcoming). Most of the shells recovered were encased in calcium concretion and their extraction proved problematic. The evidence suggests that the stream started with a fast flowing environment with well oxygenated water, and that much of the molluscan evidence may well have been washed in from upstream.

It is suggested from the molluscan analysis that the next phase, from which most of the ceramic evidence was recovered, consisted of an open flowing channel with weedy eutrophic conditions and possibly clearer, less vegetated stony substrates in the centre of the stream or possibly further upstream. Terrestrial species were also recovered indicative of local stream side environments and some rare species normally associated with woodland habitats, screes and stone walls. Other species are indicative of an open, drier, environment, possibly grassland existed close to the stream to the east.

The top of the molluscan sequence most likely indicates a slower flowing calcareous stream with a reduction in stream vegetation and overall shallower water, consistent with infilling of the stream channel.

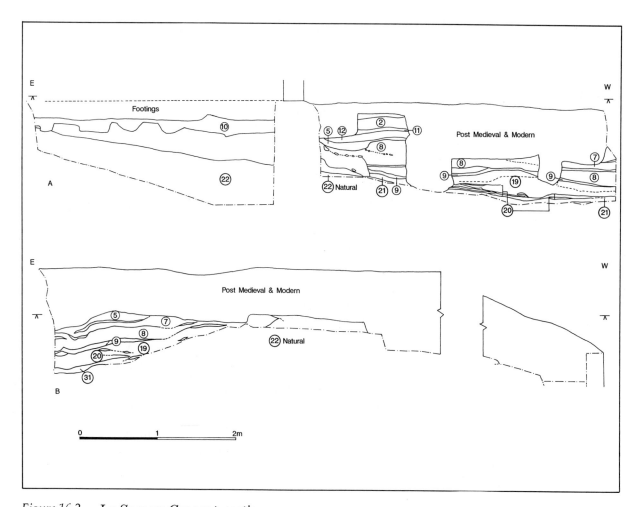

Figure 16.2   La Sagesse Convent, sections

The available evidence suggests that the archaeological materials were deposited during a relatively short space of time, perhaps no more than 20 years and certainly less than 100 years. The evidence of possibly industrial activity, consisting of iron smelting slag and possible bronzeworking (the tuyère fragment), adds significantly to our distribution of such production sites in Wessex. Bone was clearly worked on the site as evidenced from antler fragments, and the presence of loomweights suggest that weaving was a significant activity on the adjacent settlement site.

The site is located adjacent to an area of highly fertile brickearth soils where both autumn and spring sown crops could have been cultivated. The location is ideal for the exploitation of a wider range of environments and raw materials than would be available on the chalk downland.

This material from Romsey fills a very important gap in our knowledge about Early Iron Age settlement and economy in the lower Test Valley. The parallels with the lower Thames Valley are clear. The information is perhaps what should be expected from the arguments of Barrett and Bradley (1980, 181). It may be significant that since the excavation of this site a number of others have been found in the area, the evidence from which forms the basis of a separate publication (Rees in press b). The evidence from the Late Bronze Age through the Iron Age from this area suggests a pattern of continuity in an extensively farmed landscape. The material from this site gives a real hint of the evidence to be gained and helps provide a balance to the concepts produced from the prevailing extensive knowledge gained from excavations on contemporary chalkland sites.

Acknowledgements
The author would like to acknowledge that this report is a distillation of the completed excavation report and uses information provided by Helen Rees, Elaine L. Morris, Jennifer Bourdillon, and Michael J. Allen. The post-excavation work was funded by English Heritage.

17. Balksbury Camp, Andover, Hampshire

G.J. Wainwright and Susan M. Davies

Introduction

Balksbury Camp is a univallate plateau enclosure situated on a low spur at the junction of the Rivers Anton and Anna (Pillhill Brook) in the southern suburbs of Andover (SU 350 445). The enclosure has been investigated by excavation on five occasions. In 1939 the defences on the southern side were sectioned by Mrs J. Hawkes (Hawkes 1940). Further details of the defences were revealed in 1958 through investigations during house building along Rooksbury Road in the north-eastern corner of the enclosure (Thompson 1958). In 1967, ahead of the construction of the southern Andover bypass a strip through the south part of the enclosure was excavated by Dr G.J. Wainwright, who excavated a further 10 ha in the interior of the enclosure in 1973, in advance of redevelopment (Wainwright 1969). During 1981, further excavations were carried out by the Central Excavation Unit of the Department of the Environment, directed by Ken Smith, in advance of an extension of the housing development into the western and south- eastern areas previously not threatened. The latter three excavations examined some 60% of the total area of the site (Wainwright and Davies in press).

Balksbury Camp sits on a small knoll which rises gently to a height of 91 m OD and encloses a roughly triangular area of 18 ha. The low spur on which the site lies is not topographically commanding as it is overshadowed by many other hills in the area, as well as by much of the 91–110 m surface. Nevertheless, it has a good position in relation to the local river valleys and their resources, superior in fact to that of the broadly contemporary hillfort of Bury Hill which overlooks it to the south. Balksbury is ideally positioned to exploit a number of ecological zones. The low spur of downland has easy and direct access to water for animal and human consumption, and lies only 500 m from the nearest permanent water source. Many of the known Late Bronze Age and Iron Age sites in the vicinity appear to be some distance from a current permanent water supply, adjacent to valleys which are now dry. But many of these 'dry' valleys are known to have contained running water within the last half century; Balksbury is situated within watered downland, virtually surrounded by rivers and streams, and has access to four ecological zones: the river floodplain (water meadows for pasture, reeds, rushes, and willow for housing and basketry), dry downland (pasture for stock, arable fields), isolated woodlands and forest timber (for timber, pannage, and browsing for stock, and herbs and fungi).

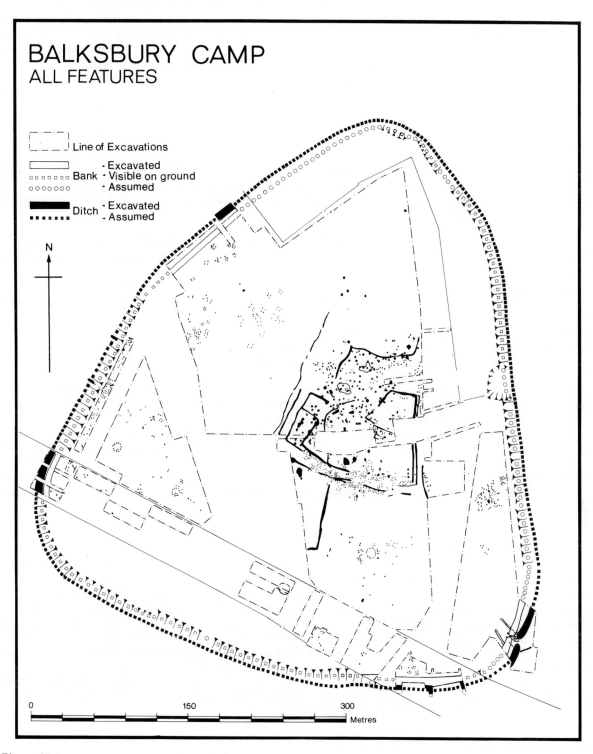

BALKSBURY CAMP
ALL FEATURES

Line of Excavations

Bank
- Excavated
- Visible on ground
- Assumed

Ditch
- Excavated
- Assumed

N

0   150   300
Metres

Figure 17.1   Balksbury Camp, all features plan

Pre-Enclosure Activity

There is slight evidence for activity in the Neolithic and Bronze Ages before the inception of the enclosure. This includes Neolithic artefacts (worked flint, a flint axe, and a Cornish axe); hearths with Beaker pottery of Domestic and Southern British Tradition, and a burial of an adolescent female, accompanied by a complete Beaker akin to Clarke's Wessex/Middle Rhine group of Lanting and van der Waals's step 2 type (calibrated date of 2131–1680 cal BC). Evidence for the Middle Bronze Age is limited to a small number of Globular Urn sherds recovered from the fills of later features.

Late Bronze Age–Earliest Iron Age (*c*. 1000–900 BC)

The inception of the enclosure

This period saw the first large-scale clearance of the dense oak woodland, with the construction of the plateau enclosure covering some 18 hectares. The enclosure had a single, gated entrance in the south-east corner, and was defined by a ditch and bank. Three phases of ditch and bank construction and modification were apparent:

a) a shallow ditch, at least 0.9 m deep, fronting a chalk and soil bank about 3 m wide which survived to a height of 0.5 m. The width of the ditch is uncertain as later modification had removed most of it.

b) the ditch was enlarged to an average depth of 1.8 m, and a width of about 7 m. The bank was widened to about 5 m, and, at least near the entrance, may have been strengthened with timber supports.

c) the ditch was enlarged again, to a depth of 3.3 m and average width of 7.3 m; the bank now enhanced with excavated material appears to have been about 6.4 m wide. At the entrance the rampart bank was wider still, producing an 8 m wide corridor from the gate.

Internal features comprise scatters of post-holes around the periphery of the site, four small pits, and a number of 4– and 5–post structures. The dating evidence for the last two groups is not extensive (pottery from a single post-hole) and they may belong to a later phase.

The period is dated by 'plain' and 'early decorated' pottery, found both on deposits associated with the defences and in the pits and post-holes excavated. A radiocarbon date of 1100–790 cal BC (one sigma) was obtained from layers associated with the second phase bank, and one of 1036–896 cal BC was obtained from a post-hole. An period of apparent neglect is suggested between refurbishment episodes two and three, and implies that this period is a lengthy one, despite the very coherent nature of the pottery assemblage.

Early Iron Age (*c*. 900–400 BC)

The first substantial evidence for settlement occurs in this phase, with the presence of at least three post-built round houses in the southern part of the enclosure and 27 storage pits, mainly in the central area. It is unclear whether the defensive circuit was still maintained and indeed the ceramic evidence supports the suggestion that it had fallen into disuse. However, it is possible that the third phase of refurbishment of defences is contemporary with at least one of the round houses, particularly if parallels at local sites such as Old Down Farm (Davies 1981, 81–163) are taken into account. Even if the ditch and bank were not being actively maintained, they would still have formed a significant boundary both for definition of 'ownership' and for stock-keeping.

The earlier part of the phase is dated by the presence of furrowed bowls and decorated jars of early All Cannings Cross type, whilst later stages include the haematite-coated scratch-cordoned bowls of Meon Hill type and other similarly decorated wares.

Middle–Later Iron Age (*c*. 400–50 BC)

Evidence for activity in this period is confined exclusively to the central area excavated in 1973. No structures were identified, but a series of 90 pits and one post-hole can be assigned to the period. There is no evidence to suggest that the enclosure was still functioning in this phase, and parallels elsewhere would suggest that it is far more likely that the settlement was an open one, or that its boundaries were defined by more ephemeral structures such as hedges or fences. It is possible that some of the interior was under cultivation at this stage, as the environmental record suggests that soils were being eroded and colluvial deposits forming. As the majority of the features of this period are central to the site, it would be quite feasible for the surrounding parts to have been under the plough.

Late Iron Age–Early Roman (c. 50 BC–AD 50)

Activity in the first centuries BC and AD was again apparently focused in the central area, although the enclosure entrance in the south-east corner of the site was also modified in this phase. Seventeen pits and a series of shallow gullies, probably small enclosures or fields, as well as 31 post-holes are attributed to the period.

The date range of this period is not well-defined, as closely datable pottery is absent. Whether the activity dates to the pre-Conquest period, or whether it commences in the mid-or late first century AD, is uncertain, but the phase may well have continued until AD 120 or later.

Late Roman

Substantial evidence was present for occupation of this period concentrated in the centre of the (out-of-use?) enclosure. A series of enclosures or fields continue the developments of the early Roman phase, suggesting that settlement was continuous, rather than disrupted as perhaps implied by the ceramics. Associated with the small enclosures are pits, hollows, post-holes forming fence-lines, a grain drier, burials, and a substantial building with ovens. The presence of painted wall plaster within the building might suggest that it was initially of some quality or pretension, though there is little else to imply anything other than a straightforward domestic structure.

Economy

The evidence for farming practices in the major periods of site occupation complements the exploitation of the suggested ecological zones. In all periods sheep/goat and cattle were the most common sources of meat, and it appears from the surviving remains that the former outnumbered the latter by a ratio of about 3:1 in all phases. This figure could be misleading, however, as the butchery, consumption, and disposal practices of the remains of the two animal types may have been radically different. Butchery evidence indicates that meat was often stripped from the bones of cattle and that sheep/goat meat may more often have been eaten on the bone. Horse and pig bones were also found throughout the Iron Age and Roman deposits, but in smaller numbers. The only new species in the Roman period was the domestic fowl.

Evidence from neonatal mortality and articulated burials of young animals indicate that in the Iron Age sheep/goat, cattle, pigs and dogs were being bred on site. However, the extent to which these burials are 'ritual' deposits, or 'Special Animal Deposits' (Grant 1984c; Hill this volume), and thus not necessarily representative of farming practice, is not clear. Wild species were never extensively hunted. The lack of exploitation of wild species at any time could be indicative of either choice, a lack of access to the resource or that Balksbury lay within a highly cultivated landscape and there was a lack of need to seek out wild species for food to any extent. Antler for boneworking, for which there is a small amount of evidence in the Iron Age phases, could have been 'traded' as a separate commodity or collected if it were shed.

The similarity of the Late Bronze/Iron Age assemblage at Balksbury to other chalkland settlement sites (as opposed to hillforts) is remarkable; in all aspects, from proportions of species exploited to mortality profiles and butchery, the assemblage shows that the farming regime at Balksbury was almost identical to those suggested for small, contemporary enclosed and open settlements in the immediate area and further afield of the Hampshire Chalk downlands. There is nothing in the animal bone assemblage to indicate that the Late Bronze Age/Iron Age settlement at Balksbury was functionally or socially different from apparently much smaller sites such as Old Down Farm, Lains Farm, High View Farm, or Winnall Down (Davies 1981; Bellamy 1991; Fasham 1985).

The archaeobotanical remains indicate the cultivation in the Iron Age of a standard range of cereals. Barley comprises 55% of the remains from the earlier part of the Iron Age, with 25% wheat and 20% unidentified. In the Middle and later Iron Age wheat became more important, at 32%, with 26% barley and 11% oats, and large numbers of querns were recovered from features dated to this period. Crops of all periods were not well-processed and there was high contamination with weed species. There is little artefactual material connected with crop-processing on a large scale, though reaping hooks are present. This contrasts markedly with the collection from Danebury hillfort (Selwood 1984, 346–9) and even with the number found at the settlement at Old Down Farm (Davies 1981), less than 2 km away and potentially exploiting the same resource area. The environmental evidence suggests some tilling of land within the site boundary, probably in the Iron Age as well as in the Roman period and it is possible that the actual settlement at Balksbury never achieved any great size and was able to support itself from within its immediate environs.

Evidence for other aspects of site economy can also be gleaned from the artefact record. Combs, weights, and spindle whorls attest textile manufacture throughout the later first millennium, in keeping with all other sites except Lains Farm, where the excavation was on a very small scale. But in the earlier period Balksbury shows a marked paucity in scale and variety of artefact type, even when compared to the partially excavated enclosure at High View Farm. However, since the range of types generally at Balksbury is very limited in this period, this may be only a reflection of a lack of substantial rubbish deposits, rather than a true reflection of site activities. There is little evidence for other craft or industrial processes, with the possible exception of pottery production in the Late Bronze or Early Iron Age, and the evidence for working, perhaps casting, copper alloy in the mid–later Iron Age, as well as production of bone and antler tools.

Much of the pottery assemblage could perfectly well be the product of on-site work, utilising 'local' clays but a small number of vessels can be identified as definite imports in the earlier Iron Age, from the Upper Thames area of the Jurassic Ridge, and possibly from Dorset. The red-slipped or 'haematite-coated' bowls, whether the earlier furrowed types or of the later scratched-cordoned style, are also likely to be imported to the sites from production centres clustering in the Avon Valley area to the west. From the Middle Iron Age the ceramic assemblage narrows in its form and fabric ranges, suggesting a formalisation of larger-scale production centres with wider-scale distribution networks. Throughout the later Bronze Age and Iron Age the ceramic groups from Balksbury show marked similarities in form, decoration, and fabric to material from other contemporary local sites in north-west Hampshire and Wiltshire, particularly the settlement sites of Old Down Farm, Lains Farm, High View Farm, Vigo Road, and Spine Road. Such similarities are symptomatic of the close relationships between the sites and of their inter-dependence.

The participation of Balksbury in the established trade networks is also shown by other imported products; the querns from a variety of sources in the Iron Age and Roman periods, briquetage, shale, and metal goods. Recent research has shown that almost all the saddle and rotary querns originate from the Lodsworth quarries in Sussex (Peacock 1987). Other sources include the Hampshire Basin, Purbeck, and, possibly, the continent. The shale and possibly the briquetage would have been imported from Purbeck, although the briquetage fabrics are not well-matched by the known Purbeck fabrics, and the metals would have come from a number of sources.

Most of the artefact assemblages from Balksbury resemble those of many other settlement sites, in quantity as well as quality, and in this respect the similarities between Iron Age hillforts and non-hillfort settlements is worth emphasising (see for example Bowden and McOmish 1987; Stopford 1987). There is nothing in the material that suggests specific functional or status variation from these settlements or that points to a site at the apex of the social structure.

Function and Status

The scale of investigation of the interior of the enclosure at Balksbury should enable a reasonably objective assessment of site organisation and function through time. Most areas within it have been explored to some extent, though perhaps the area immediately inside the line of the defences is less well covered than others. The most immediate question concerns the function of the earliest major site activity: the construction of the enclosure and its subsequent modifications and related internal features. The enclosure at Balksbury stands out from other sites, certainly on the Chalk downlands at least, because of its massive size; not because of the scale or even construction sequence of the actual defences themselves, which can be matched at much smaller enclosures such as Old Down Farm, Lains Farm, or Winnall Down, but the area enclosed, over 18 hectares. Such a vast circuit, on a fairly flat plateau, is effectively incapable of defence. Contemporaneous features or structures are few in number and do not imply extensive usage. Evidence tends towards the enclosure circuit falling into disuse relatively quickly. The construction of the enclosure ditches and accompanying banks would have required considerable effort and manpower, available not only for the initial work but for the modifications as well. It is likely that the effort to construct the enclosure was a communal one involving manpower from a wide area. This obviously implies an organised society and probably a communal need or function for the enclosed area. The physical remains from the site do not assist in interpreting this communal function though its primary role is unlikely to have been defensive. More likely is the suggestion that the main function was as a stock enclosure, ideally located close to a permanent water source and good pasture. It may have performed this role as a seasonal or periodic one, connected with annual redistribution or exchange of stock but no tangible remains would necessarily be left from such a use. However, in this scenario, the 4–post structures could be interpreted as the bases of fodder ricks (Cunliffe 1984b, 17–18), as could the 2–post 'structures'. Alternative explanations in terms of definition of social or status boundaries are equally possible, but current evidence does nothing to assist in interpretation. Whatever its intended initial function, the description of Balksbury Camp as a 'hillfort' is singularly inappropriate. Its role in display rather than defence (Bowden and McOmish 1989) may have been the more important.

After the initial use of the enclosure, most of the Iron Age activity was located in the central area of the site, with scattered structures elsewhere. All evidence points to a series of settlements, probably unenclosed or defined by fence or boundaries, of no great scale or status, with an economic base akin to that of contemporary sites in the area. It is possible that some breaks in the occupation sequence existed but it is also feasible that the apparent gaps in the ceramic sequence reflect low-key activity rather than none at all. The defences may still have had some presence, and much of the evidence would be compatible with the scant occupation of early hilltop enclosures; perhaps the most appropriate parallel would be from Winklebury, phase 1 (Smith 1977; Fischer 1985).

The nature of occupation in the Roman period similarly reflects a familiar pattern for the area, with small fields enclosed by fences, the layout amended and adapted from time to time, with associated structures and burials. The settlement function appears to be agricultural, seemingly fairly low-key. It could represent an outlying farmstead attached to a villa, though which one is not immediately obvious. The presence of the grain drier might support this, and there are a number of such driers associated with local sites, such as East Anton Crossroads and Spine Road, usually found as individual features not part of a large group on any one site. This might imply a network of small farms, processing crops mainly for their own consumption or contibuting to the needs of the villa, rather than 'industrial' scale supply, and concentrating on a pastoral (or even a market garden) regime. The continuity of site use, not only at Balksbury but at many other sites, from the Late Bronze Age and Iron Age to the Roman period argues for a stable society, exploiting the natural resources of a rich hinterland.

18. Old Down Farm, Andover, Hampshire

Susan M. Davies

The enclosure at Old Down Farm (SU 356 465) was first recognised on an aerial photograph taken in 1938, but was only explored when the threat of housing development arose in 1974 when small-scale rescue excavations were mounted by the Andover Excavation Committee before about one third of the enclosure was destroyed in road cutting. Archaeological work was resumed in 1975 under the auspices of the Test Valley Archaeological Committee, with limited funding from the Department of the Environment. The work continued until late in 1977 when housing construction commenced and eventually destroyed the site. All the work, apart from two short periods in 1976 and 1977, was undertaken on weekends by local amateur societies, the Andover Archaeological Society and members of the Lower Test Valley Archaeological Society. Without the assistance of these local groups little would have been investigated.

The site lies to the north-west of modern Andover, on a spur of Upper Chalk just above the River Anton, adjacent to an east–west track way and close by the Roman road from Silchester to Old Sarum (Fig. 18.1). The final report on the work appeared in 1981 (Davies 1981).

The settlement history may be summarised as follows:

Phase 1: Late Neolithic

Around 2500 BC there was sporadic Late Neolithic use of the area indicated by features, including pits, which contained worked flint, Peterborough Ware pottery, and hazelnut fragments.

Phase 2: Late Bronze Age/Earliest Iron Age

The site appears not to have been used for settlement again until about the eighth century BC when a shallow U–shaped ditch was dug to enclose an area of *c.* 1.2 hectares, D–shaped in plan, within which there were a few scattered pits. The enclosure entrance lay on the north-west side. The small pottery assemblage falls within the well-defined ceramic tradition of the Late Bronze Age, with distinctive slack-profiled bowl and jar forms frequently smoothed or wiped with grass. Decoration was rare and

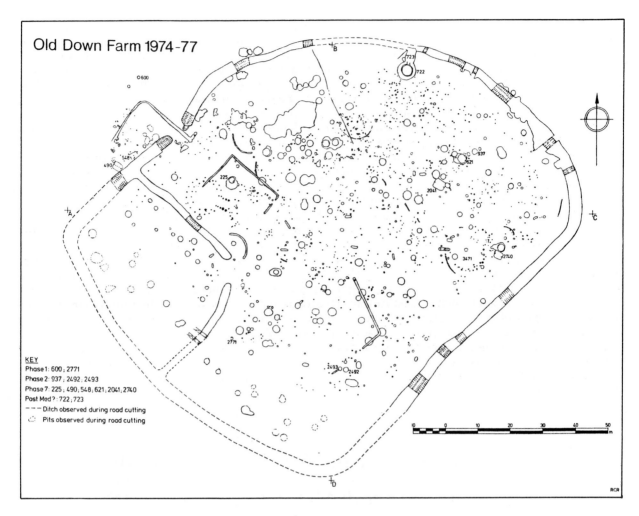

Figure 18.1   Old Down Farm, Andover, Hampshire, plan of prehistoric and Roman-British features

limited to fingertip or nail impressions, and although the pottery was crude in appearance it was well-finished and fired quite highly. Pottery fabrics indicate the exploitation of fairly local sources, but also some importation, one vessel containing Limestone ooliths from the Jurassic Beds probably in Dorset.

The animal bone from the pits indicates that sheep (or sheep/goat) were probably the most important stock comprising some 87% of the collection. However, the collection is biased by the number of bones belonging to few individual skeletons (seven from one pit) including a young lamb only a few weeks old (Maltby this volume). The other principal stock animals and those used for food included cattle (5%), horse (0.5%), pig (3%) and dog (5%); there was no evidence for the diet being enhanced by hunting.

Phase 3: Early Iron Age

In the seventh century the ditch was enlarged and deepened to 2 m. Within this enclosure lay at least one large post-built round house, close to the north-western entrance but facing away from it with the porch opening to the south-east. The extant remains of the roundhouse comprised two concentric rings of posts enclosing a floor area of 50 m², with a porch on the south-east side, 2 m wide and 3.5 m long, defined by six large post-holes; no floor levels survived because of later ploughing. Twenty-seven pits, several areas of quarry-pits, and a small number of other post-holes were contemporary with the round house.

The pottery was significantly different from the Phase 2 material with a wide variety in form and fabric. The most characteristic forms were 'haematite-coated' furrowed bowls with both short necks and tall flaring ones, and their associated coarse variants and storage vessels. Decoration was frequent. Only a single copper alloy object, a pin fragment which may be residual, was found, but the range of clay, stone, and bone/antler objects shows evidence for boneworking, weaving, and possibly fishing.

Archaeobotanical evidence for economy and diet was sparse, limited to wheat (unattributable to species), and the absence of chaff may suggest that crop processing took place off site. The animal bone indicates an increasing importance in cattle (24%), with sheep representing a similar proportion of bones but presumably less of a contribution to diet and farming regime. Horse (13%), pig (7%) and dog (28% — but including five individual skeletons) all contributed to the diet, along with grey lag goose, pheasant and mallard. There was again a lack of other wild species, apart from occasional red deer antler used for boneworking.

This period is the first from which human remains were recovered — a neonatal infant from a pit, and fragments of an adult and child (both skull pieces) from a post-hole.

Phase 4: Early Iron Age

For the next two centuries (sixth–fourth centuries BC) there is evidence for at least four round houses of varying construction, mainly gully built or gully-and-post built. The enclosure ditch had silted up by the end of this period, to about 1 m from the surrounding ground surface. The settlement could still have been defined by bank or hedge, or it may have been entirely open.

This phase was characterised by the presence of Meon Hill type cordoned bowls, frequently with footrings, and with characteristic cherry-red haematite coat and incised or burnished decoration. The coarsewares were large undecorated storage jars. The limited range of forms and lack of decoration contrasts markedly with the rich assemblage from Phase 3. Other artefacts were rare; an iron pin and blade, and a small number of bone pins and needles as well as working debris.

The stock reared, or at least eaten on site, show a marked increase in the importance of cattle (48%), with sheep still forming a significant element (31%). There is a slight rise in the number of pig bones (10%), and decrease in horse (8%) and dog (<2%). Few wild species were found, but these included red deer, roe deer and mallard. Wheat (*Triticum Spelta* and *Dicoccum*), oats and barley were all present, but the last two were probably wild varieties. Three further fragments of human skulls (two adult and one child) were found in separate pits.

Phase 4/5: Early Middle Iron Age

Sometime at the end of the fourth century there was a marked change in pottery vessel form to a predominance of proto-saucepan types, but there were no concommitant changes in fabrics. Only four pits produced such material, and it may by a false division to isolate this phase as separate from the succeeding Middle Iron Age.

Phase 5: Middle Iron Age

Occupation continued without a substantial break (if any) into the Middle Iron Age (c. third–first centuries BC) when all the evidence came from a series of storage pits; there is no evidence for any form of enclosing bank, ditch, or fence, or any structures. As in all the previous Iron Age phases there is little suggestion of internal planning or defined areas of activity within the main settlement area.

Despite the lack of structural evidence this period was the richest in terms of artefactual and economic data. The pottery assemblage, in both form and fabric, was highly standardised suggesting factory production and importation to site from Wiltshire and central Hampshire. The dominant form was the saucepan pot, frequently burnished and decorated with linear and dotted motifs characteristic of Hampshire, Wiltshire, and possibly Sussex. Other forms and decorative motifs (such as the round-bodied 'goldfish' bowls) seem more akin to Upper Thames types, and the whole assemblage gives the feeling of trade and specialisation.

A wide variety of other artefacts was found, many connected with spinning and weaving — bone pins, combs, and handles, and stone spindle whorls and weights, as well as a Greensand quern and a whetstone. This period provided the only evidence for smithing on site, and the metalwork collection includes agricultural and carpentry tools, part of a currency bar, and is suggestive of a flourishing site. A 'hoard' of metalwork was found in one pit (Fig. 18.2), concealed below a dump of triangular clay loomweights. The hoard comprised one complete and one fragmentary 'currency' bars, two bronze-coated linch pins, a socketed iron gouge, and two scraps of bronze.

Evidence for agriculture in the form of reaping hooks and sickle blades was complemented by palaeobotanical remains of wheat (spelt and emmer), oats, and barley, an increase in weed species associated with crop production, and brassica seeds, although the total absence of legumes is odd in a reasonable sized collection. The emphasis in stock was on sheep, which provided over half the animal bone assemblage, with cattle back to 20%. Horse formed a further 12% of the collection, with little pig and dog present. Wild species again form a very small proportion of the assemblage, but included red deer, hare, fox, raven, mallard, and ?pochard.

As well as fragmentary adult skull remains from two pits, one neonatal infant skeleton was found in a pit, in addition to two foetal (c. 5 months) incomplete skeletons from a post-hole, possibly the

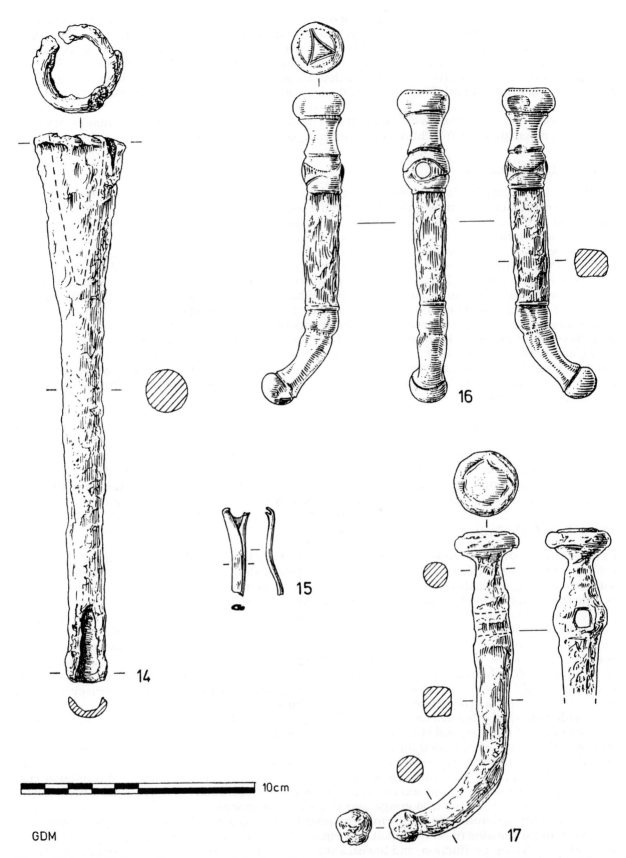

GDM

Figure 18.2   Old Down Farm, part of the Late Iron Age metalwork hoard from pit 2420. Scales 14, 16, 17, 2:3, 15, 1:3.   14 = socketed iron gouge; 15 = strip of copper alloy; 16 = iron lynch pin with copper alloy terminals; 17 = iron lynch pin with copper alloy head

burial of twins born prematurely. Two complete skeletons of young men were also found buried in pits. One, an individual aged 18–22 years, bore a number of cut marks to the rear of the skull, the neck, left arm, and torso. The cuts suggest that if a single implement was used to inflict the wounds it was long, sharp, double-edged and thin-bladed, probably with a pointed end. Most of the wounds were to the rear of the skeleton, and were slashing cuts, though some to the rib cage and thoracic vertebrae were thrusts. Though one blow, to the cervical vertebrae could have killed the man, it is impossible to determine whether the wounds were inflicted before and were the cause of death or whether the blows were inflicted as post mortem mutilation. The skeleton was buried under a pile of large flint nodules at the base of a pit with few artefacts, suggesting deliberate segregation and burial; but there is nothing else to suggest the burial was in any way different to others.

Phase 6: Late Pre-Roman Iron Age and Roman

The Phase 5 occupation seems to have ended in the early years of the first century BC, though the reasons for abandonment are not apparent. However, in the early years of the first century AD a small ditched or palisaded enclosure was constructed in the south-west corner of the early Iron Age enclosure, using the old ditch line for two of its sides. Road construction in 1974 removed virtually the whole of the interior of this enclosure and its internal layout and function are unknown but it does seem to have been short-lived, going out of use before the Roman Conquest. The whole site was used in the earlier Roman period for agricultural activity, but was then abandoned until about the sixth century AD when six early Saxon sunken-featured buildings occupied the site (Phase 7)(Davies 1980).

The limited evidence for farming and economy suggests a similar pattern to the previous phase with an emphasis on sheep and cattle, and continuing cereal production though the seed evidence is poor. The pre-Conquest pottery comprised a range of small necked and bead rim cooking jars and bowls and storage jars, with no fineware imports. Metal items included a small number of tools, reaping hooks, and knives, an iron penannular brooch, a bronze Colchester type brooch, and a plain bronze bracelet. A solid copper alloy strap junction, probably from a horse bridle, was found in the upper fills of the enclosure ditch by a metal detector user.

Discussion

The Iron Age artefactual evidence is similar to other enclosures and hillforts, with ceramics providing the largest element and contributing principally to the site dating. The earlier phases (2–4/5) produced very little metalwork, indicating either its rarity generally or its value and curation which prevented disposal as rubbish. In the later phases (5 and 6) there is a standard range of domestic and agricultural metal items, with few luxuries or personal items. The few luxury items in general seem connected with horse furniture or carts/chariots which may indicate status, site function or principal economy.

There is evidence for many of the domestic crafts and activities which might be expected; crop processing, spinning, weaving, boneworking, carpentry, hide preparation/working, potting, and smithing (but not iron smelting or bronzeworking). These activities can be recognised for all phases apart from Phase 2, and apart from smithing which is restricted to Phase 5.

The pottery (decoration and forms) in both Early and Middle Iron Age phases seems to indicate connections with several areas, mainly Wiltshire, central and north Hampshire, and the Upper Thames Valley. Petrological examination complements the observations on form and decoration. Old Down seems therefore to lie at a point of overlap between major style zones (or cultural areas), emphasising perhaps its position on good communications routes, and the centre of a highly developed and utilised landscape. A 5 km radius around Old Down takes in at least 17 contemporaneous Early Iron Age settlement sites, one large plateau enclosure at Balksbury (Davies and Wainwright this volume) and one hillfort (Bury Hill, Cunliffe this volume), or more than one site per square kilometre on present knowledge. The area was obviously prosperous between the seventh–fourth centuries (and later), and capable of support- ing a large population. Many of the sites lie on good communications routes, close to good water supplies, and it is quite feasible that some sites specialised in, for example, rearing cattle and horses whilst others farther afield on the drier downs concentrated on sheep and arable agri-culture.

The role of Old Down itself is unlikely to have been static over its period of occupation. The reason for its initial settlement in about the eighth century is uncertain, but by the seventh century the enclosure appears to be flourishing, its 'wealth' derived from stock probably rather than arable agriculture. The size of enclosure and the quality of building suggests a single, extended family perhaps of some local status, a thought reinforced by the pottery assemblage which seems to be more than merely functional. Whether the enclosure ditch was defensive is a debatable point; it would have required substantial manpower to implement any defensive strategy, so perhaps a more appropriate interpretation is as a display of wealth, prestige, and status; or a more mundane one of good stock husbandry. It is equally possible, though unprovable, that the then laws or traditions of land owner-ship required definition of boundaries to avoid disputes over trespass or other conflict.

The extent to which the settlement's prosperity continued is less certain, with the gradual erosion of the main boundary and a lack of artefactual evidence for wealth (though such prosperity cannot be defined in terms of what remains in the current sparse record). But it is likely that occupation was continuous for some seven centuries or more, which argues for at least a degree of prosperity and a stable environment. The apparent demise of the settlement in the late pre-Roman Iron Age is un-explained, but the new enclosure in the early first century AD implies fortification and follows a pattern which is widespread in the years before the Roman Conquest — presumably in response to population pressure and threat of war. Again the reasons for eventual abandonment and probable shift of settlement focus are uncertain, but are in line with evidence from other sites of a changing economic atmosphere with emphasis on the growing villa structure and even larger-scale landuse and ownership.

19. Winnall Down and Easton Lane: Settlement From the Bronze Age to the Roman Period

Peter Fasham

Two separate excavations of what proved to be a single area of settlement took place in 1976–7 and 1982–3. Over 16 hectares were investigated in both excavations located on chalkland to the east of Winchester. The fieldwork was a result of the proposal to construct the M3 motorway and an interchange at this location.

Winnall Down was the 1976–7 excavation. It was primarily the investigation of a D–shaped enclosure recorded on aerial photographs (Fasham 1985). The excavation of 1.26 hetares included a relatively small strip outside the enclosure. The 1982–3 excavation, called Easton Lane Interchange, was designed to sample a 700 m length of motorway and an interchange immediately west of Winnall Down (Fasham *et al.* 1989). A 10% sample was trenched and areas of archaeological features were cleared. The Easton Lane site covered 15 hectares, of which 5 hectares were investigated. A further 5 hectares to the west were recorded in a watching brief.

The Winnall Down excavation recording system, and particularly the computer-based post-excavation work, enabled the excavated data to be interrogated in a number of ways with particular attention being paid to the relationships between time and spatial distribution of archaeological features and artefacts. There was a detailed examination of carbonised seeds (Monk and Fasham 1980), animal bones, and terrestrial molluscs.

The chronological sequence — up to the Roman period — for both excavations is summarised in Table 19.1. The chronological summary indicates an area of settlement with the principal focus of the settlement moving around the area through time (Fig. 19.1–19.3). It is also worth considering in a little more detail the settlement activities in the area of the excavation of the D–shaped Winnall Down enclosure (Fig. 19.4).

Late Bronze Age

On the west of the enclosure were four post-built circular structures, or houses, whose distribution indicated that they could not all have been in use at the same time. This particular area of settlement was very limited when compared to the settlement pattern in the Middle Bronze Age which was dispersed over about 6 hectares and apparently located within the fields (Fig. 19.1).

Early Iron Age

A D–shaped enclosure with V–shaped ditch and internal bank was constructed immediately east of the four Late Bronze Age structures (Fig. 19.2). The entrance to the enclosure faced west. Spatial analysis of features and artefacts enabled the following suggestions to be made about areas of activity within the enclosure. Four activity areas were identified. Area 1 in the north-west corner contained a relatively elaborate gully-built circular structure and two post-built circular structures. There was a high proportion of four-post structures, a large number of loomweights, medium-sized pits and the densest concentration of animal — particularly cattle — bones. It was suggested that this area was a major family unit within the enclosure.

Table 19.1   *Chronological sequence for Winnall Down and Easton Lane*

Period	Winnall Down	Easton Lane
Neolithic	interrupted ring-ditch	ceramics
Late Neolithic	–	?circular structure, pits
Early Bronze Age	–	two cemeteries of mixed cremation and inhumation burials, groups of post-holes
Middle Bronze Age	–	rectilinear ditch system, post-built circular huts, pits, post-hole arrangements over 6 hectares on south-facing slope
Late Bronze Age	four post-built circular structures in tight group	revised ditch system
Early Iron Age	D–shaped enclosure with post-built and gully houses, pits, and post-hole arrangements	pits
Early–Middle Iron Age	–	unenclosed settlement, circular gully-built structures, post-hole clusters, pits, and burials
Middle Iron Age	unenclosed settlement with clear separation between houses and pits	pits on north-west Winnall Down settlement
Late Iron Age–early Roman	rectangular enclosures linked with track down east side; pits and burials	

Area 2 in the north-east corner had a single crude post-built circular house and one other possible circular structure. It was characterised by a series of shallow scoops and pits and was defined on its west side by fencing. It was not possible to decide what activities had taken place in this area.

Area 3 in the south-west was ill-defined with a central blank area surrounded by pits. Boneworking may have taken place within the area.

Area 4 in the south-west contained two post-built circular structures, some four-post structures and a small group of large volume pits, and a considerable volume of daub and baked clay. This area seemed to have been a second living unit, perhaps where crop-processing took place.

Early–Middle Iron Age

The settlement shifted to the west and north-west of the earlier D–shaped enclosure, the bank of which may have been pushed into the ditch on the west side (Fig. 19.2). There were 19 gully and post-built houses extending up to, but not over, the ditch system laid out in the Middle to Late Bronze Age. The settlement was arranged around four main gully-built structures which may represent living space for family units.

Middle Iron Age

By the Middle Iron Age, the bank of the D–shaped enclosure had been flattened — at least on its west side — and an unenclosed settlement developed centred on the site of the earlier enclosure (Fig. 19.3). The distinctive element of this phase was a concentration of structures into a fairly small area with clear separation of houses and pits. The pits lay in two groups: one to the east of the houses; the other to the north-west. The animal bone evidence suggested that large mammal carcasses were processed on the periphery of the settlement area.

Late Iron Age–Early Roman

Part of the site was used into the Roman period. The straight side of the D–shaped enclosure — the east side — must have still been visible as it was used as the boundary for a track on whose west side were constructed a number of small ditched enclosures (Fig. 19.3).

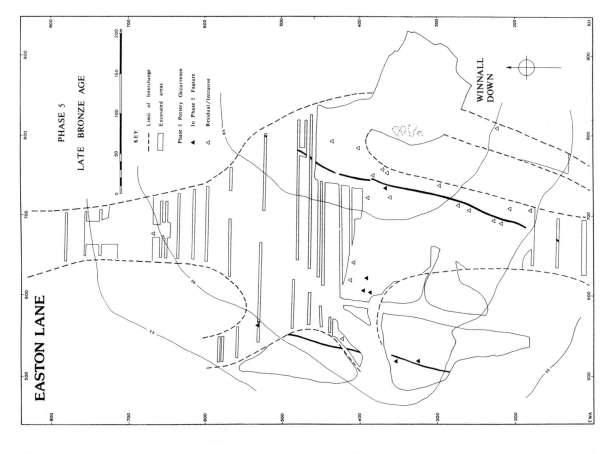

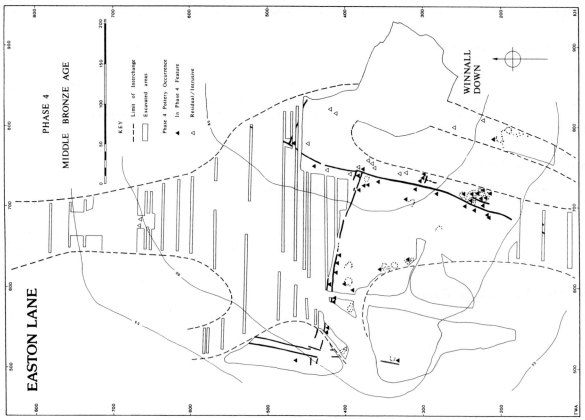

Figure 19.1   Easton Lane and Winnall Down, left: Phase 4; right, Phase 5

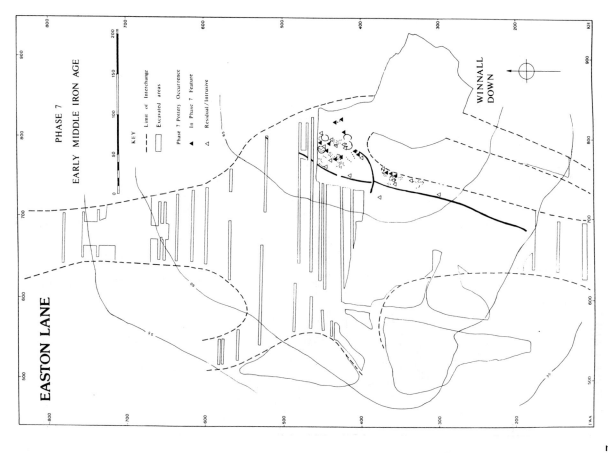

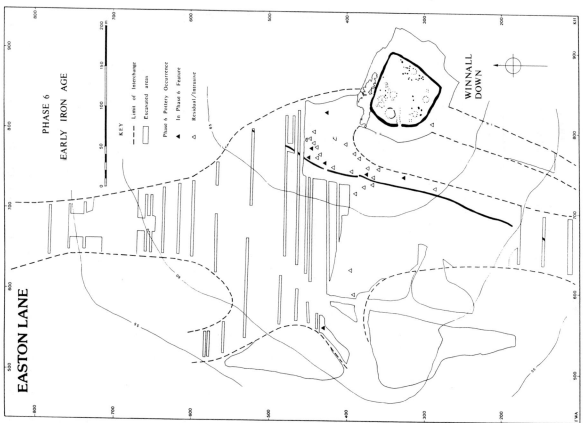

Figure 19.2   Easton Lane and Winnall Down, left: Phase 6; right, Phase 7

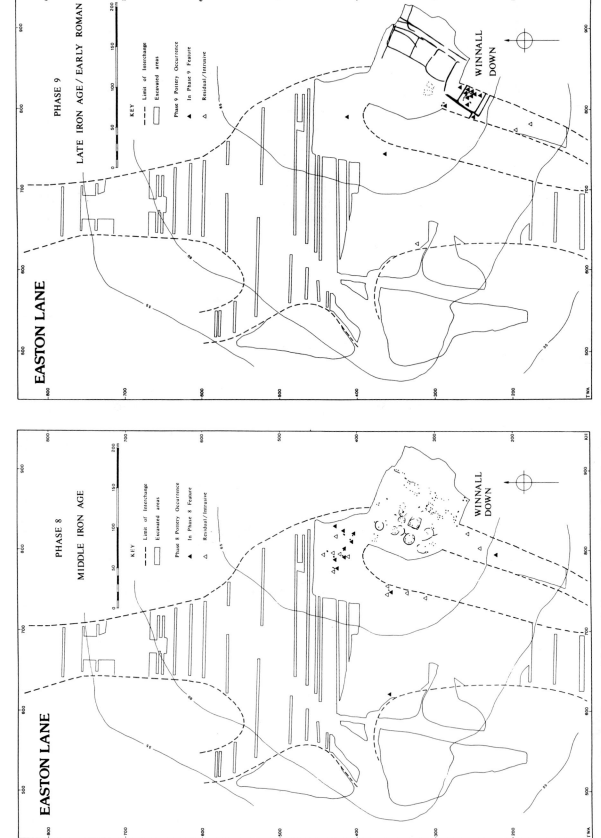

Figure 19.3   Easton Lane and Winnall Down, left: Phase 8; right, Phase 9

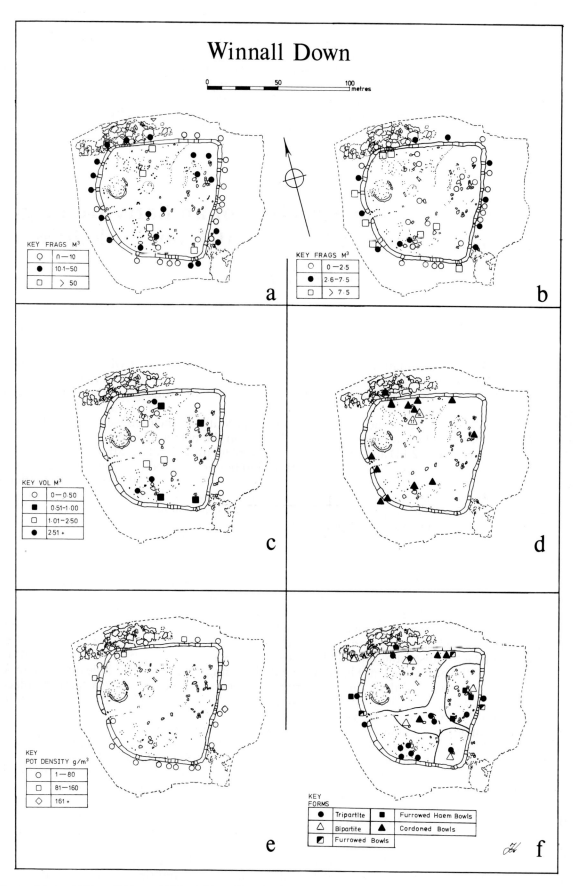

Winnall Down

KEY FRAGS M³ (a)
○	0 — 10
●	10.1 — 50
□	> 50

KEY FRAGS M³ (b)
○	0 — 2.5
●	2.6 — 7.5
□	> 7.5

KEY VOL M³ (c)
○	0 — 0.50
■	0.51 — 1.00
□	1.01 — 2.50
●	2.51 +

KEY POT DENSITY g/m³ (e)
○	1 — 80
□	81 — 160
◇	161 +

KEY FORMS (f)
●	Tripartite	■	Furrowed Haem Bowls
△	Bipartite	▲	Cordoned Bowls
▨	Furrowed Bowls		

a   b   c   d   e   f

Figure 19.4   Winnall Down, Hampshire, distribution of selected elements in the Early Iron Age: a = total density of animal bone frags per m³; b = density of cattle bone frags per m³; c = pits by volumetric range; d = triangular loomweights; e = pottery density per m³, enclosure ditch 5; f = selected pottery forms and the outlines of the four main activity areas

Discussion

Both excavations have recorded patterns of settlement mobility from the Bronze Age onwards. Dispersed settlement in fields in the Middle Bronze Age gives way to more nucleated settlement by the late Bronze Age and through the Iron Age. Sometimes the settlements were enclosed by bank and ditch but most of the time they were not so defined. Structural patterning within the settlement areas has been identified throughout the Iron Age, as has the shifting of the focal points of the settlements.

The inability to refine more precisely the chronologies of the activities either by ceramic or scientific means suggests that subtle details about structural patterning and shifting focal points have not been recovered.

20. Outside in: the Structure of an Early Iron Age House at Dunston Park, Thatcham, Berkshire

A. P. Fitzpatrick

Introduction

Following the systematic evaluation of a proposed housing development at what is now known as Dunston Park near Newbury, Berkshire (SU 523 681), excavations were undertaken in 1989 and 1991 in advance of the first stage of the development to examine an Early Iron Age settlement (Fitzpatrick *et al.* in press).

The excavations revealed evidence for a dispersed, apparently unenclosed, seventh–sixth century BC Iron Age settlement which ran up a low gravel ridge on the northern side of the Kennet valley. Only one certain house (Fig. 20.1) and one possible one were identified but a scatter of post-holes near it which contained small quantities of flint, burnt flint, and pottery may be associated with tasks away from the home. The scope of the environmental evidence was limited by the poor preservation of animal bone but the plant macrofossils show that barley was grown and may have been processed on site. It may be supposed that a typical Early Iron Age farming regime of mixed, small-scale, farming which exploited a range of habitats was practised.

At Home

Although the evidence for the settlement is otherwise limited, that from the one certain house is of particular interest in its own right. Apart from repairs to the porch only one phase in represented and the two post rings of the house give an internal diameter of 9 m and an area of 64 m². As with most Iron Age houses the entrance is aligned to the east/south-east (Hill 1993a, 66–8, fig. 3a), while the foundations display symmetry of planning (Guilbert 1982). Only relatively large features were identified in excavation; less substantial internal features such as screens, or external ones associated with the construction of the house, may not have survived ploughing. Only one post-hole does not appear to be part of the walls and, while it could be a repair, it seems more likely to be a carefully placed, non-structural internal feature. This post-hole is opposite the porch from which the post or furniture it supported would have been clearly visible.

The most striking aspect of the distribution of the finds within the house is the way in which all categories of material culture are almost exclusively restricted to the porch and the right hand side of the house (when viewed from inside looking out of the porch; Figs 20.2 and 20.3). Clearly these distributions reflect not only what objects were in use, but also the values ascribed to them which determined how they were disposed of. Decay and other formation processes, and excavation methods, also contribute. The poor preservation of bone may have reduced the representation of some finds and perishable goods such as wooden bowls, also may have been lost (Evans 1989). Even so, the discovery of a such a large number of finds from an Iron Age house is notable as most Iron Age houses seem to have been kept very clean (Hingley and Miles 1984, 63). The smaller and abraded pottery sherds from the postholes could be associated with the use of the house (e.g. Hodder 1984, 55; Blake *et al.* 1993, 111). Alternatively they could relate to the abandonment and final decay of the house; the mean sherd size is similar to that from Brighton Hill South (Morris 1992), where the house was burnt down. The clarity of these distributions does not mean that their interpretation is equally clear. For example the left side of the house may have been a living area which was kept clean and the finds in the right side may indicate storage there, or the presence of furniture under or behind which parts of broken pots accumulated. Here the distribution of finds is taken to relate to the ways in which the house was used and that the right side was a living area; the left one a sleeping one. This division may be interpreted in different ways.

If the decorated pottery assemblages of the Late Bronze Age and Early Iron Age were used to serve food individually (Barrett 1980), it is possible that there was an activity/group specific area towards the front of the house. There are also hints of more subtle patterning in that while there are no significant differences between the overall distribution of coarse and fine wares, there is a suspicion that decorated wares are restricted to the area next to the porch. The presence of burnt flint, and perhaps the fired clay, could suggest that cooking took place within the house, but there was no structural evidence for any central hearths or other evidence for any distinction between cooking and eating areas. A crucible, quern fragments, and a spindle whorl were all found close together (Fig. 20.2) but they provide insufficient evidence to suggest that there was a working area there and it might be thought unlikely that metal smelting would be undertaken inside. The only pottery from the left side of the house (three sherds of coarseware) could, however, suggest that goods were stored there or that, for example, there was a toilet there. There is no evidence to suggest how a mezzanine floor or a loft might have been used.

At another level, the social space of architecture was clearly structured. The architecture of the house and the nature and distribution of the activities which took place within it with their clear left/right distinction almost certainly incorporate cosmological referents (Fitzpatrick 1991a; Parker Pearson in press), and the precise orientation of the entrances of Iron Age houses (including Dunston Park) and enclosures towards sunrise should be emphasised (Hill 1993a). It may be that it was this orientation which helped define the left/right distinction and the single non-structural post could have signified these distinctions to people as they passed through the porch and crossed the threshold of the house, entering the household (Fig. 20.4). It is also likely that the porch was as much symbolic as structural as a liminal space which helped to define the orientation of the house, and perhaps of time, and to emphasise the threshold. It is interesting therefore that the distribution of finds

Figure 20.1   Dunston Park, Thatcham, Berkshire, the round house viewed from the north-west.
Photograph: Elaine Wakefield

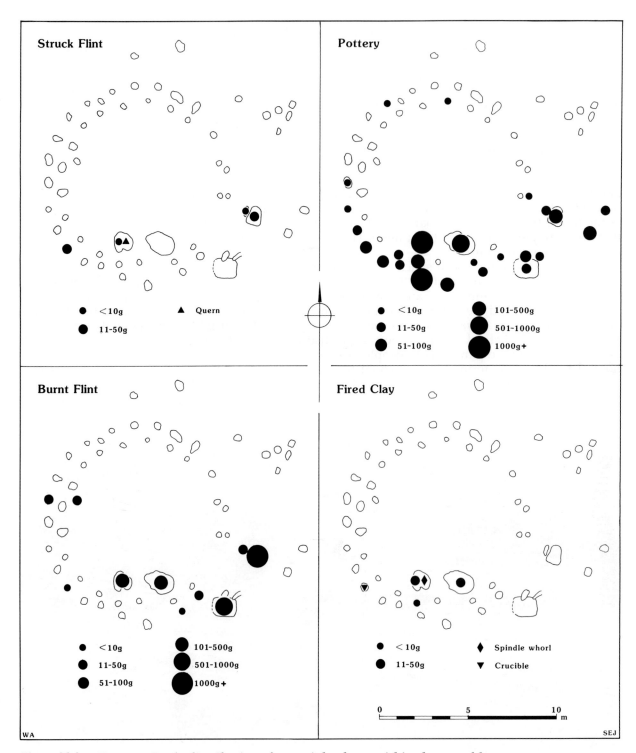

Figure 20.2   Dunston Park, distribution of material culture within the round house

in the two post-holes at the outside of the porch are reversed, with more finds from the left hand one, which may suggest a different order outside the home.

This left/right division echoes the distribution of finds from the comparable, and broadly contemporary house (eighth–seventh century BC) at Longbridge Deverill Cow Down, Wiltshire. The double (or less likely triple) ring house was burnt down and the distribution of finds within it indicated that all the 'domestic refuse was confined to this [right] side of the house' (Chadwick 1960, 19), The finds included pottery, querns, bone tools, burnt flint, animal bones, spindle whorls, and, perhaps, a loom. Chadwick-Hawkes's also interprets this as a separate living area and sleeping quarters. A small amount of pottery was also found in the left side of the house (S. Chadwick-Hawkes pers. comm.). Although this evidence from Wessex is limited, it does not support Hingley's suggestion of a central 'public' area in round houses (Hingley 1990c, 128–35).

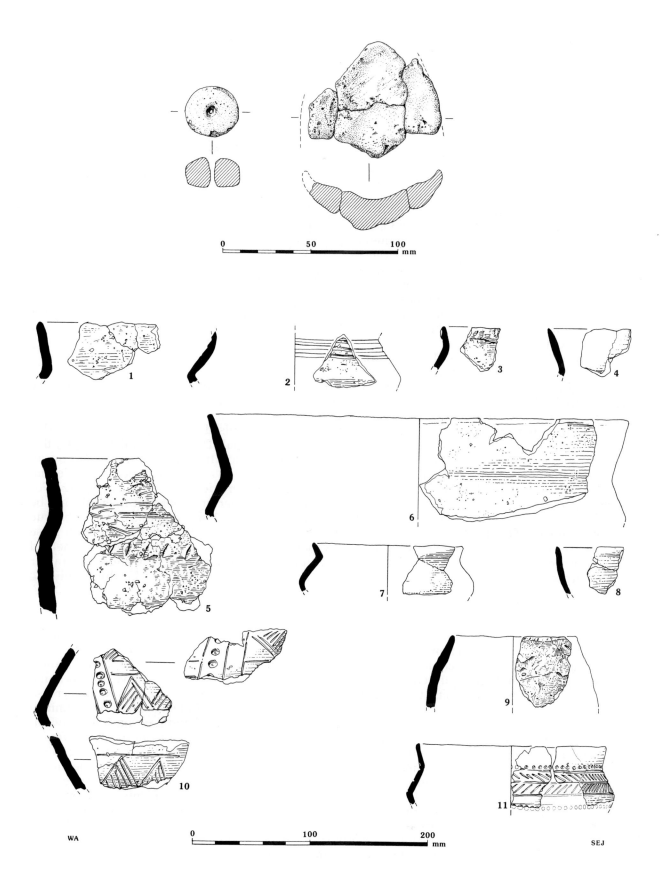

Figure 20.3   Dunston Park, finds from the round house; a spindle whorl, crucible, and pottery. Pots 10 and 11 are from a pit to the east of the round house

Figure 20.4   Dunston Park, possible uses of the round house and its cosmological referents

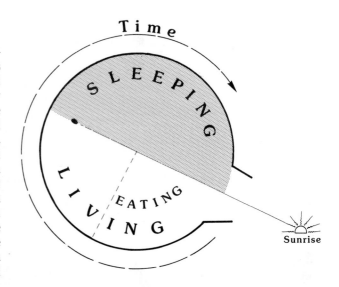

House and Home

While the Dunston Park house is of a well-known general type, the best parallels for its very large size and clearly recognisable second ring are in Wessex (Guilbert 1981). Closely comparable houses are known at Pimperne (Harding *et al.* 1993) in Dorset, Brighton Hill South, Site X/Y (Coe and Newman 1993, 10–13, fig. 5; R. Newman this volume) and Old Down Farm (Davies 1981, 102, fig. 14; this volume) in Hampshire, Little Woodbury House II (Bersu 1940), and Longbridge Deverill Cow Down in Wiltshire, all of which date between the seventh and fifth centuries BC with the emphasis on the seventh century. It is now possible to emphasise the short time for which these houses were in fashion, and they are found in both enclosed and unenclosed sites (McOmish 1989, 102–3).

The size of these houses should also be emphasised. In comparison with most houses of Middle Bronze Age or Middle–Late Iron Age date, the type is very large (Hill 1984, fig. 2; Strang 1991) and contrasts clearly with the smaller buildings of the Middle–Late Bronze Age which have been suggested to occur in pairs as a standard settlement module; one building being residential, the other ancillary for more specialised uses (e.g. Ellison 1987). This module might also occur at some Early Iron Age sites, e.g. Winnall Down (Fasham 1985, 142; this volume). It may be that the increased size reflects a change in the location of activities which now all took place under one roof, or it may reflect a different categorisation and presentation of residential groups, such as some of the ways in which gender and lineage were defined (Barrett 1989, 312). For example, groups might now have lived as extended families under one roof, but it should not be forgotten that ancillary buildings might still exist at this time (Fisher 1985), and this may also be true for Dunston Park. Few Iron Age houses appear to have been rebuilt and this is the case with these large houses suggesting that the style of house and perhaps also the living arrangements it helped enact spanned a comparatively short time when the emphasis was on encompassing household rather than incorporating clan. This change to larger houses may have affected the ways in which daily life was organised within it and it may not be coincidental that the houses at Brighton Hill South X/Y, Dunston Park, and Longbridge Deverill Cow Down all appear to have been abandoned without indications of major repairs or renewal.

Although their contemporaneity and association should not be pressed, these changes in domestic architecture and the construction of social space occurred at approximately the same time as other changes in Wessex. These included an increase in the deposition of the products of the 'bronze industry', greater emphasis on the enclosure of settlements, even though they may have been as much symbolic as functional constructs (Bowden and McOmish 1987), the appearance of iron, an increase in the number of hillforts (Thomas 1989, 274), and the creation of vast middens such as All Cannings Cross, East Chisenbury (Brown *et al.* this volume) and Potterne (Gingell and Lawson 1985; Lawson this volume). The association of hillforts with earlier 'ranch boundaries' dividing parts of the Wessex landscape, perhaps into domestic and agricultural areas, has been well rehearsed (e.g. Cunliffe 1990).

The reasons for these changes and their relationships — if any — are not clearly understood. Population pressure and in particular an increase in agricultural productivity have been suggested (e.g. Barrett and Bradley 1980, 202–4). However, the redefinition of land, settlements, and houses as well as an increased emphasis on decorative motives on other sorts of material culture suggests a major shift in the social order and its presentation. The similarities between Dunston Park and Longbridge Deverill show that these changes were enacted precisely over considerable distances (*c.* 80 km). It is in this context that the evidence for intra-site patterning within the Dunston Park settlement should be seen.

Acknowledgements
The work was funded by Trencherwood Homes Ltd. I am grateful to Sonia Chadwick-Hawkes for information concerning Longbridge Deverill Cow Down in advance of her own publication and to J.D. Hill and David McOmish for their comments on the draft excavation report. The photograph is by Elaine Wakefield and the drawings by Liz James.

21. Recent Excavations at Brighton Hill South, Basingstoke, Hampshire

Richard Newman

The Basingstoke area contains a remarkable concentration of Iron Age sites. The majority of the settlements are single farmsteads, some enclosed, some not, and include such published sites as Cowdrey's Down, Rucstalls Hill, and Viables Farm. These sites have generally been recognised through aerial photography, which has proved a successful discovery technique for cropmarks in the area because of the predominantly chalk geology of the Basingstoke environs. Opportunities to investigate the sites have arisen because of the rapid expansion of the town since the 1960s; that these opportunities have been taken and the results disseminated has been in no small part the result of the dedicated endeavours of the local amateur archaeological group, the Basingstoke Historical and Archaeological Society. It is the fortuitous combination of archaeological circumstances, favourable geology, urban expansion and an enthusiastic and capable local group that has probably caused the mapped concentration of Iron Age sites in the Basingstoke area, rather than it being representative of an unusual concentration of Iron Age activity.

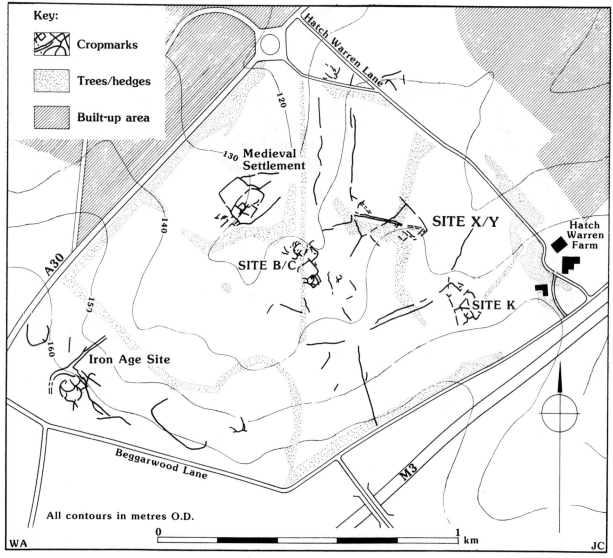

Figure 21.1   Brighton Hill South, Basingstoke, Hampshire, the evidence from aerial photographs

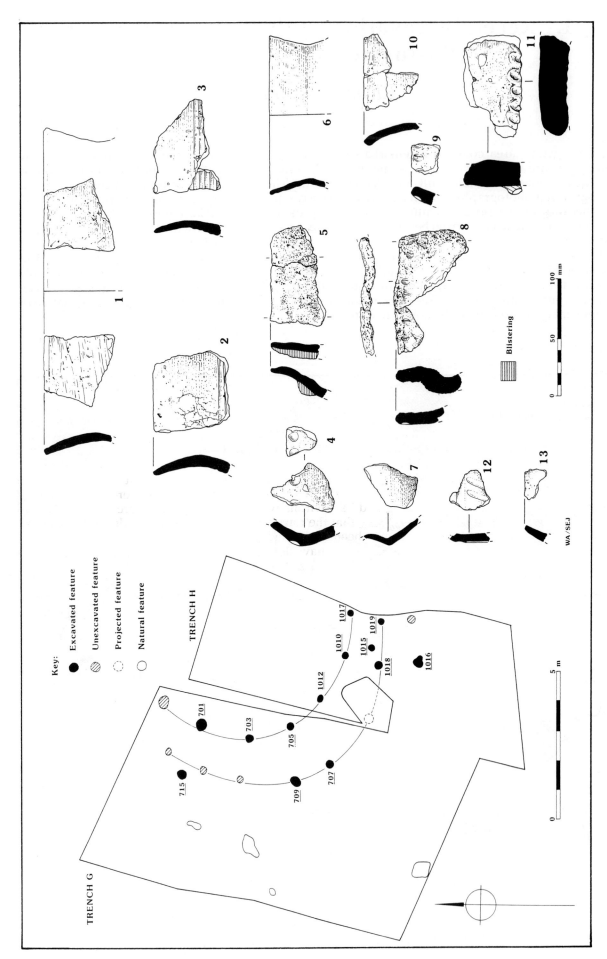

Figure 21.2   Brighton Hill South Site X/Y, the burnt timber round house and pottery from its post-holes

Between 1984 and 1986 Wessex Archaeology ran a Manpower Services Commission scheme which carried out a series of excavations on cropmark sites within a proposed development area known as Brighton Hill South on the southern outskirts of Basingstoke (Fig. 21.1). Four cropmark sites, all identified from aerial photographs, were initially assumed to be of an Iron Age date, and all were investigated to varying degrees. Two sites proved to be Iron Age enclosures, one a deserted medieval settlement and the fourth, known as site X/Y, was considered to have only limited archaeological potential.

Site X/Y appeared on aerial photographs to be a possible double-ditched enclosure with associated field systems and a trackway. It was evaluated by means of a phosphate survey and two test pits. The results were not encouraging so further work concentrated during the 1980s on the other cropmark sites. In 1990 the proposed imminent development of part of site X/Y presented an opportunity to investigate this site further. Excavation was carried out as initial site clearance was taking place. Seven linked trenches were excavated, totalling 602 m^2. The nature of the work was limited, being constrained by time and available finance, but it was assisted by generous loans of the developer's plant.

The excavations (Coe and Newman 1992) revealed the supposed Iron Age enclosure to be of a possible Late Iron Age–early Roman date in origin, with usage continuing into the later Roman period. The near total absence of features suggestive of structure from within the enclosed area and the paucity of artefacts, indicated that the area was not used for any long-term settlement and that the enclosure probably had an agricultural function. To the north of the enclosure, within an area previously demonstrated as having relatively high phosphate levels. but outside of the cropmark complex, an Early Iron Age round house was identified (Fig. 21.2). This structure was not within the area originally defined for investigation but was revealed during the developer's clearance of topsoil and subsequently included in the excavation area. A similar coincidental relationship between a principally Romano-British enclosure lacking in structural evidence and an earlier Iron Age round house had been noted at Cowdrey's Down. Here again attention had initially been focused on the perceived potential of the enclosure.

The Early Iron Age round house revealed at Site X/Y is the earliest settlement evidence thus far discovered in the Brighton Hill South development area. Relatively large numbers of pot sherds were recovered from the investigated post-holes, a number of these sherds were vitrified. Two explanations have been advanced to account for this evidence. The round house could have been destroyed by fire, the pottery being vitrified as a result of being inside the building at the time of the fire. The sherds could then have finished up in the post-holes as a result of site clearance. Alternatively it is possible that the distorted and blistered pottery was deposited in the post-holes deliberately, perhaps a symbolic act. Too little of the building and its environs were excavated to do more than tentatively hint at the possibilities and it is quite likely that the round house represented a wider settlement but we do not know this, and the site has now been developed.

The recent excavations at Brighton Hill South have demonstrated some of the difficulties inherent in basing site targeting on aerial photographic evidence, a practice that has been very common in Iron Age studies on the southern English Chalks and gravels. Investigations targeted on the basis of aerial photographic evidence can lead to important elements in the archaeological landscape being overlooked. Many of the rectilinear features so noted at Brighton Hill South appear to represent the sub-surface remains of field boundaries. Over reliance on aerial photographic evidence can lead to a concentration of attention on field systems at the expense of settlements. It is clearly a mistake to assume that all enclosures are settlements, or contemporary; they are often the visible relics of wider feature systems spatially but not chronologically related, existing in a multi-period, largely invisible, palimpsest.

22. Rooksdown Hospital, Basingstoke, Hampshire

C.A. Butterworth

Introduction

Part of an Iron Age settlement, probably a farmstead, was excavated during a second-stage archaeological assessment in the grounds of the former Rooksdown Hospital, Basingstoke, Hampshire. Although not continuous, activity on the site extended from the Early Iron Age through into the early Roman period.

Background

The site, in an area of known archaeological potential, lay within a proposed new housing development area. On the advice of the County Archaeologist (Hughes this volume), Hampshire County Council, as the local planning authority, asked the developer, Basingstoke and District Health Authority, to commission an archaeological evaluation before planning permission could be granted. An

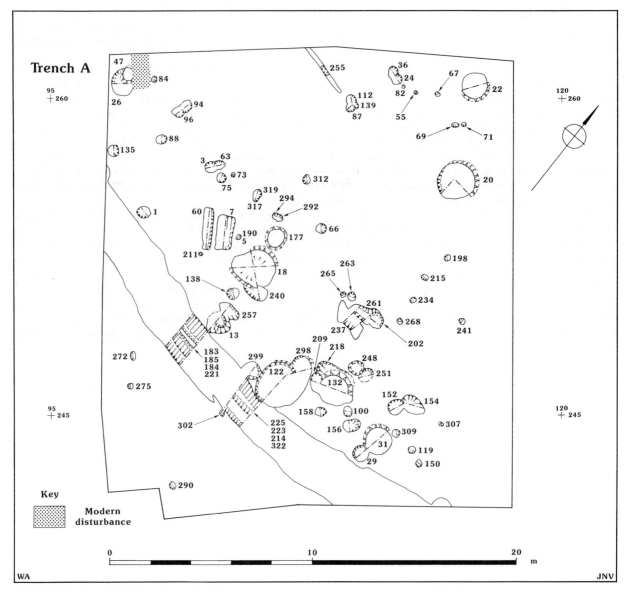

Figure 22.1   Rooksdown Hospital, Basingstoke, Hampshire, plan of Trench A

initial evaluation, undertaken by the Oxford Archaeological Unit, covered an area of c. 6 hectares with a grid of widely spaced machine-excavated trial trenches, within which, where present, a sample of potential archaeological features was recorded and manually excavated. A spread of Iron Age activity extending over c. 1.5 hectares north-east of the former main hospital building was thus defined and, within this area, a focus of archaeological deposits was recorded immediately north-east of Rooksdown. As a result of the first broad evaluation, the County Council asked the developer to commission a second assessment to provide further information about the more closely defined area of archaeological deposits. The second-stage evaluation was put out to tender, won and subsequently undertaken by Wessex Archaeology in October and November 1989.

The Setting

The site lies on Chalk and is on high ground on the north-western outskirts of Basingstoke, c. 1 km north-west of a large univallate hillfort at Winklebury (Smith 1977). Many other Iron Age settlement sites are known in the Basingstoke area (Oliver 1992, fig. 1), and details about several have come as a result of archaeological assessment and excavation before and during development of former green-field sites on the town's expanding perimeter (Coe and Newman 1992; Millett and James 1983; Millett and Russell 1984; Oliver 1992; Oliver and Applin 1979; Fasham and Keevill in press). Cropmarks in the fields north-west of the Rooksdown site are also thought to be of Iron Age date. The Roman road between *Venta Belgarum* (Winchester) and *Calleva Atrebatum* (Silchester) passed less than 100 m to the south-east of the site and a Roman settlement lay nearby to the south-west.

The Settlement Evidence

For the second evaluation, two trenches, A and B, separated by an access road, were cleared of topsoil by machine; the excavation had a total area of c. 13652 m^2 (Figs 22.1 and 22.2). After being cleaned and planned, a sample of the ditches and all other features were sectioned by hand and recorded. Although some truncation or erosion of shallow deposits or features had occurred, stratified deposits survived well within the deeper features.

The excavation revealed two distinct sequences of recut ditches on the site, one in each trench and on different but converging alignments, as well as a number of pits, post-holes and other features. The greatest density of features lay north of a probable enclosure ditch in the northern trench, Trench A, and, since evidence of Early Iron Age activity was only found in this area, may indicate that the settlement moved or expanded southwards during the Middle and Late Iron Age. Few features of early Roman date were recorded, but early Romano-British pottery was found in the upper levels of features in both trenches.

The earliest ditch of the northern sequence could be dated to the Early Iron Age; three later recuts on almost exactly the same alignment were dated to the Early/Middle, Middle and Late Iron Age or early Roman periods respectively. Much of the area immediately inside the ditch was occupied by pits and there was no recognisable evidence of a bank, although some post-holes near the inner edge of the ditch may have been associated with a timber-laced rampart.

The sequence and purpose of the southern ditch in Trench B was less certain, although the later recuts, of which again there were three, were thought to be of Middle and Late Iron Age date. An area of quarry hollows extended southward from the ditch, but, unlike the interior of the northern ditch, no other features were close by.

No evidence of houses or other structures was recorded in either trench, although a few, possibly related clusters of post-holes were noted. The majority of pits, eight of twelve, were north of the northern ditch; four were south of the Trench B ditch and only one in the area between the ditches (although part of this area was beneath the access road). No evidence of the pits' original uses had survived; the bottom of one pit showed possible signs of tool marks, but the bases of many were smooth, suggesting that they had been cleared and reused more than once (Fig. 22.3). All appeared to have been deliberately backfilled, partly with rubbish but predominantly with loose chalk rubble. Several contained large amounts of burnt flint and much iron slag was recovered from one. In addition to pottery, spindle whorls, clay loomweights and a weaving comb were also found, together with much animal bone; sheep/goat and cattle were the species most commonly represented. Recovered from the bases of separate pits were the articulated skeletons of a young pig and, except for the legs, which had been removed, a horse. Environmental evidence, seeds and chaff (the former including at least two cereal types), charcoal, and land snails, were also recovered from a small number of environmental samples.

Discussion

The second-stage assessment showed that the site at Rooksdown preserves features with well-stratified deposits containing valuable artefactual and environmental evidence. The importance of the

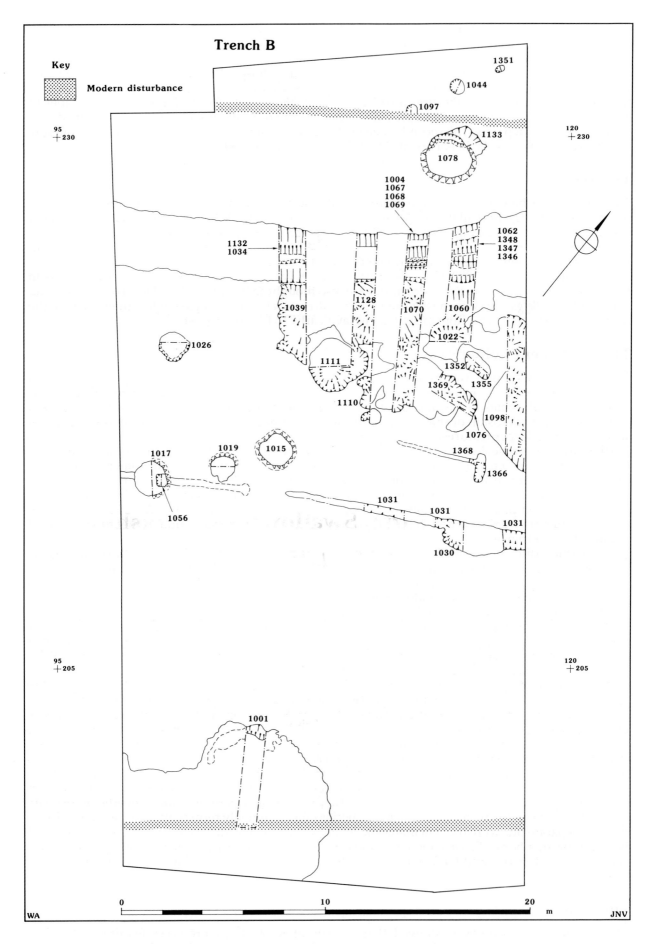

Figure 22.2   Rooksdown Hospital, plan of Trench B

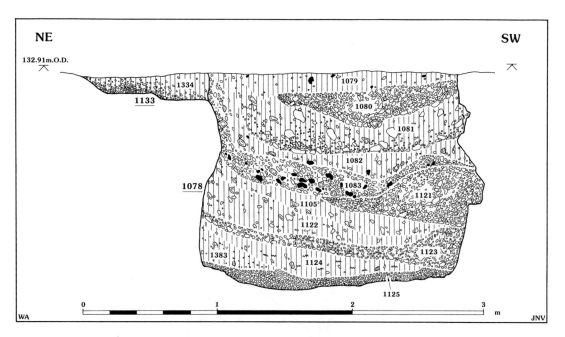

Figure 22.3   Rooksdown Hospital, section of pit 1078, Trench B

site can be enhanced both by the knowledge already derived from known Iron Age sites in the Basingstoke area and by the additional contribution this site can make to that knowledge. Although, at the time of writing, houses have been built on part of the development area, the site of the Iron Age settlement remains undeveloped. It is hoped that further excavation can be carried out and that the site will fulfill its potential.

23. Riseley Farm, Swallowfield, Berkshire

S.J. Lobb

Riseley Farm lies on a broad stretch of gravel on the floodplain of the Blackwater River (SU 735 636) on the Hampshire/Berkshire border. The ground is poorly drained and liable to flooding in the winter months. Aerial photographs taken in 1975 by the Royal Commission on Historical Monuments identified complex and apparently nucleated settlement features, consisting of compounds with round houses and possible field systems, with more dispersed, and sometimes poorly defined, features in the surrounding area (Gates 1975, map 1). In 1981, because of a potential threat to the archaeology of the site from gravel extraction, sample excavations were carried out to assess the date, nature, and state of preservation of the archaeological deposits. This work was carried out by Wessex Archaeology and funded by English Heritage. A full report was submitted to the Berkshire Archaeological Society in 1989 and will appear in due course in the *Berkshire Archaeological Journal*. The features visible on the aerial photographs in the southern part of the farm form a fairly coherent and definable group which had already been recommended for preservation. (Fig. 23.1). The excavation therefore concentrated on enclosures and features which were peripheral to the apparent focus of the settlement. Two enclosures were investigated which are of relevance to this volume, a rounded enclosure and a rectangular one.

The rounded enclosure

A possible enclosure defined by a curvilinear ditch was visible on the aerial photographs, even though it was fairly indistinct in places. This enclosure contained a T–shaped hearth and very few other features. The hearth was lined with burnt flint and large quantities of charcoal and contained pottery

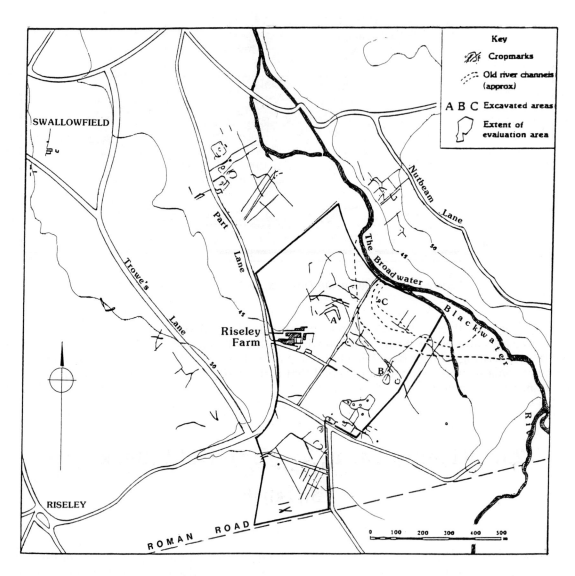

Figure 23.1   Riseley Farm, Swallowfield, Berkshire, the evidence from aerial photographs

with burnt clay attached. There was slight evidence that the feature may have had a clay super-structure. Charcoal from the central area was filled with alternate layers of silt and clay containing dense burnt flint and charcoal, interspersed with lenses of ash. Charcoal from the primary deposit produced a radiocarbon date of 2250±60 BP (HAR 9157).The specific function of this feature was not clear, but it may have been connected with the drying of pottery prior to firing. The lack of cereal remains in the carbonised material from this feature precludes its interpretation as a corn dryer. Other features to the north of the hearth contained fairly large quantities of burnt flint as well as some iron smithing slag, possibly suggesting ironworking activities in this enclosure. The pottery was entirely hand built and dominated by sandy and organic wares. The forms mainly reflect influences from the south Midlands and the upper Thames region, and suggest a date in the Middle Iron Age date which fits well with the radiocarbon date.

The rectangular enclosure

A double ditched enclosure visible on the aerial photographs to the north-east of the modern farm buildings, was associated with ditches which probably represent two different field systems. Three small trenches were excavated across the ditches and into the interior of the enclosure allowing a complex sequence of ditches with evidence for recutting and replacement to be defined. Two broad phases are suggested by the pottery, although the total length of occupation in the first half of the first century AD appears to have been fairly short. The second phase of activity dates to the mid-first century AD. In its final phase after the silting up of the ditches the enclosure may have been formed by a fence.

It was difficult to relate the internal features to particular phases of occupation but two possible structures were identified within the excavated areas. On the south-eastern side of the enclosure a trampled floor area was lined by post-holes suggesting the existence of a rectangular building. On the opposite side of the enclosure were the remains of a more flimsy structure which was defined by small stakes driven into a shallow ring gully; fragments of wattle and daub from the ditch close by may have come from this structure. Large quantities of burnt material including iron slags, burnt flint, and charcoal were recovered from the eastern side of the enclosure suggesting that both iron smelting and smithing were carried out. Finds from the features of the rectangular structure included the remains of a possible hearth or kiln, providing further evidence for industrial activity in this part of the enclosure. By contrast the northern part of the enclosure appears to have been kept clean with very little dumping of waste material and a domestic function for the structure in this area seems likely.

The pottery types from this enclosure include local imitations of imported wares and examples of imported wares which had a wide distribution in the south and south-east at this time, as well as grog-tempered fabrics and the flint-tempered Silchester ware of the period. This reflects the proximity and influence of the late Iron Age oppidum at Silchester. Riseley Farm is adjacent to the Roman road running eastwards towards Staines and London, 9 km from Silchester. It is possible that the same road network was used prior to the Roman period for the distribution of commodities, both locally and further afield, to and from the important market and commercial centre at Silchester.

The evaluation excavations examined only a small sample of two enclosures within an extensive archaeological landscape and suggested the importance of the site, while posing other questions. The apparent nucleus of the site, suggested by the aerial photographs, lies on higher ground to the south of the two enclosures investigated and its morphology is in marked contrast to the more rectangular enclosures and associated field systems of the later Iron Age settlements in the area. However, there is some resemblance to the Middle Iron Age sites in the upper Thames Valley, perhaps indicating an early date for the occupation of a large part of the site. Since the investigations the interest in extracting gravel from the site has been dropped, and the extensive archaeological landscape at the site remains, for the time being, intact.

24. An Iron Age settlement at Ashton Keynes, Wiltshire

Caron Newman

Introduction

The village of Ashton Keynes lies between Swindon and Cirencester in north Wiltshire close to the border with Gloucestershire. It is situated on a first level terrace of alluvium and gravel within the Upper Thames valley, close to the headwaters of the River Thames at c. 83 m OD. Although the Thames is little more than a brook at this point, the area is subject to regular and periodic flooding. The area around Ashton Keynes is a major centre of gravel extraction. One of the main characteristics of the local landscape, therefore, is the large number of water-filled quarries which almost surround Ashton Keynes, and the village is the focus for the Cotswold Water Park.

The Upper Thames valley is an area of intensive archaeological activity, and archaeological survey and excavation over many years has demonstrated that Ashton Keynes and its environs has an extremely rich archaeological resource. A survey which covered the Upper Thames valley in Gloucestershire and Wiltshire mainly using aerial photographic evidence was undertaken in 1983–4 (Hingley 1984b). It defined several archaeological sites, the earliest of which was a series of cropmarks described as a complex of possible Bronze Age date including a broad linear ditch and settlement enclosure to the north-east of Ashton Keynes. This was designated a site of national importance, as was an area of cropmarks and earthworks, covering c. 5 hectares at Cleveland Farm, to the east of the village. Many other areas of cropmarks were identified, most of which are thought to be Iron Age or Roman.

Many of the sites identified in the survey have now disappeared because of gravel extraction, permission for which has been long-standing and therefore contained no provision for archaeological

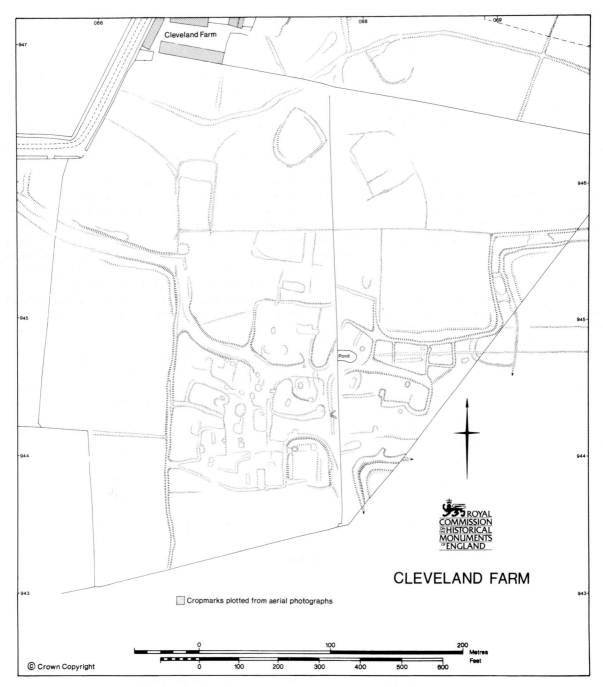

Figure 24.1   Ashton Keynes, Cleveland Farm, Wiltshire, hachured survey of the Iron Age and Romano-British earthworks and plot of evidence from aerial photographs. Crown Copyright

recording. In recent years, however, archaeologists have been given the opportunity to survey and excavate sites in advance. These have included some of the areas of interest identified by Hingley, most significantly the complex of cropmarks and earthworks to the south and east of Cleveland Farm, Ashton Keynes.

Cleveland Farm

Cleveland Farm was part of an area of proposed gravel extraction under a long standing planning permission granted to English China Clays Ltd (ECC Ltd). Following the identification of the potential importance of the site in Hingley's survey, an evaluation survey and limited excavation was carried out by the Trust for Wessex Archaeology in 1984 (Coe *et al.* 1991). This demonstrated the excellent state of preservation of much of the site, and indicated a date within the earlier part of the Roman period for those features which were sampled. However, because of the extant planning permission, by the time the importance of the site had been adequately documented, the opportunity for preservation had gone. A plan of recording and survey was drawn up, funded by the developer and English Heritage. In 1988 work begun with a detailed survey of the earthworks (Fig. 24.1) by the Royal Commission for Historic Monuments (England). This was followed by a programme of further evaluation, small-scale targeted excavations, geophysical survey and watching briefs carried out between 1988 and 1991.

The work revealed evidence for both Iron Age and Romano-British settlement. A series of four Iron Age enclosures were defined, as were a number of unenclosed hut circles, four-post structures, pits, ditches and gullies (Fig. 24.2). Generally, the Iron Age features tended to be grouped in the northern half of the site and the Romano-British occupation to the south. A long linear feature, running east–west across the site, roughly formed a boundary between the two, possibly marking the northern edge of the Roman settlement area.

Enclosure 1 lay to the north of the other Iron Age enclosures (Fig. 24.1) (Wessex Archaeology 1989). Three sides of the subrectangular enclosure were revealed, with a series of later ditches probably marking the original line of the north end. The ditch contained well-preserved organic materials, and showed evidence of repeated scourings, indicating that one of its main functions was drainage. Within the enclosure was the remains of a round house, approximately 10 m in diameter, consisting of two partially preserved concentric gullies. Finds indicated that the round house and enclosure dated to the Late Iron Age and possibly early Roman period.

Enclosure 2 lay directly to the south of Enclosure 1 (Fig. 24.2). This was the most complex enclosure, being nearly square with one slightly curving side. There was no evidence for contemporary round houses within the enclosure, which dated to the Middle Iron Age, although later hut circles were recorded. Two 4–post structures, pits and a number of post-holes do appear to be contemporary (Coe et al. 1991).

Enclosure 3 lay to the west of Enclosure 2 (Fig. 24.2). It was subrectangular, with three straight sides and a semi-circular south-western end. It contained the remnants of a possible round house, c. 13 m in diameter, and several post-holes. A further 'exclamation mark'–shaped feature was identified within this enclosure, and contained large quantities of burnt Limestone. It cuts across, and is therefore later than, the round house. The round house and enclosure ditch produced Middle Iron Age pottery.

Enclosure 4 was roughly rectangular, and was marked on its southern boundary by the long east–west boundary (Fig. 24.2). There was some evidence for a round house within the enclosure, all of which is dated by pottery towards the end of the Late Iron Age, c. 50 BC – c. AD 50.

Aside from the enclosures, ten unenclosed hut circles were recorded, as well as five further sections of curving gully which may have been the remains of hut circles. Pottery from the gullies varied from the Middle–Late Iron Age.

Rixon Gate

Further excavations, funded by ECC Ltd, were carried out to the south-west of Cleveland Farm, in an area known as Rixon Gate to the east of Ashton Keynes (Wessex Archaeology 1992). The work was undertaken as a salvage excavation following the discovery of Iron Age and Roman features during topsoil stripping (Fig. 24.3). The site lay on a slight rise within the low-lying and marshy ground next to the River Thames and deeper cut features produced plentiful waterlogged environmental evidence, such as organic waste which included floor coverings and animal faeces as well as wetland plants.

Evidence for at least two separate round houses was discovered, the larger of which was at least 13 m in diameter. The smaller round house appeared to have a related curved gully to the north-east, with a large terminal post-hole at its western end, and possibly represents a working area. An Iron Age enclosure ditch survived as a section of curved ditch, forming the north-west corner of the settlement. Several other sections of curved ditch towards the periphery of the settlement area may indicate part of the route followed by the enclosure boundary ditch, but they could not be examined in the time available. Other isolated features were dated to the late Iron Age within the settlement area. It must be assumed that the remainder of the evidence for the Iron Age settlement was removed and/or reused during the later Romano-British settlement which directly overlay the Iron Age settlement.

Discussion

Rixon Gate was made up of at least a single farmstead with successive occupations on the same site from the Late Iron Age to the late Roman period. The settlement to the north at Cleveland Farm, however, seems to have comprised several farmsteads, with slight shifts in location from the Middle to Late Iron Age and into the Roman period. Although neither site was fully excavated, it does appear that the southern boundary of the Cleveland Farm settlement was defined although it continued outside the excavation area to the north and west. The Rixon Gate settlement, however, almost certainly continued to the east and north, an area extracted for gravel some years before. It is likely that the two areas of occupation are part of an agglomerated settlement pattern, made up of single

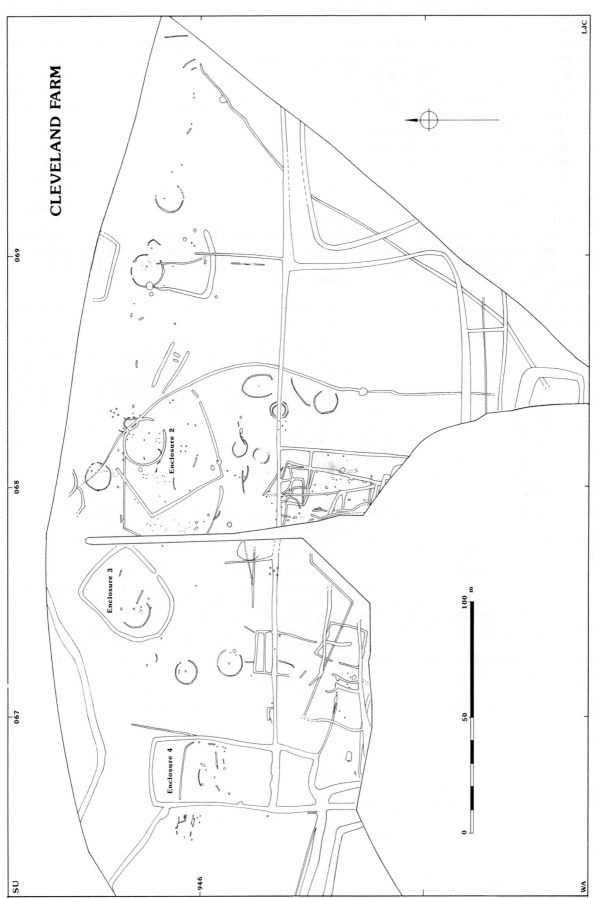

Figure 24.2   Ashton Keynes, Cleveland Farm, plan of observed archaeological features

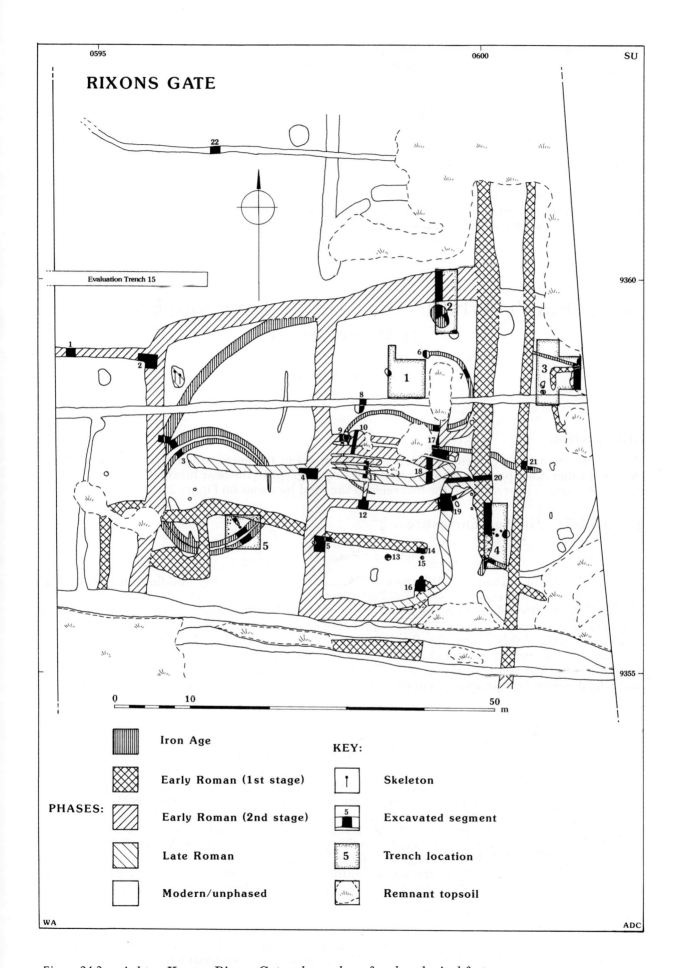

Figure 24.3   Ashton Keynes, Rixons Gate, phase plan of archaeological features

farmsteads or, as at Cleveland Farm, small groups of farms forming loose complexes. This settlement type has been described as a 'girdle pattern', and is a well-established type in the Fens (Hingley 1989, 95). Hingley has identified other parts of Britain where the girdle pattern characterises the Iron Age settlements, and which may include the Upper Thames valley (Hingley 1989, 100). Generally the settlements within this pattern are not more than 500 m apart. Although Rixon Gate and Cleveland Farm are about 1 km apart, there is evidence from local people that the area between the two did contain archaeological remains which have now been destroyed. Clearly the area was quite densely settled, though probably not unusually so. Any such settlement pattern would probably have evolved as a means of sharing rights to areas of arable and pasture.

Both sites have shown considerable evidence for continuity from the Iron Age up to late Roman period. There is little indication that the imposition of Roman rule was socially disruptive in this area but further work is needed to exploit the environmental data, examine the relationship between the enclosures and the field systems and to investigate the slight shifts in settlement pattern during the Iron Age.

25. Oram's Arbour: the Middle Iron Age Enclosure at Winchester

R. Whinney

Introduction

This article summarises current knowledge and ideas about the enclosure at Oram's Arbour, Winchester; a fuller description and justification will be published in the near future (Qualmann *et al.* in press). The figures in brackets in the text refer to sites and locations on Figure 25.2.

The Middle Iron Age Enclosure

Location

The Oram's Arbour enclosure at Winchester was constructed during the Middle Iron Age, on the western side of the Itchen valley (SU 4780 2975 centre), at a significant narrowing of the floodplain (Fig. 15.1). In the floodplain itself was a low island or knoll. Together, these natural features formed a favourable position for a crossing point — probably a ford — of the river. For some distance to the north and south of this island, the floodplain probably formed a broad barrier to all east–west movement in the area; as a consequence, the ford may have become a focus of communications for much of central and southern Hampshire. The ford was approached by an east–west route that ran along the downland ridges and by a north–south route along the western edge of the floodplain.

Dating

The dating of the construction of the enclosure is difficult to establish precisely, but it appears that the ditch was excavated and the bank built during the Middle Iron Age. Datable material derived from the primary fills of the ditch is rather scarce, as most recently excavated sections showed evidence of recuts or cleaning. At New Road (45), several recuts were identified, but a near-complete profile of a Middle Iron Age saucepan pot was recovered from the fill of the earliest surviving recut.

The dating evidence for the disuse of the enclosure is slightly less equivocal. At Trafalgar House (42), and at Assize Courts North (37), large scale levelling of the ditch and its associated bank appeared to be of pre-Flavian and early Flavian date. To this evidence may be added the possibility that the 'earthwork' sealed by Claudian buildings, at St George's Street was really the remains of the enclosure rampart (16, 17, 19). It seems likely that the enclosure had ceased to function as such by the end of the Iron Age, but that parts of its line were adapted for other purposes during the Roman period and later.

The defensive circuit

The defences have been located on the north, south, and west sides of the enclosure, but the eastern limit has not been definitely identified (Fig. 25.2). Middle Iron Age material has been recovered just

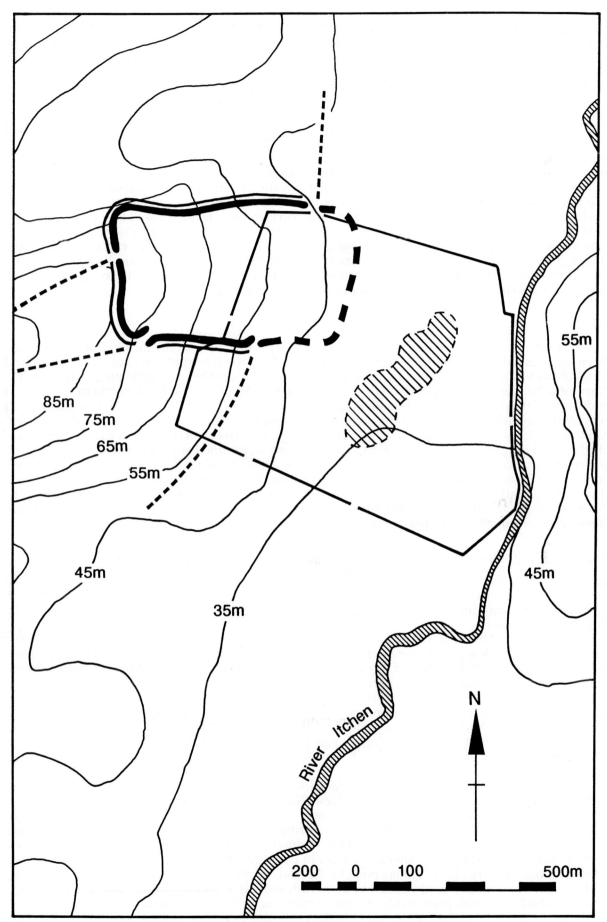

Figure 25.1   Location of Oram's Arbour, Winchester, Hampshire, enclosure in relation to the natural topography and the later Roman defences. The island or raised knoll is shaded

to the east of St Peter's Street (27), suggesting that the enclosure may have extended up to this line. Other watching briefs and small scale excavation in this area (54, 38) all suggest a substantial natural slope. In these circumstances, neither ditch nor rampart may have been required, as the marshy conditions of the floodplain might have provided ample protection.

The circuit of the defences has been traced over a length of about 1.125 km; however, if the enclosure extended to a line just east of St Peter's Street, the total length of the defensive circuit was about 1.650 km, enclosing an area of some 20 hectares.

Excavated sections through the ditch reveal a V–shaped profile that has usually been much altered by later recuts, cleaning and quarrying. Where it is not truncated, the ditch has usually been found to be 3.5–4.0 m deep, although a depth of 4.8 m has been recorded (33). The original width was apparently between 7–7.5 m, although the weathered profile is usually 9–10 m wide.

Nothing of the associated rampart survives in the modern landscape, although some evidence from the Carfax site (61) suggests a basal width of about 8.0 m. Near the south-eastern corner of the enclosure, at St George's Street (16), an 'earthwork' survived to a height of about 1.8 m. These layers sealed pre-Roman deposits and were themselves overlain by Claudian timber buildings. It may be that this 'earthwork' represents a survival of the enclosure rampart either *in situ* or in a slighted state, although this interpretation was not favoured in the published account (Cunliffe 1964, 21–2). As no structural components of the rampart — timbers or stone walls for instance — have been identified, it is assumed to have been of glacis or simple dump construction.

Entrances

Several entrances into the enclosure are either known or postulated. but only the western entrance has been investigated in any detail (33). Here, the defensive ditch was interrupted by a causeway of natural chalk about 8 m wide. The northern arm of the ditch turned inward before terminating. A track, in the form of a hollow way, passed through the entrance (Biddle 1968, 251–5). A northern entrance is indicated by the pre-Roman north–south hollow way identified at Victoria Road (53). This led towards a point in the enclosure defences later occupied by the north gate of the Roman and medieval town. On the south, excavations and a watching brief at Trafalgar House (42) revealed that the enclosure ditch turned inwards at that point, perhaps representing an inturned entrance. There may have been a further entrance near the south-western corner of the enclosure at a point where a hollow way, later to form the Roman road from Winchester to Old Sarum, crossed the line of the enclosure defences. There are indications that the hollow way was contemporary with, or earlier than, the enclosure (51). No evidence for an entrance into the east side of the enclosure has been recovered. Any such entrance here would presumably have been linked to the ford across the river Itchen.

Internal Occupation

Less than 3% of the interior of the enclosure has been excavated. Of this 3%, a third produced no evidence of pre-Roman activity save the occasional residual pottery sherd. Therefore, based on such a small sample, any interpretation of the interior organisation and associated activities must be considered tentative.

Where present, Middle Iron Age occupation was represented by shallow ditches, drainage gullies, post-holes, and shallow scoops, but often insufficient areas were available to provide a coherent plan. At Staple Gardens (60), Middle Iron Age occupation consisted of a four-post structure and a possible stake-built circular building or pen, partly surrounded by drainage gullies. Another Middle Iron Age round house was excavated at Tower Street (25). On both of these sites, the remains may represent no more than a single phase of Middle Iron Age occupation. At the Westgate Car Park (13) and the Sussex Street sites (48–50), Middle Iron Age occupation was represented by several phases of intercutting ditches, gullies and postholes, suggesting a longer period of use. Middle Iron Age occupation deposits were also recovered from the Carfax and New Road sites (61, 45) immediately to the rear of the rampart.

The presence of plough soils immediately outside the enclosure, and at least two four-post storage structures, together with quernstones from New Road (45), suggests that some cultivation, storage and processing of grain was carried out on or near the site. The evidence of the plant remains is in keeping with other sites in the Winchester area during the Middle Iron Age period, with barley and spelt wheat predominating over emmer wheat. Animal husbandry also appears to have conformed fairly closely with practices elsewhere, as far as can be judged from such a small sample. The absence of very young and very old sheep may point to seasonal occupation. The main diet of sheep/goat, pig, cattle, and horse was also supplemented by both fresh and salt water fish. The discovery of briquetage shows that salt was used, presumably as a preservative as well as a seasoning.

There are a few hints that certain parts of the enclosure were reserved for specific activities; the large number of querns recovered from a single feature at New Road (45) may suggest this.

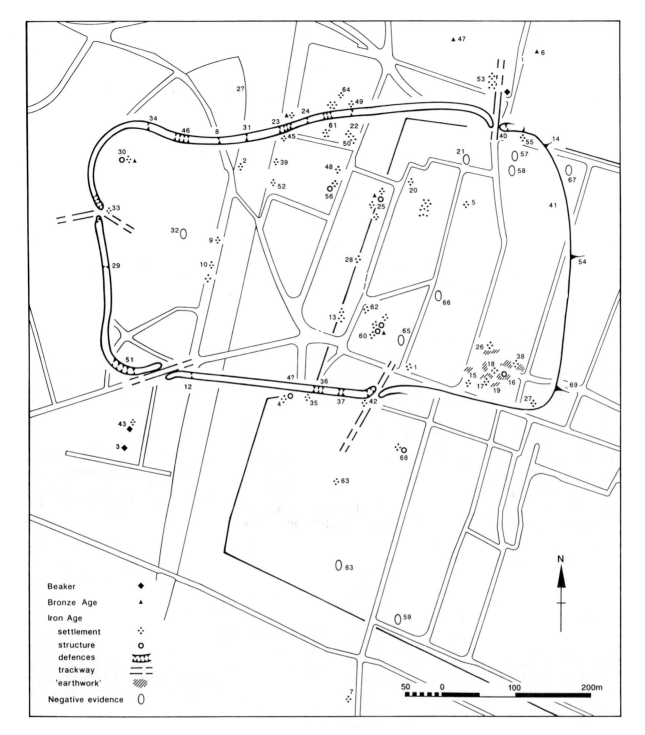

Figure 25.2   Oram's Arbour enclosure, showing location of prehistoric sites, watching briefs, and other discoveries. Not all sites shown are mentioned in the text. The line of the later Roman town defences is shown for reference

Summary

The structural, artefactual and environmental evidence gives the impression that Middle Iron Age occupation within the enclosure was widespread but patchy, and either very short-lived or rather sporadic. Some of the activities normally associated with Middle Iron Age sites in central Wessex may not have been carried out here, but the lack of evidence for others may be merely fortuitous. In other respects, the site appears to have been perfectly normal. There are hints that occupation was seasonal, perhaps taking place during the late summer and early autumn.

The Role and Function of Oram's Arbour Enclosure

It is evident from the foregoing description of the Middle Iron Age enclosure that the surviving evidence, except perhaps for that pertaining to the enclosure defences, is generally rather limited. Because of this, it is not possible to be very certain about the character and extent of Middle Iron Age occupation. Equal uncertainty therefore exists in postulating a *raison d'être* for the construction of the enclosure. However the following observations may be pertinent.

Strategic location

The valley-side location and the command of a major ford and crossroads all suggest that the Oram's Arbour enclosure was very distinct from the majority of the hillforts and other enclosed settlements of Iron Age Wessex. As already indicated, this uniqueness cannot at present be fully explained. It is perhaps the physical location of the enclosure rather than the character of the interior occupation that provides the best clues as to its function.

The siting of the enclosure was such as to compel users of all known routes approaching the area to either enter the enclosure, or pass immediately below the southern defences. North–south traffic would of necessity have used the entrances at Northgate and Trafalgar House. Traffic from the west and south-west used either the entrance at Oram's Arbour, or the entrance in the south-west corner. Either route lead eventually to the ford across the Itchen. This implies that the defences not only enclosed the junction of the east–west and north–south routes, but also controlled the western approaches to the ford. Similarly, all traffic crossing from the eastern bank of the river would have been compelled to pass through, or very near to, the enclosure.

It appears that these routes were a major consideration in the siting of the enclosure during the Middle Iron Age. However, from what is known of the spatial relationships between the defences and Late Iron Age occupation phases within the enclosure, it is difficult to assess whether this situation persisted until the close of the Iron Age.

Contact, distribution, and exchange

Despite the overall paucity of the Middle Iron Age artefactual assemblage, the evidence for contact over a wider area of central Wessex is relatively good. For instance, the presence of sea fish indicates at least occasional exploitation of coastal resources for food. That querns probably manufactured at Lodsworth, in Sussex, were in use at Oram's Arbour occasions no surprise, as they are common in the Winchester area generally, especially during the Middle Iron Age.

It is also becoming increasingly clear that whereas some types of Iron Age pottery were manufactured for very local consumption, others were the objects of regional exchange. Some of the pottery from Oram's Arbour may have been supplied from two (or more) regional industries — at least one producing glauconitic sandy wares and the other, flint-tempered wares in the St Catherine's Hill–Worthy Down style. Although accurate definition of the fabrics is difficult and more work is necessary to locate the sources of manufacture of these wares, it should be possible to assess the nature of the regional pottery supply in the near future.

This evidence for exchange, between groups using the Oram's Arbour enclosure and others, seems to conform quite closely with that from other sites in Hampshire. The presence of sea fish is slightly unusual, but this may be the result of preservation and sampling strategy rather than a genuine reflection of past human behaviour. It should be noted, however, that quite substantial contact with the coast seems to be indicated, although the nature of Middle and Late Iron Age settlement in the nearest of these areas, around the Solent, is poorly understood.

Oram's Arbour in a Wider Context

It appears that the enclosure was occupied at the same time as the unenclosed Middle Iron Age phase of settlement at Winnall Down/Easton Lane, and was also contemporary with the construction and occupation of the hillfort on St Catherine's Hill. The proximity of Oram's Arbour to this 'typical' Middle Iron Age hillfort — St Catherine's Hill is only 2 km to the south-east — has been commented upon many times. It is also contemporary with the dense late period occupation at Danebury (ceramic phases 6–7).

It is possible to envisage a scenario which places Oram's Arbour in the centre of the Middle Iron Age 'St Catherine's Hill–Worthy Down' ceramic style zone (Cunliffe 1984a, 257). It could be argued that the Oram's Arbour enclosure, apparently unique in the region, was a new creation, built by the inhabitants of the style zone in the Middle Iron Age, in a more accessible valley-side location. The new enclosure, in the geographic — and possibly the socio/economic centre — of the style zone, was strategically dominant, and may have exploited on behalf of the local 'St Catherine's Hill–Worthy

Down' community, the increasingly profitable trade routes that were developing as a result of contact with the Romanised continent of Europe. It dominated at least one important north–south route from the coast up the Itchen valley, into the heart of the country. It was thus in an almost ideal situation to exploit any movement of goods and peoples.

As already noted, there is some evidence for external trade and communications into and probably through the enclosure. Salt, quernstones and some ceramics have already been cited. Biddle has highlighted the concentration of both native and exotic coin finds (1983, 108; but see Haselgrove this volume) which, together with the small but growing number of fragments of Dr 1 amphorae from the immediate area, for example at Owslebury (Collis this volume) and, Berwick Field, Winchester, could be cited as pointing to a wider series of national and international contacts.

If these factors, albeit some of them speculative, are taken together, it is possible to make a case for the Oram's Arbour enclosure functioning as a focus of exchange and communications (and possibly ceremony) for the area of central Hampshire. By virtue of its dominant yet accessible location, local, regional, national, and perhaps even international traffic was almost forced to pass through the enclosure, thereby contributing to the success and wealth of the local community as a whole, and perhaps sowing the seeds for the development of Winchester as an socio-economic centre in later times.

The strategic advantages enjoyed by the site, and the trade routes and contacts already in place may have allowed the late Iron Age inhabitants of the area to maintain and develop their local and perhaps regional dominance. Contact with, or indeed absorption into, the 'core zone', may have resulted in Oram's Arbour becoming (or indeed continuing as) the centre of 'a socio-economic zone' in the period 50 BC–AD 10 (Cunliffe 1991, 132 and fig 7.2). Indeed the enclosure has again been described as an oppidum, serving the southern Atrebatic peoples (Cunliffe 1991, 154).

Whatever the precise function of the Oram's Arbour enclosure, its strong strategic position, and its central role in local socio-economic matters must have been key factors in the establishment of the early Roman town in the middle of the first century AD.

26. Maiden Castle, Dorset

Niall Sharples

The Iron Age settlement at Maiden Castle is the best known and also the most physically impressive period of occupation on this Dorset hilltop. However, this needs to be placed in the context of a history which stretches from an Early Neolithic enclosure to a modern farming landscape. The construction of the Neolithic enclosure defined the hilltop as a special centre and it is unlikely that it ever lost this significance even during long periods in the later Bronze Age and medieval period when the hilltop appears to have been largely abandoned.

Archaeological investigation of the hilltop began in a haphazard fashion in the late nineteenth century, but the first significant excavation was started in 1934. This excavation was directed by Sir Mortimer Wheeler who was then the pre-eminent archaeologist working in the British Isles and even today remains one of Britain's most famous archaeologists. He carried out four seasons of excavation which lasted all summer and employed large numbers of people. At the time they were the most extensive excavations undertaken in Britain employing the best archaeologists and utilising the best techniques currently available. It is only in comparatively recent times that their scale has been surpassed. These excavations gave a very clear picture of the sequence of occupation on the hilltop and still provide the basis for any understanding of the Iron Age occupation. However, in 1985 and 1986 further excavations were undertaken which have added a considerable amount of information which was inaccessible to Wheeler (Sharples 1991a; 1991b).

The Iron Age occupation began with the construction of a small, 6.4 hectare, enclosure which seems to have been built in a pastoral landscape, probably on the boundaries of two adjacent territories. The size and location of this enclosure is very similar to large numbers of hillforts found in south central England dating from the fifth–fourth centuries BC. These enclosures are defined by a single ditch and bank whose substantial depth and height is assumed to indicate a defensive function. At Maiden Castle the distance from the base of the ditch to the top of the rampart was over 8.4 m. The rampart was a simple dump of chalk and clay excavated from the adjacent ditch, but on either side of the entrance this was elaborated by the construction of a timber faced revetment to create a vertical wall 5 m high. Access to the hillfort was by two entrances facing east and west. The eastern entrance was a unique

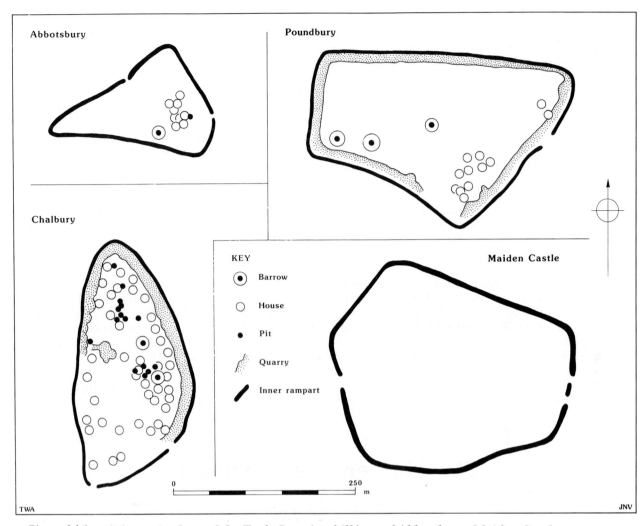

Figure 26.1   Schematic plans of the Early Iron Age hillforts of Abbotsbury, Maiden Castle, Poundbury, and Chalbury, Dorset

double gateway which may have been constructed to respect an existing territorial boundary running along the crest of the hill.

Unfortunately we know very little about the occupation of this hillfort as much of the settlement evidence is confused with the later Iron Age occupation. Comparison with similar nearby hillforts such as Poundbury, Chalbury, and Abbotsbury (Fig. 26.1) suggests that there would have been a small con- centration of circular houses somewhere in the interior with associated subterranean granary pits and above ground storage buildings. These nucleated settlements mark a radical departure from previous settlements in the region which were dispersed farmsteads.

In the 400–500 years between the establishment of the first Iron Age settlement and the Roman invasion of southern England, occupation in Maiden Castle was continuous and permanent. The form and significance of the hillfort, however, changed considerably during this period and the number of people living permanently and temporarily inside it fluctuated dramatically not only from decade to decade but from season to season.

One of the principal activities visible in the archaeological record for the first 300 years was the construction, modification and reconstruction of the enclosing banks and ditches. The original 6.4 hectare enclosure was extended to the west to enclose a further 12.6 hectares. Then further external ramparts and ditches were constructed and the original inner bank was heightened. By the second century BC an area of 19 hectares was enclosed by three to four lines of banks and ditches with the inner bank being over 5.5 m high. At both entrances a maze of overlapping banks and ditches formed an imposing access to two double gateways (Fig. 26.2).

The work involved in this activity would have been enormous and labour requirements suggest that this was a seasonal activity undertaken by a large influx of people in the summer when the crops could be left unsupervised. This work established the importance of the community occupying the hillfort. The ramparts not only symbolised the community's prestige but also provided an occasion whereby this prestige could be demonstrated by the mobilisation of an enormous labour force which might otherwise be employed fighting for the community or rebelling against it. Control over this

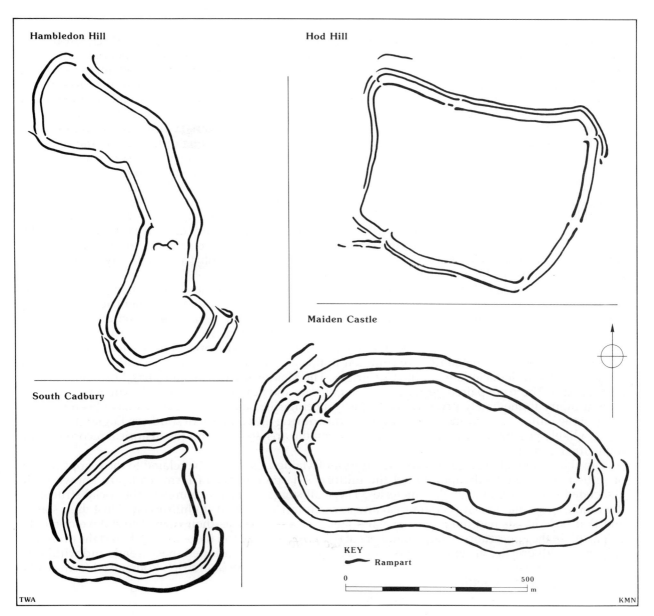

Hambledon Hill

Hod Hill

Maiden Castle

South Cadbury

KEY
Rampart

0   500
                                          m

TWA   KMN

Figure 26.2   Schematic plans of the developed hillforts of Maiden Castle, Hambledon Hill, Hod Hill (Dorset), and South Cadbury (Somerset)

labour force was possible only through control over agricultural produce. The bulk of the grain harvested in the surrounding countryside was stored in underground grain silos which are found in large numbers across the hilltop. Storage above ground is also represented by distinctive 4–post structures.

At first this large area was only sparsely occupied. Dispersed groups of houses, pits and ancillary structures are found scattered across the hilltop. Gradually the number of buildings constructed grew and the population increased as people moved in from neighbouring settlements. Around 250 BC, at the end of the principal period of rampart building, a major reorganisation of this settlement appears to have occurred. Rows of houses adjacent to routes ran across the hilltop from east to west.

Excavations in the south-west corner of the hilltop revealed three well preserved examples of these houses in the hollow immediately behind the inner rampart. These houses all had individual peculiarities such as stone foundations, an enclosing gully or a terraced floor but they were similar in size (6.7–8.2 m in diameter, relatively small in comparison to Late Bronze Age houses), probably looked almost identical when roofed, and were all completely rebuilt once. Inside these houses was a hearth placed almost centrally and often accompanied by a domed oven. The distribution of ash from this fire indicates that the floor to the back right was kept clean and may have been used for sleeping whereas the floor to the front and left was covered in ash and was possibly where food preparation and other domestic activities took place.

Large quantities of artefacts and ecofacts were recovered from this Middle Iron Age period of occupation providing a detailed picture of the economy and social life of the inhabitants. The agricultural economy of the inhabitants was dominated by the cultivation of spelt and six-row barley. Animal husbandry seems to have been largely concerned with the production of wool but cattle were also present in large numbers, probably as traction animals, and pigs were kept for meat. Craft activities in the hillfort included textile production, small scale metalworking and, in the early part of the period, pottery manufacturing . These activities all seem to have taken place in households and there is no evidence for specialisation or large scale surplus production for trade at this period.

Towards the end of the Middle Iron Age various aspects of the material culture changed dramatically. This is best exemplified in the ceramic assemblage. In the beginning of the period the ceramics were large almost undecorated jars and bowls with a simple shouldered form and very rough surface finish. Similar vessels could be found all over southern England. At the end of the period a distinct regional assemblage of ceramic forms was available. This ranged from small bowls to large jars and included fine vessels with elaborate decoration and carefully burnished surfaces. Most of the later assemblage was imported to Maiden Castle from large workshops in the Poole Harbour region of east Dorset (Hearne and Cox this volume). Other changes are visible in the quantity and quality of the items available to the inhabitants of the hillfort and this appears to be related to the creation of a number of specialist production centres that manufactured a range of objects specifically used to create a regional identity for the inhabitants of Dorset.

In the Late Iron Age there was a dramatic reorganisation of the settlement in Maiden Castle. Most of the area enclosed was abandoned with a concentration of the remaining settlement activity around the eastern entrance. The basic structures used, however, appear to remain the same; circular houses and pits. Immediately outside the eastern gateway was an extensive area of metalworking debris which is the remains of a smith's workshop. Further out in the earthworks of the eastern entrance was a large cemetery. Such cemeteries are common in this area in the Late Iron Age and form one of the defining cultural characteristics of the Durotriges. The Maiden Castle cemetery has, however, various peculiarities. There are paired burials, extended burials and burials of individuals who have suffered violent injury immediately prior to death. These peculiarities and other features have been used to suggest the hillfort was stormed by the Roman army during the conquest of southern England. Though this is a likely possibility, a detailed linkage between the archaeology and the historical record is both unjustified and unnecessary.

The abandonment of large areas of the interior of Maiden Castle can be related to the reappearance of settlement in the landscape around the hillfort. A large number of farmsteads are known with associated enclosures and small cemeteries. These all suggest a major change in the social structure. It would appear that the large communal and agricultural settlements in hillforts had lost their status and that individuals had the power to claim land and resources as their own. These developments help explain the appearance of large numbers of pieces of jewellery on the settlements and the presence of burials with prestigious grave goods. The Roman occupation continued these trends and within 50 years Maiden Castle was abandoned for the new town of *Durnovaria* and rich Romanised farmsteads began to appear at the settlements established in the Late Iron Age.

27. Danebury, Hampshire

Barry Cunliffe

The hillfort of Danebury has been the scene of an extended campaign of excavation spanning twenty field-work seasons (1969–1988) during which time 57% of the main enclosed area has been excavated and the defences and gates examined (Cunliffe 1984a; Cunliffe and Poole 1991).

The earliest enclosure of the hilltop took place in the eighth or seventh century BC when a V–shaped ditch was dug around the hill enclosing an area of 16.2 hectares. At least three entrances have been discovered. One, dominating the main approach to the hill, was linked to a linear earthwork which can be traced running eastwards for a distance of some 2 km. Within the enclosure several large 'ritual' pits were traced, sited roughly on a contour concentric with the ditch: they are undated and may precede the enclosure or be broadly contemporary with it.

Within this arc of pits, the main defences of the hillfort were erected in the sixth century. The rampart overlaid several 4–post structures which must, therefore, belong to the pre-hillfort occupation. One possibility is that the hillfort defences were preceded by a palisaded enclosure (removed by the hillfort ditch except at the entrance where gate posts survive) and that the 4–post storage structures lay within this enclosure.

Figure 27.1   Aerial photograph of Danebury, looking north

The earliest defences of the hillfort enclosed an area of 5 hectares. In the initial stage the rampart was strengthened by a box-like structure of vertical timbers. These will have rotted within 20–30 years. No attempt was made to replace them but the rampart was subsequently increased in size (most substantially in the mid-fourth century) by the addition of tips of soil and chalk on the inner slope. The fort originally had two gates but that on the south-west side was blocked in the fourth century leaving the eastern gate to form the only entrance thereafter. It was later provided with massive forward-projecting hornworks and remodelled to create, in its final phase, a narrow corridor leading to a double gate.

The hillfort was occupied on an increasingly intensive scale from the sixth century to the beginning of the first century BC when the gate was burnt and intensive occupation ceased. Thereafter the site continued to be used into the first century AD but on a much reduced scale.

The principal occupation can be divided on the basis of pottery typology into five 'ceramic phases' designated cp 3–cp 7 spanning the period *c.* 550–*c.* 100 BC: against this framework it is possible to examine the developing social and economic systems within the fort. The essential points, which deserve emphasis, are that occupation appears to have been continuous throughout the period, the system of roads created at the beginning serving to control the structure of the settlement until its final abandonment. For the most part houses occupied the peripheral zone behind the rampart, the central area being reserved largely for storage (in storage pits and 4–post and 6–post 'granaries'). A complex of small structures which may be shrines lay towards the centre of this zone.

Throughout the period of occupation there is clear evidence of increasing intensification, demonstrated by the increasing number and variety of artefacts and by greater quantities of animal bones. Raw materials, such as ingots of iron and salt, were brought to the fort from outside the hinterland presumably for redistribution in cycles of exchange which may have involved local surpluses of corn and wool.

There is also ample evidence of complex belief patterns involving the deposition of a wide range of items, most notably animal carcasses in whole or in part, in the storage pits after their primary use as grain silos had ended. It is suggested that these deposits are propitiatory, belonging to a belief system which involved control by the chthonic deities of the community's seed corn (Cunliffe 1992).

In a note as constrained in size as this, it is impossible to do justice to the rich array of data obtained. Detailed reports on the excavation have been published (Cunliffe 1984a; Cunliffe and Poole 1991). A

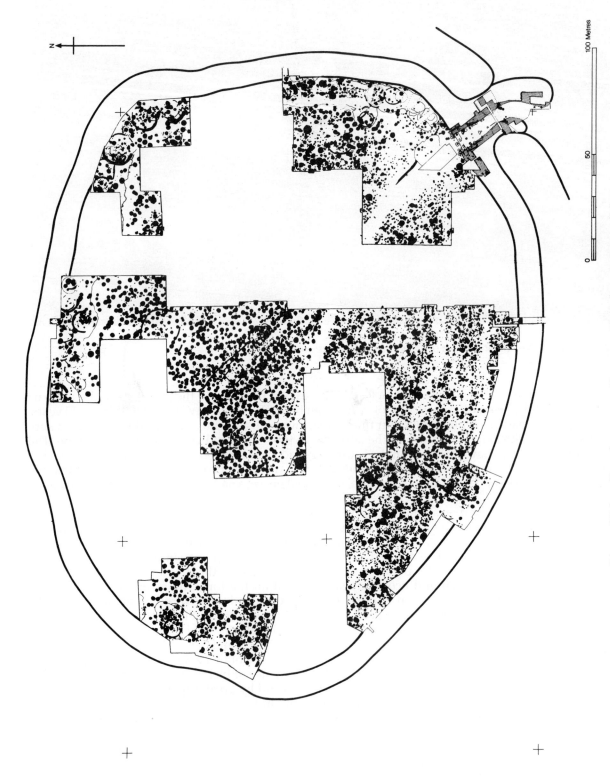

Figure 27.2   Danebury, overall exacavation plan showing all features

100 Metres

50

0

Figure 27.3   Danebury, general excavation view, with round house in the lee of the rampart and pits in the foreground

final volume, considering the broader implications of the Danebury data, is in preparation (Cunliffe forthcoming). A general summary of the site and its context and an overview of the research design have also been published (Cunliffe 1993a; 1993b) while the Danebury Environs Project is discussed elsewhere in this volume.

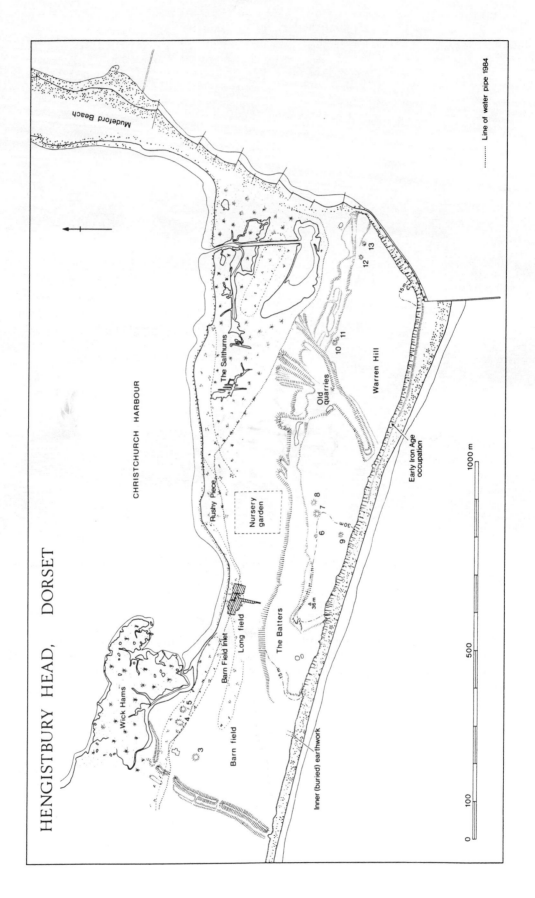

Figure 28.1   Hengistbury Head, showing position of area excavated (numbers refer to Bronze Age barrows)

28. Hengistbury Head, Dorset

Barry Cunliffe

Hengistbury Head is a promontory scoured on one side by the harsh tides of the English Channel whilst protecting, on the other, the almost land-locked harbour of Christchurch Bay into which flow two major Wessex rivers, the Avon and the Stour (Fig. 28.1). The headland is therefore admirably sited to serve as a port of entry on the Solent coast linking the Atlantic sea routes with the heartland of Wessex. As might be expected it was extensively occupied in the prehistoric period first by Palaeolithic and Mesolithic hunting bands (Barton 1992) and later in the Neolithic and Bronze Ages.

The topography of the site in the first millennium can be reconstructed with reasonable limits of certainty. The headland was then more than twice its present size probably with a steeply sloping cliff

Figure 28.2   Hengistbury Head, general view of the northern part of the excavation, 1983, showing structures on the old shoreline

Figure 28.3   Hengistbury Head, the palisaded enclosures, 1981

facing the sea and with three gravel banks extending out into the harbour to the north. These gravel bars would have provided convenient strands upon which to beach ships.

The headland was protected from the mainland by a double bank and ditch system which has not been examined by excavation and is undated, although likely to belong to the Middle or Late Iron Age. Another bank and ditch, now obscured by blown sand, was noted in a cliff section 200 m east (i.e. inside) of the Double Dykes. It too is undated but is probably of Early Iron Age date.

Knowledge of the Iron Age settlement comes from excavations undertaken by Bushe Fox in 1911–12 (Bushe Fox 1914), St George Gray 1918–1924 (unpublished) and by the writer in 1979–85 (Cunliffe 1987).

The earliest Iron Age occupation, dating largely to the sixth century, covered an area about 400 m from end to end spreading along the lee of the headland. In the areas excavated in 1979–85, a number of circular houses were discovered some with drainage ditches around them (Fig. 28.2).

Judging from the quantity of pottery recovered, Middle Iron Age occupation was much less extensive and less intense and it could indeed be that the site was only reoccupied late in the Middle Iron Age some time towards the end of the second century BC or early in the first century BC. From then on activity was continuous into the Roman period, including the construction of a palisaded enclosure complex occupying much the same area as the Early Iron Age settlement (Fig. 28.3),

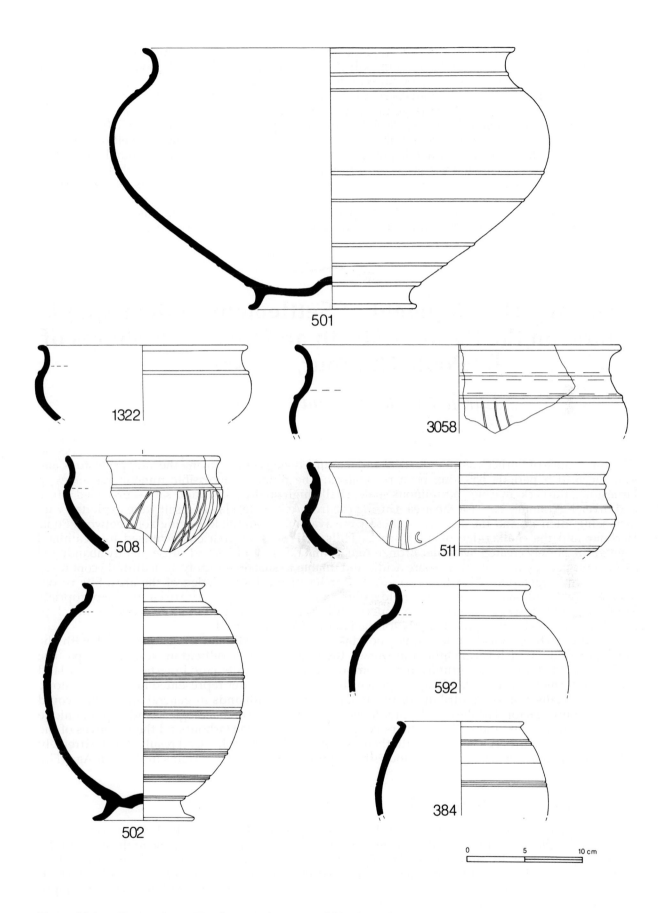

Figure 28.4   Hengistbury Head, typical imported black cordoned ware. Scale 1:3

becoming particularly intensive in the first half of the first century BC. It was at this time that the natural inlet between Barnfield Bar and Limekiln Bar was modified with tips of gravel and the digging out of silt to provide better docking for ships of deeper draught.

The intensification of activity in this period is directly associated with evidence of maritime contact along the Atlantic sea-ways. Very large numbers of pottery vessels from the Armorican peninsula were being carried to Hengistbury (Fig. 28. 4) together with quantities of Dr 1 amphorae (90% of those which could be identified belonging to the earlier 1A variety), blocks of purple and yellow glass, and figs. Material gathered on the headland, quite possibly to make up return cargos, included gold, silver, tin, copper, iron, and shale, and also possibly cattle (or hides) and corn. It may even be that the archaeo-logically invisible slaves and hunting dogs mentioned by Strabo as British exports, passed through the port.

By the middle of the first century BC, the period of intensive trading had passed though some overseas contact remained. Thereafter Hengistbury seems to have functioned more as a regional centre.

29. The Development of Settlement, Industry and Trade on the Purbeck Heath and Southern Shores of Poole Harbour, Dorset

Carrie M. Hearne and Peter W. Cox

The importance of Purbeck as an industrial and manufacturing centre during the later prehistoric and Romano-British periods has long been recognised. The range of accessible mineral resources — Limestone, Purbeck 'marble', bituminous shale, chalk, high quality clays, and salt — provided a firm and diverse economic base for the area. During the Iron Age shale, clay and salt were exploited with increasing intensity and the last two of these were available from the low-lying zone between Poole Harbour and the chalk ridge of the Purbeck Hills. This was an area characterised by heathland vegetation, largely created by earlier Bronze Age farming communities and subsequently abandoned as the soils became progressively more acidic and unable to sustain a purely agricultural economy.

The same vegetation cover has also affected archaeological knowledge of the area. Site recon-naissance by traditional means such as fieldwalking and aerial photography are largely inappropriate to a heathland landscape. As a result an understanding of settlement patterns and economic develop-ment has remained elusive, particularly for the later prehistoric period.

A major archaeological project was undertaken between 1987 and 1990, associated with the expansion of the Wytch Farm Oilfield in Dorset, the largest onshore oilfield in western Europe. The project provided a rare opportunity for a comprehensive and systematic investigation of lowland heath and former heath — a landscape type which is generally under represented in later prehistoric studies. Specialisation is an attribute of the archaeology of heathlands in general and, some would argue, a limiting factor. The Purbeck heaths, however, represent an archaeological landscape of unique importance in Wessex, and beyond. Their juxtaposition with Poole Harbour and the resources of the uplands of south Purbeck combined with their own mineral reserves have all resulted in a extremely diverse and rich history of settlement, industry and trade which had its origins in the Iron Age (Fig. 29.1).

Late Bronze Age/Early Iron Age

Although there is good evidence that the Limestone uplands of south Purbeck were occupied by agricultural settlements throughout the Late Bronze and Early Iron Ages, the zone to the north of the Chalk ridge can now be shown to be largely devoid of settlement. The Wytch Farm project has, however, produced important new vegetational data (through the analysis of terrestrial pollen) which sheds some light on the nature of Late Bronze Age/Early Iron Age exploitation of the seemingly unpopulated northern zone.

Following the widespread establishment of the heath on acidic soils (podzols) during the earlier Bronze Age, the pollen record demonstrates an expansion of heathland (ericaceous) vegetation, a constant and high percentage of grasses, and no evidence for woodland regeneration during the centuries following Bronze Age abandonment and prior to Middle Iron Age recolonisation (see below).

The implication of this is that, even if the area was abandoned for settlement purposes, it continued to be 'managed' since heathland represents a stage in a cycle of vegetational change which will revert to woodland unless actively maintained. Such management is likely to have resulted from a combination of stock grazing, turf cutting for fuel, and burning — both controlled and accidental.

Utilisation of the heath as a resource in this way was, in all likelihood, executed from a settlement base at the foot of the northern side of the Chalk ridge. This zone, on the fringes of the heath, benefited from more fertile, Chalk-derived soils and is known to have been densely occupied in the later Iron Age.

Middle Iron Age

For the zone at the base of the ridge, continuity and expansion of settlement may be envisaged during the Middle Iron Age. The project coincided with this zone in only one area (West Creech) but the discovery of a multi-phase Middle to Late Iron Age settlement here would appear to be an indication of the intensity of exploitation to which this zone was subjected. Further north, on the heath proper, the project has demonstrated that a settlement and agricultural base was re-established during the later part of the Middle Iron Age. This is of considerable importance in both a local and regional context. Prior to the project, the inclusion of a few Middle Iron Age sherds amongst the unstratified collections from the Fitzworth Peninsula and Shipstal Point on the shores of the harbour were not in themselves sufficient to suggest any coherent level of activity.

However, the evidence for second century BC occupation on Furzey Island demonstrates that the impetus for Iron Age recolonisation *pre-dated* the early first century BC trading contacts (see below). Consequently, it is now proposed that the other unexcavated sites mentioned above were also recolonised in the Middle Iron Age. The 'pioneer' nature of these settlements is illustrated by the vegetational data from Furzey Island which shows that the site was implanted into an area where relict stands of indigenous Scots Pine still existed.

Furzey, Fitzworth, and Shipstal Point all lie on the fringes of the harbour, located on prominent peninsulae with access to main harbour channels and the more saline waters of the neap tides. It is suggested that the apparent focus or even confinement of Middle Iron Age occupation to the harbour fringe was closely linked with the extraction and production of salt for wider transport and exchange. This hypothesis may be viewed alongside evidence from Iron Age sites in south Purbeck which are known to have been involved in salt production. At Rope Lake Hole, for example, a dramatic increase in the level of salt production occurred from the Middle Iron Age (Woodward 1987b). If, as seems likely, this reflects an increasing demand for salt and/or the increasing specialisation of its production during the Middle Iron Age, it is not unexpected that the uninhabited southern shores of Poole Harbour would become an equally important zone for salt production. The sheltered bays and creeks of the harbour shoreline offered more accessible and favourable conditions than the high cliffs and narrow or non-existent beaches of the south coast of Purbeck.

The potential for salt production is, therefore, a major factor in the recolonisation of the southern shores of Poole Harbour during the Middle Iron Age. It is possible that the subsequent development of large scale pottery production in the area had its origins in these settlements and the goods they were producing (see below). That these settlements were also successful agricultural communities is attested by the pollen record from Furzey Island. Overall, a scenario of permanent but small agricultural settlements, engaged in part-time salt production (i.e. during the summer and early autumn), shale working and domestic potting may be envisaged. Such a scenario of non-specialist production sites emerging during the Middle Iron Age has been identified elsewhere in Wessex.

Late Iron Age

The Late Iron Age may be characterised as a period of large scale intensification of interest in and exploitation of the area, linked both with internal resources and external contacts. Although an industrial component to the sites on the harbour fringe was already established, the expansion of existing settlements and the establishment of new ones indicate that the level of manufacturing output was on a much increased scale and linked to a modified economic basis. Moreover the appearance of a range of imported wares dated from the early first century BC onwards signals involvement in extended trading networks.

The chronology of Late Iron Age activity correlates with the sequence established for Hengistbury Head by reference to the imported ceramics, that is an initial 'contact' phase dated 100–50 BC (LIA1) and a later phase (LIA2) dated c. 50 BC–AD 43 (Cunliffe 1987; and this volume).

The scale and location of activity for each phase is particularly interesting, not least for the light it sheds on the chronological development of Hengistbury Head and Poole Harbour in Late Iron Age trading contacts. Evidence for LIA1 activity is limited to Furzey Island, Green Island and Hamworthy. On Furzey Island it represents the most intensive phase of Late Iron Age occupation, but also an apparently short-lived one. The amount of Armorican Black Cordoned Ware and Dressel 1 amphora

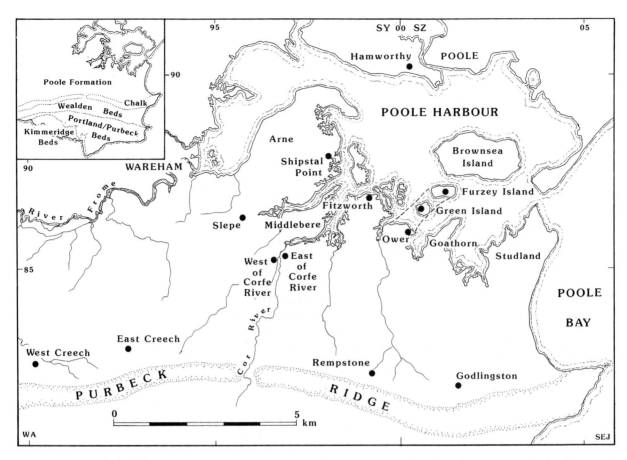

Figure 29.1   The Wytch Farm, Dorset, study area, showing sites mentioned in the text

from Furzey Island is minimal in comparison to that at Hengistbury Head where LIA1 represents the peak of that site's involvement in foreign exchange. The present evidence therefore suggests that during the early first century BC sites around Poole Harbour were in a subordinate role, receiving their imported goods via Hengistbury Head (Cunliffe 1987, 341; Woodward 1987a, 68–9).

The sudden decline in Furzey's fortunes along with its role in cross-Channel trade appears to be linked with rising sea levels. Cox's suggestion that it was around this time that Furzey was detached from the head of a peninsula formerly linking it with present day Green Island and Ower Peninsula — as shown in Figure 29.1 (Cox 1989a, 70) — still seems the best explanation for the abandonment of the settlement and the rise to prominence of a major new settlement, industrial and trading complex on Ower Peninsula only 1500 m to the south-west, as discussed below.

The main phase of Late Iron Age activity was in the decades which followed (LIA2). The energy and resources which were invested in the area during the second half of the first century BC is attested by an increased density of occupation of the area and the size of settlements established. Ower Peninsula and East of Corfe River approximate to 10 hectares and 9 hectares respectively and the striking layout of the enclosures at the former (Woodward 1987a, fig. 31A) gives every indication of a 'planned' settlement rather than an agglomerative development. The data available for Fitzworth indicate that that site was comparable in size. The chance discovery of a further (if smaller) site at Slepe by aerial reconnaissance during the Wytch Farm project points to the potential for the discovery of yet further sites on the southern shores of Poole Harbour.

These sites were primarily industrial: shale working, potting, salt production and metalworking are attested, to varying degrees, on all excavated sites. The production of carved objects of bituminous Kimmeridge shale (from the south coast of Purbeck) is readily identifiable in the archaeological record. Ower Peninsula in particular appears to have functioned as a production centre. On the other sites shale working is certainly less intensive and may have served as a 'supplementary' activity, perhaps during the winter when saltworking and potting were not being undertaken.

Direct evidence for pottery production is still rather enigmatic for the Late Iron Age, although assemblages from sites across the Durotrigian tribal area testify to the increasing importance of Poole Harbour ceramics. The lack of firmly identifiable pre-Conquest firing structures is not entirely unexpected given the technological evidence from the Black Burnished Ware (BB1) production site at Worgret, near Wareham which suggests that pit clamps were still in use during the later first and early second centuries AD (Hearne and Smith 1991). Insubstantial archaeological traces such as the probable clamps at East and West of Corfe River are all that are likely to survive from open or partly-sunken firings. The range of fired clay objects from most of the sites are likely, in part at least, to be associated with pottery production.

The production of salt is well represented by briquetage — in particularly large quantities at East of Corfe River. There can be little doubt that the extraction of salt for off-site consumption was closely linked with the manufacture of ceramic vessels as containers for their transport. The links between saltworking and the utilisation of the local clays may even have been more fundamental. The recolonisation of the harbour shores in the Middle Iron Age, coupled with the need to utilise the local clays (for both domestic potting and for ceramic containers for salt boiling and transport) would have lead to a wider appreciation of the high quality of the local Eocene clays. A recognition of the area's potential for large-scale pottery production leading to the development of an intensive ceramic industry may therefore have had its origins in the recolonisation of the area during the second century BC.

Ironworking and, at Ower Peninsula at least, non-ferrous metalworking, was also an economic component of the sites but the scale of metalworking appears to be comparable to that which took place on most Late Iron Age settlements.

Ower Peninsula's additional role among this network of contemporaneous sites is evidenced by a range of imports dating from the later first century BC onwards. During this period at Hengistbury Head it is suggested that 'long distance trade was maintained but on a much reduced scale' (Cunliffe 1987, 345). By contrast, the Ower Peninsula assemblage contains elements relatively poorly represented at Hengistbury Head, notably the containers of those goods which appear to have superseded the import of Italian wine, in particular Dr 1–Pascual 1 amphorae and, later, Dr 20. Furthermore, the relative proportions of Dr 1–Pascual 1 (within the total amphora assemblage) at the two sites — 3% at Hengistbury Head and 83% at Ower Peninsula — strongly suggests that Poole Harbour superseded Hengistbury as a leading point of entry for imported goods in the region.

Although activity was increasingly focused on the shores of the harbour during the Late Iron Age, it did not shift wholesale from the well-established settlement and agricultural base at the foot of the Chalk ridge. Prior to the Wytch Farm project the evidence for Late Iron Age settlement in this zone was largely confined to small unstratified collections from Godlingston, Rempstone, and East Creech. The excavations at West Creech have enhanced this background noise, demonstrating that such settlements continued to function as agricultural units, cultivating spelt wheat, oats and barley. The only 'industrial' component is low level shale carving and iron smithing and this is typical of most Late Iron Age sites in Purbeck away from the main industrial centres.

A simple model of the two distinct zones of occupation housing different economic activities (i.e. settlement and agriculture at the foot of the ridge and non-residential, industrial 'estates' adjacent on the harbour shores) is not sustainable. The evidence for arable and pastoral agriculture on the Late Iron Age sites on the harbour shores is most important in this respect. Interestingly there appears to be variation between the sites. Arable agriculture, including the cultivation of rye (which would have been more tolerant of the local acidic soils), is evidenced at Slepe and East of Corfe River. West of Corfe River and Ower Peninsula are, conversely, characterised by a lack (or very limited scale) of arable agriculture and over-grazed grasslands. Even given the lack of need, economically, for these sites to be self-sufficient, the realisation that they were participating in agriculture at some level precludes their interpretation as seasonal, exclusively industrial, centres. It is likely that arable agriculture was only viable because of the large amounts of ash generated by potting and saltworking which would have provided a valuable and ready-made fertiliser.

Acknowledgements
The Wytch Farm Oilfield is operated by BP Exploration on behalf of a group of development partners which also includes ARCO British Ltd, Premier Consolidated Oilfields PLC, Purbeck Exploration Ltd, Clyde Petroleum (Dorset) Ltd, and Goal Petroleum PLC. The archaeological field project and post-excavation programme were funded by the Wytch Farm Partners. This article is drawn from the project publications (Cox and Hearne 1991; Hearne and Cox 1992).

30. An Iron Age and Roman Cemetery at Owslebury, Hampshire

John Collis

The excavation of the Iron Age and Roman farming settlement at Owslebury near Winchester was carried out between 1961 and 1972; a rescue excavation due to the effects of deep ploughing, it was the first large scale excavation of such a site in Hampshire (Collis 1968; 1970). The earliest phase dates to about the fourth–third century BC with a short-lived banjo enclosure. This was succeeded by a period when the settlement was unenclosed except for the redigging of the ditches around the former entrance. In the late second–early first century BC, when St Catherine's Hill style saucepan pots were in vogue, the site was completely remodelled, with a series of ditched enclosures approached by ditched trackways. Bell-shaped storage pits were in use until the end of the saucepan pot period, but other than two 9–post 'granaries' belonging to the Late Iron Age, few traces of buildings were found. The ditches of this phase silted in during the mid-late 1st century BC, producing a rich assemblage of Late Iron Age pottery. Subsequently, shortly before the Roman Conquest the ditches were redug on a larger scale.

Throughout the Late Iron Age and early Roman period, the site was relatively wealthy (Collis 1990). Amphorae of Dr 1A type from Italy were imported, and later in the first century BC so too were Pascual 1 from Spain (Williams 1981). From a later Roman deposit there was a Gallo-Belgic E gold stater. In the mid-first century AD there were silver coins of Tincommius and Verica, and a rich assemblage of imported Gallo-Belgic and, later southern and central Gaulish fine pottery. However, in the second century AD the site declined, and it never acquired stone buildings like nearby villa sites before finally being abandoned towards the end of the fourth century AD.

The majority of burials excavated on the site were found within the settlement area, especially infant burials, but there were also later Roman cremations and inhumations (Collis 1977a). As is usual in the British Iron Age, few burials were found dating to the Middle Iron Age but included two infant burials found in a storage pit. The cremated remains of a child also from this phase which were

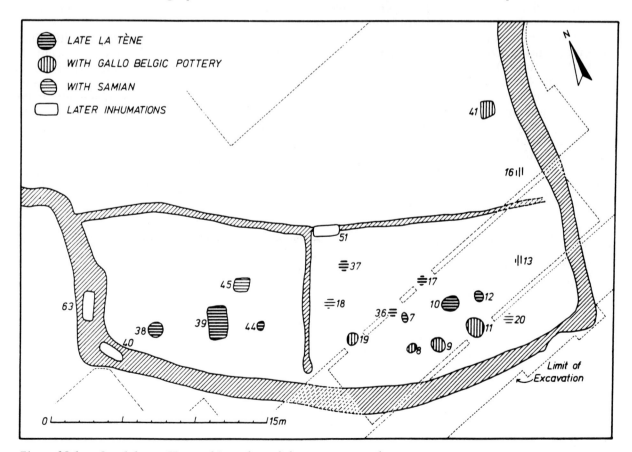

Figure 30.1   Owslebury, Hampshire, plan of the cemetery enclosures

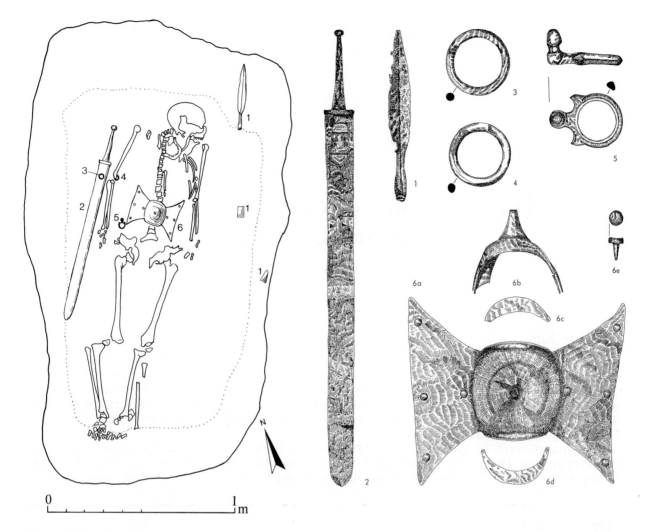

Figure 30.2   Owslebury, plan of burial 39

accompanied by two fragmented pots and a burnt bronze bracelet with a large glass bead threaded on to it, were found in the upper filling of the northern antenna ditch of the banjo enclosure. The lack of burials at this period could be due to two factors; firstly the ephemeral nature of a burial such as this, and secondly that it comes from a part of the settlement which is rarely excavated, outside the entrance. During the Late Iron Age and early Roman periods infant burials, mainly new born, continued to be buried in ditches and pits within the settlement. At least 14 belong to this period, a high number for such a small settlement. One adult male crouched inhumation may also belong to this period.

The Middle–Late Iron Age remodelling of the settlement incorporated two enclosures on the eastern slope of the spur on which it was sited (Fig. 30.1). Both enclosures contained central burials, with other burials grouped around them, but a couple of burials were also found outside the enclosures. With one exception all were cremations. Later, three unaccompanied inhumations were cut through the enclosure ditches.

The central burial of the earlier enclosure was an extended inhumation of a man accompanied by weapons (Fig. 30.2)(Collis 1973): a sword, a bronze shield boss, and a spear with an iron butt end and a bronze strip wrapped around the shaft (Fig. 30.2). The sword, in a wooden scabbard, seems to have been suspended from a baldric to which it was attached by a leather strap and two bronze rings; the baldric was buckled by a belt hook of continental type made of bronze with a high tin content. Both the shield boss and the belt hook are types which date on the continent to La Tène D1, and so belong to the first half of the first century BC.

At the centre of the later enclosure was a cremation in a large urn with a lid (Collis 1977a, fig. 6), and accompanied by six accessory vessels and lids, mostly wheel-turned, and dating to an early phase of the local Late Iron Age. Another early cremation was contained within a wooden box along with four small pottery vessels, one handmade. Later burials belonging to this early phase contained pedestal jars with cordoned necks.

In the latest Iron Age and early Roman graves Gallo-Belgic wares appeared, including plates of *terra nigra* and *terra rubra*, and a Colchester 113 butt beaker (Collis 1977, fig. 8); another contained two grog-tempered pedestal vessels of Aylesford–Swarling type, and a local platter. Burial 19 had a whetstone or pendant, and an iron razor. Only two burials contained brooches; both had the back plates of rosette brooches; one of them also had two late Colchester brooches, and was accompanied by Neronian samian. The latest burial of this phase contained a Hadrianic samian bowl.

Several of the burials were highly disturbed by ploughing, and it is possible that some had been completely destroyed by ploughing. The total of 70 burials covering just over 150 years indicates a small group, perhaps a couple of nuclear families.

31. The Late Iron Age Cremation Cemetery at Westhampnett, West Sussex

A.P. Fitzpatrick

Introduction

The construction of the A27 Westhampnett Bypass, 3 km east of Chichester was preceded by a systematic evaluation of the route which revealed a range of sites dating from the Late Glacial to the Romano-British period. Collectively these sites provided the first major multi-period results from the Sussex Coastal Plain and a number of them were excavated in early 1992 (Fitzpatrick 1992). Two adjacent cemeteries; one of Late Iron Age date, the other Romano-British, comprised the single most important area examined.

The two cemeteries lay on a small gravel knoll, which in the relatively low-lying landscape of the Coastal Plain would have been a significant local landmark. Approximately 170 features were initially identified as graves of Iron Age date in the fieldwork and the limit of the cemetery was defined on three sides (Fig. 31.1). On the fourth side it appeared to extend under the current A27 road. The small early Roman cremation cemetery containing *c.* 25 burials was sited close by, but at present there does not appear to be continuity between the cemeteries, and most of the burials are spatially discrete.

The Late Iron Age Cemetery

The size of the Iron Age cemetery was unanticipated as prior to its excavation only a small number of Late Iron Age cremation burials were known from historic Sussex (Whimster 1981, 389; Foster 1986, 181–4, fig. 44). The burials were usually unurned cremations placed on the bottom of a small, circular, grave. As very few graves intercut, it is likely that they were marked in some way. A whole earth sampling strategy was employed in the fieldwork and preliminary post-excavation work on those samples has shown that goods were frequently burnt on the pyre with the corpse (*pyre goods*; Flouest 1993; Roymans 1990, 219-20). Offerings of *grave goods* were also made, usually in the form of one or two pots and/or their contents, one of which was often a pedestal urn. Although the burials are very similar in some respects to the 'Aylesford' burials found principally in south-east England (Whimster 1981), there is an important difference in that the ashes are unurned rather than urned (although at least some unurned cemeteries are known in south-east England (e.g. Mucking; Going 1993, 20)).

As well as the recognition of pyre good and grave goods, there is important evidence for other stages in the burial rites. A series of small rectangular slots, occasionally occurring as crosses, may have been dug to provide the updraught for the cremation pyres (Fig. 31.2). Shallow scoops containing either burnt wood or fired clay as well as cremated bone, may be the bases of pyres, material cleared from the pyres themselves, pyre graves, or separate votive deposits (e.g. Abegg 1989). The charcoal from these deposits is predominantly of oak but there are also significant quantities of hazel. This is the first time that such a range of associated features has been confidently identified at a cemetery in this period in southern England.

In addition a group of small rectangular enclosures was sited to the east of the cemetery. The date of these enclosures is not yet known but it seems unlikely that all of them were associated with the Roman cemetery. The largest enclosure had post-holes at each corner and contained inhumation grave-like features. The acidity of the soil makes it possible that inhumation burials could have disappeared entirely, but it is possible that these were mortuary enclosures used as part of the funerary rituals.

Figure 33.1   Hayling Island temple, Hampshire, aerial photograph of the Romano-British temple before excavation seen as a cropmark from the north-west on 16 July 1976. Photograph: Grahame Soffe

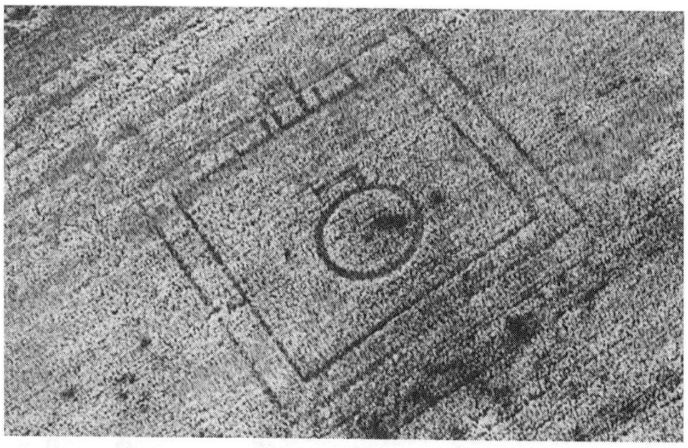

backfilled pit. Central pits are known from other Iron Age temples, e.g. Gournay-sur-Aronde, Oise (Brunaux *et al.* 1985, 94–124), and in the case of Hayling Island, it is the only feature apart from the associated finds assemblage that distinguishes the circular building from its secular contemporaries.

Just to the east of the porch structure of the circular shrine was an enclosure of trapezoidal plan. This is probably contemporary with the circular building, and seems to have been a fence made of squared posts and vertical planks set in a post-trench. Its purpose was probably to separate the entrance to the shrine from the rest of the enclosure, perhaps with a view to restricting access, for the ground inside appears to be less disturbed than in the courtyard generally. It is likely that different ritual activities took place inside and outside this fenced area. Most of the votive offerings found were in the zone between the fenced area and the outer boundary of the site: their density of deposition varied, however, with concentrations of artefacts on the eastern side, particularly in the south-east corner where amorphous groups of stake-holes and burnt patches were located. These groups of features probably represent ritual activities repeated a number of times.

Surrounding the outer enclosure was a boundary made up of a shallow ditch and post-holes. It was of at least two phases, and probably took the form of a fence with a drainage ditch around it. In various places there were gaps, the most obvious being the main entrance on the east side. The ditch on the south side of this entrance terminated in a large rectangular hole, 1.5 m by 1.2 m, the profile of which is suggestive of a stone-hole, possibly for one of the large sarsens that are found as erratic boulders in the region. Large stones are known to have been held sacred in Celtic religion, most notably at Triguères (Horne and King 1980, 482–3), where a small menhir entirely occupies the cella of a small Romano-Celtic temple.

The main courtyard and its outer boundary contained a great many finds. Amongst these were pieces of shield-binding, belt loops, strap unions, chain mail, spearheads, horse harness, bridle bits, terret rings, linch pins, nave hoops, and other material that can be associated with the trappings of an Iron Age warrior and his vehicle. In addition there were brooches, finger rings, bracelets, glass, and amber beads, tankards, amphorae, currency bars, and *c.* 170 Celtic coins. The coins are of considerable interest, as the assemblage includes many continental issues and many relatively early types, which suggests a period of fairly prolific coin-offering in the mid-first century BC, which tails off towards the early/mid-first century AD (Briggs *et al.* in press; also Haselgrove 1987, 129–30, 402–6). It is not known at present whether this reflects the general history of the temple, or simply a change in the pattern of votive offerings. An important feature of the coin assemblage are some coins which are in silver or gold over bronze cores, i.e. non-standard or unofficial issues. An explanation for this may be that the more valuable solid gold or silver coins were not left in the ground as votive deposits, but were displayed. Their fate would thus have been to be dispersed when the temple site eventually lost its sanctity.

The finds assemblage demonstrates fairly clearly that the outer courtyard was the main area where votive offerings were made, and that objects and utensils were brought to the site to be left there, probably because they were deemed sacred once they had played their part in a sacrifice or ritual. A number of the artefacts were bent or broken, perhaps to prevent their reuse or to sacrifice them symbolically to a deity. In addition to the metal objects, the pottery, marine shell, and animal bone finds also represent the remains of offerings. Most of the pottery vessels were food containers, and the bones were almost exclusively of sheep and pig, unlike contemporary local settlement sites. Also of interest was a small number of human bones from a couple of individuals. These were mixed with the other finds and probably also represent the remains of offerings, but it is not possible to say from the bones themselves that human sacrifices definitely took place.

The Roman Temple

At the time of the Roman Conquest of AD 43, the Iron Age temple was still in use. Little appears to have changed, probably because the establishment of a client kingdom in the area ensured a peaceful transition to Roman rule. In *c.* AD 60–70, however, a radical transformation took place, with the removal of the old structure and the setting up of a large stone temple in its place. This transformation,

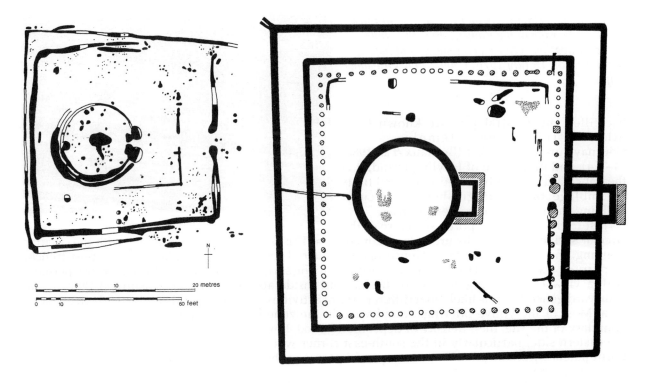

Figure 33.2   Hayling Island, left: Late Iron Age and right: Romano-British phases of the temple

relatively soon after the Conquest compared with other temples in Britain, reflects the rapid pace of Romanisation in the client kingdom. The proto-palace at Fishbourne, the Hayling Island temple and various other building projects in the Chichester area were all begun at about the same time, and use similar, probably Gallic, expertise. For the worshippers at Hayling Island, the large new temple, at least twice the volume of the old one, and in a different and very new building style, must have decisively altered the cult from one that was almost purely Celtic to one that was now Romano-Celtic. The change marks a new emphasis on the structure of the temple rather than on the votive offerings, which had been relatively more in evidence in the Iron Age phase (King 1990). A notable change in the votive offerings is the rapid decline in metalwork that could be associated with the warrior element in pre-Roman society. This probably reflects the downgrading of 'warrior culture' after the Roman Conquest, and its replacement by new forms of status display that included the construction of conspicuously Roman-style buildings, of which Hayling Island Roman phase is a testament.

The new temple was not, however, a complete break with the past, since its plan was substantially the same as its predecessor. A galleried temenos replaced the Iron Age courtyard enclosure, and the open space within continued to be the main zone of ritual depositional activity. In the centre stood a circular cella, 13.8 m in diameter, with a porch on the east side. Evidence suggests that it had a tiled roof, red external plaster, and polychrome plaster and a flagged floor inside. It was probably similar to examples still surviving as standing structures in Gaul, notably at Périgueux and Villetoureix (Horne and King 1980, 446, 490–1; Fauduet 1993, 54–5; Downey *et al.* 1980). If so, it would have had a tower-like shape higher than the overall diameter, and a blank windowless wall except possibly for small windows over the entrance.

The existence of Gallic parallels is of some interest, for it appears that Hayling Island is the only British representative of a distinctive group of large circular temples set in rectilinear courtyards. They are mostly located in western Gaul, and one, Allonnes, has yielded inscriptions to Mars Mullo and a suite of votive offerings very similar to that at Hayling Island (Horne and King 1980, 374–5). It is therefore possible to suggest that Hayling, too, was dedicated to a Romano-Celtic Mars. Allonnes also has evidence for a pre-Roman phase, and it is likely that the others also had Iron Age origins. Hayling Island Iron Age temple may provide an exemplar for their form.

References

Abegg, A., 1989, 'Die Aschengrube 82/28', in Haffner, A. (ed.), *Gräber: Speigel des Lebens*, Trier, Schriftenrh. Rheinischen Landesmus. Trier 2.

Alcock, L., 1980, 'The Cadbury Castle sequence in the first millennium BC', *Bull. Board Celtic Stud.* 28, 656–718.

Aldsworth, F.G., 1987, 'Prehistoric and Roman Selsey', *Sussex Archaeol. Collect.* 125, 41–50.

Allen, D.F., 1965, 'Les pièces d'argent minces du comté de Hampshire', *Rev. Numis* 6 Ser., 7, 80–93.

Allen, D.F., 1967, 'Iron currency bars in Britain', *Proc. Prehist. Soc.* 33, 307–35.

Allen, M.J., forthcoming, 'The stream and terrestial environment; mollusca and sediments', in Green *et al.*, forthcoming.

Anthony, I.E., 1968, 'Excavations in Verulam Hills Field, St Albans, 1963–4', *Hertfordshire Archaeol.* 1, 9–50.

Armour-Chelu, M., 1991, 'The animal bones', in Sharples 1991b, 139–51.

Arnold, D.E., 1981, 'A model for the identification of non-local ceramic distribution: a view from the present', in Howard and Morris 1981, 31–44.

Arnold, D.E., 1985, *Ceramic Theory and Cultural Process*, Cambridge, Cambridge Univ. Press.

Austin, D. and Thomas, J., 1990, 'The "proper study" of medieval archaeology', in Austin, D. and Alcock, L. (eds), *From the Baltic to the Black Sea: Studies in Medieval Archaeology*, London, One World Archaeol. 18, 43–78.

Barrett, J.C., 1980, 'The pottery of the later Bronze Age in lowland England', *Proc. Prehist. Soc.* 46, 297–319.

Barrett, J.C., 1989, 'Food, gender and metal: questions of social reproduction', in Sørensen and Thomas 1989, 304–20.

Barrett, J.C. and Bradley, R.J., 1980, 'Later Bronze Age settlement in south Wessex and Cranborne Chase', in Barrett, J.C. and Bradley, R.J. (eds), *The British Later Bronze Age*, Oxford, Brit. Archaeol. Rep. Brit. Ser. 83, 181–208.

Barrett, J.C., Bradley, R. and Green, M., 1991, *Landscape, Monuments and Society, the Prehistory of Cranborne Chase*, Cambridge, Cambridge Univ. Press.

Barton, R.N.E., 1992, *Hengistbury Head, Dorset, Vol. 2: the Late Upper Palaeolithic and Early Mesolithic sites*, Oxford, Oxford Univ. Comm. Archaeol. Monog. 34.

Bayley, J., 1990, 'The production of brass in antiquity with particular reference to Roman Britain', in Craddock, P.T. (ed.), *2000 Years of Zinc and Brass*, London, Brit. Mus. Occas. Pap. 50, 7–28.

Bean, S.C., 1991, 'The "Sons of Commius" reconsidered', *Celtic Coin Bull.* 1, 1–6.

Bedwin, O., 1984, 'Aspects of the Iron Age in Sussex', in Cunliffe and Miles 1984, 46–51.

Bedwin, O. and Holgate, R., 1985, 'Excavations at Copse Farm, Oving, West Sussex', *Proc. Prehist. Soc.* 51, 215–45.

Bellamy, P.S., 1991, 'The investigation of the prehistoric landscape along the route of the A303 road improvement between Andover, Hampshire and Amesbury, Wiltshire 1984–1987', *Proc. Hampshire Fld Club Archaeol. Soc.* 47, 5–81.

Bersu, G., 1940. 'Excavations at Little Woodbury, Wiltshire, part I: the settlement as revealed by excavation', *Proc. Prehist. Soc.* 6, 30–111.

Biddle, M., 1968, 'Excavations at Winchester, sixth interim report', *Antiq. J.* 48, 250–84.

Biddle, M., 1975, 'Ptolemaic coins from Winchester', *Antiquity* 49, 213–5.

Biddle, M., 1983 'The study of Winchester: archaeology and history in a British town', *Proc. Brit. Acad.* 69, 94–135.

Biringuccio, V., 1942, *The Pirotechnia*, (trans. Smith, C.S. and Teach, M.), New York, Amer. Inst. Mining Metall. Eng.

Blackmore, C., Braithwaite, M. and Hodder, I., 1979, 'Social and cultural patterning in the Late Iron Age in southern England', in Burnham, B.C. and Kingsbury, J. (eds), *Space, Hierarchy and Society*, Oxford, Brit. Archaeol. Rep. Int. Ser. 59, 93–111.

Blagg, T. and Millett, M. (eds), 1990, *The Early Roman Empire in the West*, Oxford, Oxbow Monog. 6.

Boast, R. and Evans, C., 1986, 'The transformation of space: two examples from British prehistory', *Archaeol. Rev. Cambridge* 5, 193–205.

Bourdillon, J., forthcoming, 'The animal bones', in Green *et al.*, forthcoming.

Bowden, M. and McOmish, D., 1987, 'The required barrier', *Scott. Archaeol. Rev.* 4, 76–84.

Bowden, M. and McOmish, D., 1989 'Little boxes: more about hillforts', *Scott. Archaeol. Rev.* 6, 12–16.

Bowden, M., Mackay, D. and Topping, P. (eds), 1989, *From Cornwall to Caithness; Some Aspects of British Field Archaeology*, Oxford, Brit. Archaeol. Rep. Brit. Ser. 209.

Bowen, C., 1990, *The Archaeology of Bokerley Dyke*, London, HMSO.

Bradley, R., 1975, 'Salt and settlement in the Hampshire Sussex hinterland', in de Brisay and Evans 1975, 20–5.

Bradley, R., 1990, *The Passage of Arms; an Archaeological Analysis of Prehistoric Hoards and Votive Deposits*, Cambridge, Cambridge Univ.Press.

Bradley, R., 1992, 'Roman salt production in Chichester Harbour: rescue excavations at Chidham, West Sussex', *Britannia* 23, 27–44.

Briggs, D., Haselgrove, C.C. and King, C.E., in press, 'Iron Age and Roman coins from Hayling Island temple', *Brit. Numis. J.*

Brisay, K.W., de, and Evans, K.A., (eds), *Salt: the Study of an Ancient Industry*, Colchester, Colchester Archaeol. Group.

Brown, L., 1987, 'The late prehistoric pottery', in Cunliffe 1987, 207–66.

Brown, L., 1991, Later prehistoric pottery, in Sharples 1991b, 185–203.

Brunaux, J.–L., Meniel, P. and Poplin, F., 1985, *Gournay 1: les Fouilles sur le Sanctuaire et l'Oppidum (1975–1984)*, Amiens, Rev. Archéol. Picardie No. Spec.

Burnett, A. and Cowell, M.R., 1988, 'Celtic coinage in Britain II', *Brit. Numis. J.* 58, 3–10.

Bushe-Fox, J.P., 1914, *Excavations at Hengistbury Head, Hampshire in 1911–12*, London, Rep. Res. Soc. Antiq. London 3.

Chadwick, S., 1960, 'Early Iron Age enclosures on Longbridge Deverill Cow Down, Wiltshire', in Frere, S.S. (ed.), *Problems of the Iron Age in Southern Britain*, London, Inst. Archaeol. Univ. London Occas. Pap. 11, 18–20.

Champion, T. and Champion, S., 1981, 'The Iron Age in Hampshire' in Schadla-Hall, T. and Shennan, S.J. (eds), *The Archaeology of Hampshire*, Winchester, Hampshire Fld Club Monog. 1, 37-44.

Champion, T.C. and Collis, J.R. (eds), in press, *The Iron Age in Britain and Ireland: Recent Trends*, Sheffield, Univ. Sheffield.

Clarke. D.L., 1972, 'A provisional model of an Iron Age society and its settlement system', in Clarke, D.L. (ed.), *Models in Archaeology*, London, Duckworth, 801–69.

Cleal, R.M.J., 1991, 'Briquetage', in Cox and Hearne 1991, 143–9.

Cleal, R.M.J., 1993, 'Prehistoric pottery and briquetage', in Smith, R.J.C., *Excavations at County Hall, Dorchester, Dorset, 1988*, Salisbury,Wessex Archaeol. Rep. 4, 41.

Cleere, H.F., 1981, *The Iron Industry of Roman Britain*, Unpublished, Ph.D. thesis, Univ. London.

Cliquet, D., Remy-Watte, M., Guichard, V. and Vaginay, M. (eds), 1993, *Les Celtes en Normandie: les Rites Funéraires en Gaule (IIème — Ier siècle avant J.-C.)*, Rennes, Rev Archéol. Ouest Supple. 6.

Coe, D. and Newman, R., 1992, 'Excavations of an Early Iron Age building and Romano-British enclosure at Brighton Hill South, Hampshire', *Proc. Hampshire Fld Club Archaeol. Soc.* 48, 5–21.

Coe, D., Jenkins, V. and Richards, J., 1991, 'Cleveland Farm, Ashton Keynes: second interim report; investigations May–August 1989', *Wiltshire Natur. Hist. Archaeol. Mag.* 84, 40–50.

Collis, J.R., 1968, 'Excavations at Owslebury, Hants: an interim report', *Antiq. J.* 48, 18–31.

Collis, J.R., 1970, 'Excavations at Owslebury, Hants: a second interim report', *Antiq. J.* 50, 246–61.

Collis, J.R., 1973, 'Burials with weapons in Iron Age Britain', *Germania* 51, 121–33.

Collis, J.R., 1977a, 'Owslebury (Hants) and the problem of burials on rural settlements', in Reece 1977, 26–34.

Collis, J.R., 1977b, 'Pre-Roman burial rites in north-western Europe', in Reece 1977, 1–13.

Collis, J.R., 1990, 'L'impact des processus d'urbanisation sur les sites ruraux: le cas de Owslebury, Hants, Angleterre', in A. Duval, J.-P. le Bihan and Y. Menez, (eds), *Les Gaulois d'Armorique: la Fin de l'Age du Fer en Europe Tempéreé, (Actes du 12ème colloque de l'Association Française d'Etude de l'Age du Fer, Quimper 1988)*, Rennes, Rev. Archéol. l'Ouest Supp. 3, 209–22.

Colt Hoare, Sir R., 1810, *Ancient Wiltshire*, Vol. 1, London.

Coombs, D., 1979 'The Figheldean Hoard', in Burgess, C.B. and Coombs, D. (eds), *Bronze Age Hoards: Some Finds Old and New*, Oxford, Brit. Archaeol. Rep. Brit. Ser. 67, 253–68.

Corney, M.C., 1989, 'Multiple ditch systems and Late Iron Age settlement in central Wessex', in Bowden, Mackay and Topping 1989, 111–28.

Cottrell, P., 1986, 'An Early Iron Age pit at Regent's Park, Southampton', *Proc. Hampshire Fld Club Archaeol. Soc.* 42, 23–33.

Cowell, M.R., 1992, 'An analytical survey of the British Celtic gold coinage', in Mays 1992, 207–34.

Cox, P.W., 1989, 'Excavation and survey on Furzey Island, Poole Harbour, Dorset, 1985', *Proc. Dorset Natur. Hist. Archaeol. Soc.* 110, 49–72.

Cox, P.W. and Hearne, C.M., 1991, *Reedemed from the Heath: the Archaeology of the Wytch Farm Oilfield (1987–90)*, Dorchester, Dorset Natur. Hist. Archaeol. Soc. Monog. 9.

Coy, J.P., 1982a, 'The animal bones', 68–73, in Gingell, C., 'The excavation of an Iron Age enclosure at Groundwell Farm, Blunsdon St Andrew, 1976–7', *Wiltshire Archaeol. Natur. Hist. Mag.* 76, 33–75.

Coy, J.P., 1982b, 'Woodland mammals in Wessex — the archaeological evidence', in Bell, M. and Limbrey, S. (eds), *Archaeological Aspects of Woodland Ecology*, Oxford, Brit. Archaeol. Rep. Int. Ser. 146, 287–96.

Coy, J.P., 1987, 'Animal bones', in Fasham 1987, 45–53.

Coy, J.P. and Maltby, M., 1987, 'Archaeozoology in Wessex: vertebrate remains and marine molluscs and their relevance to archaeology', in Keeley, H.C.M. (ed.), *Environmental Archaeology: a Regional Review*, Vol. 2, London, Hist. Build. Monuments. Comm. Eng. Occas. Pap.1, 204–51.

Crumley, C.L., 1987, 'A dialectical critique of hierarchy', in Patterson, T.C. and Gailey, C.W. (eds), *Power Relations and State Formation*, Washington, D.C., Amer. Anthropol. Assoc., 155–69.

Crummy, P., 1993, 'Aristocratic graves at Colchester', *Current Archaeol.* 11 (12), 492–7.

Cunliffe, B., 1964, *Winchester Excavations 1949–1960*, Vol. 1, Winchester, City of Winchester.

Cunliffe, B., 1974, *Iron Age Communities in Britain*, London, Routledge and Keegan Paul (1st edn).

Cunliffe, B., 1984a, *Danebury, an Iron Age Hillfort in Hampshire. Vol. 1: the Excavations 1969–1978: the Site; Vol. 2: the Excavations 1969–1978: the Finds*, London, Counc. Brit. Archaeol. Res. Rep. 52.

Cunliffe, B., 1984b, 'Iron Age Wessex: continuity and change', in Cunliffe and Miles 1984, 12–45.

Cunliffe, B., 1987, *Hengistbury Head, Dorset, Vol.1: the Prehistoric and Roman, Settlement, 3500 BC–AD 500*, Oxford, Univ. Oxford Comm. Archaeol. Monog. 13.

Cunliffe, B., 1990, 'Before hillforts', *Oxford J. Archaeol.* 9, 323–36.

Cunliffe, B., 1991, *Iron Age Communities in Britain*, London, Routledge and Keegan Paul (3rd edn).

Cunliffe, B., 1992, 'Pits, preconceptions and propitiation in the British Iron Age', *Oxford J. Archaeol.* 11, 69–84.

Cunliffe, B., 1993a, *Danebury*, London, English Heritage/Batsford.

Cunliffe, B., 1993b, 'Danebury: the anatomy of a hillfort re-exposed', in Bogucki, P. (ed.), *Case Studies in European Prehistory*, Boca Raton, 259–86.

Cunliffe, B., forthcoming, *Danebury, an Iron Age Hillfort in Hampshire. Vol. 6: the Hillfort and its Context*, London, Counc. Brit. Archaeol. Res. Rep.

Cunliffe, B. and Brown, L., 1987, 'Production, trade and exchange, in Cunliffe 1987, 303–21.

Cunliffe, B. and Poole, C., 1991, *Danebury, an Iron Age hillfort in Hampshire, Vol. 4: the Excavations 1979–88: the Site; Vol. 5: the Excavations 1979–88: the Finds*, London, Counc. Brit. Archaeol. Res. Rep. 73.

Cunliffe, B. and Miles, D. (eds), 1984, *Aspects of the Iron Age in Central Southern Britain*, Oxford, Oxford Univ. Comm. Archaeol. Monog. 2.

Cunnington, M.E., 1923, *The Early Iron Age Inhabited Site at All Cannings Cross Farm, Wiltshire*, Devizes, George Simpson.

Davies, S.M , 1980, 'Excavations at Old Down Farm, Andover, part I: Saxon', *Proc. Hampshire Fld Club Archaeol. Soc.* 36, 161–80.

Davies, S.M., 1981, 'Excavations at Old Down Farm, Andover, part II: prehistoric and Roman', *Proc. Hampshire Fld Club Archaeol. Soc.* 37, 81–163.

Davies, S.M., 1987, 'The coarse pottery', in Woodward 1987b, 150–8.

Done, G., 1980, 'The animal bone', in Longley, D., *Runnymede Bridge 1976: Excavations on the Site of a Late Bronze Age Settlement*, Guildford, Surrey Archaeol. Soc. Res. Vol. 6, 74–9.

Down, A., 1989, *Chichester Excavations 6*, Chichester, Phillimore.

Downey, R., King, A. and Soffe, G., 1980, 'The Hayling Island temple and religious connections across the Channel', in Rodwell 1980, 289–304.

Ehrenreich, R.M., 1985, *Trade, Technology, and the Ironworking Community in the Iron Age of Southern Britain*, Oxford, Brit. Archaeol. Rep. Brit. Ser. 144.

Ehrenreich, R.M., 1990, 'Considering the impetus for the Bronze-to-Iron Transition in prehistoric Britain', *J. Metals* 42 (7), 36–8.

Ehrenreich, R.M., 1991, 'Metalworking in Iron Age Britain: hierarchy or heterarchy?', in Ehrenreich, R.M. (ed.), *Metals in Society: Theory Beyond Analysis*, Philadelphia, MASCA (Univ. Mus. Archaeol. Anthropol. Univ. Pennsylvania), 69–80.

Ellison, A., 1982, 'Group 1: prehistoric pottery', in Leach, P., *Ilchester Vol. 1*, Bristol, Western Archaeol. Trust Excav. Monog. 3, 124–6.

Ellison, A., 1987, 'The Bronze Age settlement at Thorny Down: pots, post-holes and patterning', *Proc. Prehist. Soc.* 53, 385–92.

Ellison, A. and Williams, D.F., 1987, 'Fabrics', 249–59, in Ellison, A. and Rahtz, P., 'Excavations at Hog Cliff Hill, Maiden Newton, Dorset', *Proc. Prehist. Soc.* 53, 223–69.

Evans, C.J., 1989, 'Perishable and worldly goods — artifact decoration and classification in the light of wetlands research', *Oxford J. Archaeol.* 8, 179–201.

Farrar, R.A.H., 1975, 'Prehistoric and Roman saltworks in Dorset', in de Brisay and Evans, 14–20.

Fasham, P.J., 1983, 'Fieldwork in and around Micheldever Wood, Hampshire, 1973–80', *Proc. Hampshire Fld Club Archaeol. Soc.* 39, 5–45.

Fasham, P.J., 1985, *The Prehistoric Settlement at Winnall Down, Winchester*, Winchester, Hampshire Fld Club Monog. 2.

Fasham, P.J., 1987, *A Banjo Enclosure in Micheldever Wood, Hampshire*, Winchester, Hampshire Fld Club Monog. 5.

Fasham, P.J. and Keevill, G., in press, *Excavations at Brighton Hill South*, Salisbury, Wessex Archaeol. Rep. 7

Fasham, P.J., Farwell, D.E. and Whinney, R.J.B., 1989, *The Archaeological Site at Easton Lane, Winchester*, Winchester, Hampshire Fld. Club Monog. 6.

Fauduet, I., 1993, *Les temples de tradition celtique en Gaule Romaine*, Paris, Errance.

Fisher, A.R., 1985, 'Winklebury hillfort: a study of artefact distributions from subsoil features', *Proc. Prehist . Soc.* 51, 167–80.

Fitzpatrick, A.P., 1985, 'The distribution of Dressel 1 amphorae in north-west Europe', *Oxford J. Archaeol.* 4, 305–40.

Fitzpatrick, A.P., 1991a, 'Everyday life in the later Iron Age of European Britain', Paper presented to the 5th 'Archaeology in Britain' conference of the Institute of Field Archaeologists, Univ. Birmingham.

Fitzpatrick, A.P., 1991b. 'Death in a material world: the Late Iron Age and Romano-British cemetery at King Harry Lane, St Albans, Hertfordshire', *Britannia* 22, 323–7.

Fitzpatrick, A.P., 1992. *Westhampnett: From the Ice Age to the Romans*, Salisbury, Wessex Archaeology.

Fitzpatrick, A.P., Barnes, I. and Cleal, R.M.J., forthcoming, 'An Early Iron Age Settlement at Dunston Park, Thatcham, Berkshire', in Wessex Archaeol. Rep. 6

Flouest, J.-L., 1993, 'L'organisation interne des tombes à incinération du IIème au Ier siècle avant J.-C.: essai de description méthodique', in Cliquet *et al.* 1993, 201–9.

Foster, J., 1980, *The Iron Age Moulds from Gussage All Saints*, London, Brit. Mus. Occas. Pap. 12.

Foster, J., 1986, *The Lexden Tumulus: a Re-appraisal of an Iron Age Burial from Colchester, Essex*, Oxford, Brit. Archaeol. Rep. Brit. Ser. 156.

Foster, S., 1989, 'Transformations in social space: the Iron Age of Orkney and Caithness', *Scott. Archaeol. Rev. 6*, 34–54.

Gale, F.E., 1979, 'The ceramic fabrics, in Wainwright 1979, 49–56.

Galliou, P., 1984, 'Days of wine and roses?; early Armorica and the Atlantic wine trade', in Macready and Thompson 1984, 24–36.

Gates, T., 1975, *The Middle Thames Valley: an Archaeological Survey of the River Gravels*, Reading, Berkshire Archaeol. Comm. Pub. 1.

Gingell, C. and Lawson, A.J., 1984, 'The Potterne project: excavation and research at a major settlement of the Late Bronze Age', *Wiltshire Archaeol. Natur. Hist. Mag. 78*, 31–4.

Gingell, C. and Lawson, A.J., 1985, 'Excavations at Potterne, 1984', *Wiltshire Archaeol. Natur. Hist. Mag. 79*, 101–8.

Going, C.J., 1993, 'The Iron Age', in Clarke, A., *Excavations at Mucking, Vol. 1: the Site Atlas*, London, English Heritage Archaeol. Rep. 20, 19–20.

Grant, A., 1984a, 'Animal husbandry, in Cunliffe 1984a, 496–548.

Grant, A., 1984b, 'Animal husbandry in Wessex and the Thames Valley', in Cunliffe and Miles 1984, 102–19.

Grant, A., 1984c, 'Survival or sacrifice?; a critical appraisal of animal burials in the Iron Age', in Grigson, C. and Clutton-Brock, J., (eds), *Animals and Archaeology: 4, Husbandry in Europe*, Oxford, Brit. Archaeol. Rep. Int. Ser. 227, 221–8.

Grant, A., 1991, 'Animal husbandry', in Cunliffe and Poole 1991, 447–87.

Green, C.M., 1980, 'Handmade pottery and society in Late Iron Age and Roman East Sussex', *Sussex Archaeol. Collect. 118*, 69–86.

Green, F.J., Allen, M.J., Bourdillon, J., Morris, E.L., and Rees, H., forthcoming, 'Early Iron Age Stream deposits, Romsey, Hampshire: excavations in the grounds of the La Sagesse Convent, 1988'.

Grinsell, L.V., 1957, 'Archaeological gazetteer', in Pugh, R.B. and Crittall, E. (eds), *Victoria County History of Wiltshire*, 1 (1), Oxford, 21–279.

Groves, A.W., 1952, *Wartime Investigations into the Haematite and Manganese Ore Resources of Great Britain and Northern Ireland*, London, Min. of Supply Permanent Rec. Res. Devel. Monog. 20–703.

Guilbert, G., 1981, 'Double-ring roundhouses, probable and possible, in prehistoric Britain', *Proc. Prehist. Soc. 47*, 299–317.

Guilbert, G., 1982, 'Post-ring symmetry in roundhouses at Moel y Gaer and some other sites in prehistoric Britain', in Drury, P.J. (ed.), *Structural Reconstruction: Approaches to the Interpretation of the Excavated Remains of Buildings*, Oxford, Brit. Archaeol. Rep. Brit. Ser. 110, 67–86.

Halstead, P., Hodder, I. and Jones, G., 1978, 'Behavioural archaeology and refuse patterns: a case study', *Norwegian Archaeol. Rev. 11*, 118–31.

Hamilton, S., 1980, 'The Iron Age pottery', 196–203, in Bedwin, O., 'Excavations at Chanctonbury Ring, Wiston, West Sussex 1977', *Britannia 11*, 173–222.

Hamilton, S., 1984, 'Earlier first millennium pottery from the Excavations at Hollingbury Camp, Sussex, 1967–9', *Sussex Archaeol. Collect. 122*, 55–61.

Hamilton, S., 1985, 'Iron Age pottery', in Bedwin and Holgate 1985, 220–8.

Harcourt, R., 1979, 'The animal bones', in Wainwright 1979, 150–60.

Harding, D.W., Blake, I.M. and Reynolds, P.J., 1993, *An Iron Age Settlement in Dorset: Excavation and Reconstruction*, Edinburgh, Univ. Edinburgh Dept. Archaeol. Monog. 1.

Haselgrove, C.C., 1987, *Iron Age Coinage in South-East England: the Archaeological Context*, Oxford, Brit. Archaeol. Rep. Brit. Ser. 174.

Haselgrove, C.C., 1989, 'The later Iron Age in southern Britain and beyond', in Todd, M. (ed.), *Research on Roman Britain 1960–89*, London, Britannia Monog. 11, 1–18.

Haselgrove, C.C., 1993, 'The development of British Iron Age coinage', *Numis. Chron. 153*, 31–64.

Haselgrove, C. C., in press, 'Late Iron Age society in Britain and north-west Europe; structural transformation or superficial change?', in Arnold, B. and Gibson, D.B. (eds), *Celtic tribe: Celtic State*, New York, Cambridge Univ. Press.

Hastdorf, C., 1991, 'Gender, space and food in prehistory', in Gero, J. and Conkey, M. (eds.), *Engendering Archaeology*, Oxford, Blackwell, 132–62.

Hawkes, C., 1954, 'Archaeological method and theory: some suggestions from the Old World', *Amer. Anthrop. 56*, 158–68.

Hawkes, J., 1940, 'The excavations at Balksbury, 1939', *Proc. Hampshire Fld Club Archaeol. Soc. 14*, 291–337.

Hawkes, J.W., 1985, 'The pottery', in Fasham, 1985, 57–76.

Hawkes, J.W., 1987, 'The briquetage', in Woodward 1987b, 158–9.

Hayden, B. and Cannon, A., 1983, 'Where all the garbage goes: refuse disposal in the Maya highlands', *J. Anthrop. Archaeol. 2*, 117–63.

Hearne, C.M. and Cox, P.W., 1992, *Living with the Heath: Archaeology and the Wytch Farm Oilfield*, Poole, BP Exploration.

Hearne, C.M. and Smith, R.J.C., 1991, 'A Late Iron Age settlement and Black Burnished Ware (BB1) production site at Worgret, near Wareham, Dorset (1986–7)', *Dorset Natur. Hist. Archaeol. Soc. Proc. 113*, 1991 (1992), 54–105.

Hill, J.D., 1989, 'Rethinking the Iron Age', *Scott. Archaeol.Rev.* 6, 16–24.

Hill, J.D., 1993a, 'Can we recognise a different European past?; a contrastive archaeology of later prehistoric settlements in southern England', *J. European Archaeol.* 1, 57–75.

Hill, J.D., 1993b, *Ritual and Rubbish in the Iron Age of Wessex: a Study on the Formation of a Particular Archaeological Record*, Unpublished Ph.D. thesis, Univ. Cambridge.

Hill, J.D., in press, 'Hillforts and the Iron Age of Wessex', in Champion and Collis, in press.

Hill, P.H., 1984, 'A sense of proportion; a contribution to the study of double-ring roundhouses', *Scott. Archaeol. Rev.* 3, 80–6.

Hingley, R., 1984a, 'Towards social analysis in archaeology: celtic society in the Iron Age of the Upper Thames Valley', in Cunliffe and Miles 1984, 72–88.

Hingley, R., 1984b, *An Archaeological Strategy for the Upper Thames Gravels in Gloucestershire and Wiltshire*, Gloucester and Trowbridge, Unpublished report, Gloucestershire County Council and Wiltshire County Council.

Hingley, R., 1989, *Rural Settlement in Roman Britain*, London, Seaby.

Hingley, R., 1990a, 'Iron Age "currency bars": the archaeological and social context', *Archaeol. J.* 147, 91–117.

Hingley, R., 1990b, 'Boundaries surrounding Iron Age and Romano–British settlements', *Scott. Archaeol. Rev.* 7, 96–103.

Hingley, R., 1990c, 'Domestic organisation and gender relations in Iron Age and Romano-British households', in Samson, R. (ed.), *The Social Archaeology of Houses*, Edinburgh, Edinburgh Univ. Press, 125–47.

Hingley, R., and Miles, D., 1984, 'Aspects of Iron Age settlement in the Upper Thames Valley', in Cunliffe and Miles 1984, 52–71.

Hodder, I., 1984, *Wendens Ambo: the Excavation of an Iron Age and Romano-British Settlement*, London, Archaeol. of M11 1.

Hodder, I. and Orton, C., 1976, *Spatial Analysis in Archaeology*, Cambridge, Cambridge Univ. Press.

Hodson, R., 1964, 'Cultural grouping within the British pre-Roman Iron Age', *Proc. Prehist. Soc.* 30, 99–110.

Holgate, R., 1986, 'The Chichester Entrenchments at the Richmond Arms Hotel, Goodwood, West Sussex', *Sussex Archaeol. Collect.* 124, 255–6.

Horne, P. and King, A., 1980, 'Romano-Celtic temples in continental Europe: a gazetteer of those with known plans', in Rodwell 1980, 369–555.

Howard, H., 1983, *The Bronze Casting Industry in Later Prehistoric Britain: a Study Based on Refractory Debris*, Unpublished Ph.D. thesis, Univ. Southampton.

Howard, H. and Morris, E.L., (eds), *Production and Distribution: a Ceramic Viewpoint*, Oxford, Brit. Archaeol. Rep. Int. Ser. 120.

Jones, M.J., 1986, *England before Domesday*, London, Batsford.

Kaloyeros, A. and Ehrenreich, R.M., 1991, 'The distribution of phosphorus in Romano-British ironwork', in Vandiver, P.B., Druzik, J. and Wheeler, G.S. (eds), *Materials Issues in Art and Archaeology* 2, Pittsburgh, Materials Res. Soc. Proc. 185, 725–30.

King, A., 1990, 'The emergence of Romano-Celtic religion', in Blagg and Millett 1990, 220–41.

Knight, D., 1984, *Late Bronze Age and Iron Age Settlement in the Nene and Great Ouse Basins*, Oxford, Brit. Archaeol. Rep. Brit. Ser. 130.

Lambrick, G., 1984, 'Pitfalls and possibilities in Iron Age pottery studies — experiences in the Upper Thames Valley', in Cunliffe and Miles 1984, 162–77.

Lancley, J. and Morris, E.L., 1991, 'Local coarsewares', in Cox and Hearne 1991, 122–36.

Laubenheimer, F., 1985, *La Production des Amphores en Narbonnaise*, Paris, Ann. Litt. Univ. Besançon 327 / Ser. Centre Hist. Anc. 66.

Lobb, S.J. and Morris, E.L., in press, 'Investigation of Bronze Age and Iron Age features at Riseley Farm, Swallowfield, Berkshire', *Berkshire Archaeol. J.*

Macready, S. and Thompson, F.H. (eds), 1984, *Cross-Channel Trade between Gaul and Britain in the Pre-Roman Iron Age*, London, Soc. Antiq. London Occas. Pap. (NS) 4.

Maltby, M., 1981, 'Iron Age, Romano-British and Anglo-Saxon animal husbandry: a review of the faunal evidence', in Jones, M. and Dimbleby, G. (eds), *The Environment of Man: the Iron Age to the Anglo-Saxon Period*, Oxford, Brit. Archaeol. Rep. Brit. Ser. 87, 155–204.

Maltby, M., 1985a, 'Patterns in faunal assemblage variability', in Barker, G. and Gamble, C. (eds), *Beyond Domestication in Prehistoric Europe*, London, Academic Press, 33–74.

Maltby, M., 1985b, 'The animal bones', in Fasham 1985, 25, 97–112 and 137–8.

Maltby, M., 1989, 'The animal bones', in Fasham *et al.* 1989, 122–31.

Maltby, M. and Coy, J.P., 1991, 'The animal bone analyses on the M3 project', in Fasham, P.J. and Whinney, R.J.B., *Archaeology and the M3*, Winchester, Hampshire Fld Club Monog. 7, 97–104.

Manning, W., 1974, 'Excavations on Late Iron Age, Roman and Saxon Sites at Ufton Nervet, Berkshire, in 1961–1963', *Berkshire Archaeol. J.* 67, 1–61.

Martin, G. and Foley, V., 1979, 'Weyland the Smith: some findings', *Hist. Metall.* 13, 38–9.

Mays, M. (ed.), 1992, *Celtic Coinage in Britain and Beyond; the Eleventh Oxford Symposium on Coinage and Monetary History*, Oxford, Brit. Archaeol. Rep. Brit. Ser. 222.

McOmish, D., 1989, 'Non-hillfort settlement and its implications', in Bowden, Mackay and Topping 1989, 99–110.

Megaw, J.V.S. and Megaw, M.R., 1991, 'The earliest insular Celtic art: some unanswered questions', *Études Celtiques* 28 1991 (1993), 283-307.

Meniel, P., 1993, 'Les animaux dans les practiques funéraires des Gaulois', in Cliquet *et al.* 1993, 285–90.

Mepham, L.N. and Morris, E.L., forthcoming, 'The pottery', in Fitzpatrick *et al.* forthcoming.

Middleton, A., 1987, 'Technological investigation of the coatings on some 'haematite-coated' pottery from southern England', *Archaeometry* 29, 250–61.

Millett, M., 1987, 'An early Roman burial tradition in central southern England', *Oxford J. Archaeol.* 6, 63–8.

Millett, M., 1993, 'A cemetery in an age of transition: King Harry Lane reconsidered', in Struck, M. (ed.), *Römerzeitliche Gräber als Quellen zu Religion, Bevölkerungsstruktur und Sozialgeschichte*, Mainz, Archäol. Schr. Inst. Vor-u. Frühgesch. Johannes Gutenberg-Univ. Mainz 3, 255–82.

Millett, M. and James, S., 1983, 'Excavations at Cowdery's Down, Basingstoke, Hampshire, 1978–81', *Archaeol. J.* 140, 151–279.

Millett, M. and Russell, D., 1984, 'An Iron Age and Romano-British site at Viables Farm, Basingstoke', *Proc. Hampshire Fld Club Archaeol. Soc.* 40, 49–60.

Miró, J., 1986, 'Une inscription peinte avec date consulaire sur une amphore Dressel 1B de l'oppidum de Burriac (Cabrera de Mar, Barcelone)', *Doc. Archéol. Méridionale* 9, 201–5.

Monk, M.A. and Fasham, P.J., 1980, 'Carbonised plant remains from two Iron Age sites in central Hampshire', *Proc. Prehist. Soc.* 46, 321–44.

Morris, E.L., 1982, 'Petrological report on briquetage container material from excavations at Trafalgar House, Winchester, Hampshire', Unpublished archive report, Winchester Historic Resources Centre.

Morris, E.L., 1985, 'The briquetage', in Fasham 1985, 76.

Morris, E.L., 1987a, 'Briquetage', in Fasham 1987, 39–40.

Morris, E.L., 1987b, 'Later prehistoric pottery from Ham Hill', *Somerset Archaeol. Natur. Hist.* 131, 27–47.

Morris, E.L., 1991a, 'Ceramic analysis and the pottery from Potterne: a summary', in Middleton, A. and Freestone, I., (eds), *Recent Developments in Ceramic Petrology*, London, Brit. Mus. Occas. Pap. 81, 277–86.

Morris, E., 1991b, 'The pottery', in Bellamy 1991, 17–28.

Morris, E.L., 1992, 'The pottery', in Coe and Newman 1992, 13–23.

Morris, E.L., in press, 'Artefact production and exchange in the British Iron Age', in Champion and Collis in press.

Morris, E.L., forthcoming a, 'Pottery production and resource locations: an examination of the Danebury collection', in Cunliffe forthcoming.

Morris, E.L., forthcoming b, 'The pottery', in Green *et al.* forthcoming.

Musson, C.R., Britnell, W.J., Northover, J.P. and Salter, C.J., 1992, 'Excavations and metalworking at Llwyn Bryn-dinas hillfort, Llangedwyn, Clwyd', *Proc. Prehist. Soc.* 58, 265–83.

Neal, D.S., 1980, 'Bronze Age, Iron Age, and Roman settlements at Little Somborne and Ashley, Hampshire', *Proc. Hampshire Fld Club Archaeol. Soc.* 36, 91–144.

Needham, S.P., 1991, *Excavation and salvage at Runnymede Bridge, 1978: the Late Bronze Age Waterfront Site*, London, British Mus. Press/ English Heritage.

Niblett, R., 1992, 'A Catuvellaunian chieftain's burial from St Albans', *Antiquity* 66, 917–29.

Northover, J.P., 1984, 'Iron Age bronze metallurgy in central southern Britain', in Cunliffe and Miles 1984, 126–45.

Northover, J.P., 1987, 'Non-ferrous metallurgy', in Cunliffe 1987, 186–96, M7: A3–B4.

Northover, J.P., 1988a, 'Late Bronze Age metalwork: general discussion', 75–85; 'Aspects of Iron Age bronze metallurgy', 85–6, in Cunliffe, B., *Mount Batten, a Prehistoric and Roman Port*, Oxford, Oxford Univ. Comm. Archaeol. Monog. 26.

Northover, J.P., 1988b, 'Copper, tin, silver and gold in the Iron Age', in Slater, E.A. and Tait, J.O. (eds), *Science and Archaeology, Glasgow, 1987*, Oxford, Brit. Archaeol. Rep. Brit. Ser. 196, 223–33.

Northover, J.P., 1991a, 'Non-ferrous metalwork and metallurgy', in Sharples 1991b, 159–65.

Northover, J.P., 1991b, 'Non-ferrous metalwork and metallurgy', in Cunliffe and Poole 1991, 407–12.

Northover, J.P., 1992, 'Materials issues in the celtic coinage', in Mays 1992, 235–99.

O'Connor, B., 1980, *Cross-Channel Relations in the Later Bronze Age*, Oxford, Brit. Archaeol. Rep. Int. Ser. 91.

Northover, J.P. and Salter, C.J., 1991, 'Decorative metallugy of the celts', *Mat. Characterisation* 25, 47–62.

Oliver, M., 1992, 'Excavation of an Iron Age and Romano-British Settlement site at Oakridge, Basingstoke, Hampshire, 1965–6', *Proc. Hampshire Fld Club Archaeol. Soc.* 48, 55–94.

Oliver, M. and Applin, B., 1979, 'Excavation of an Iron Age and Romano-British settlement at Ructstall's Hill, Basingstoke, Hampshire, 1972–5', *Proc. Hampshire Fld Club Archaeol. Soc.* 35, 41–92.

Oswald, A., 1991, *A Doorway on the Past: Round-House Orientation and its Significance in Iron Age Britain*, Unpublished B.A. dissertation, Univ. Cambridge.

Palmer, R., 1984, *Danebury, an Iron Age Hillfort in Hampshire, Vol. 3: an Aerial Photographic Interpretation of its Environs*, London, Roy. Comm. Hist. Monum. Eng. Suppl. Ser. 6.

Parker Pearson, M., in press, 'Food, fertility and front doors in the first millennium BC', in Champion and Collis, in press.

Pascual Guasch, R., 1962, 'Centros de produccion y difusion geographica de un tipo ánfora', *VII Congreso Nacional de Arqueologia, Barcelona, 1960*, Zaragoza, 334–45.

Pascual Guasch, R., 1977, 'Las ánforas de la Layetania', in *Méthodes Classiques et Méthodes Formelles dans l'Étude des Amphores*, Rome, Coll. École Franç. Rome 32, 47–96.

Peacock, D.P.S, 1968, 'A petrological study of certain Iron Age Pottery from western England', *Proc. Prehist. Soc.* 34, 414–27.

Peacock, D.P.S., 1969, 'A contribution to the study of Glastonbury Ware from south-western Britain', *Antiq. J.* 49, 41–61.

Peacock, D.P.S., 1977, 'Roman amphorae in pre-Roman Britain', in Jesson, M. and Hill, D. (eds), *The Iron Age and its Hill-Forts*, Southampton, Southampton Univ. Monog. Ser. 1, 161–88.

Peacock, D.P.S., 1982, *Pottery in the Roman World: an Ethnoarchaeological Approach*, London, Longman.

Peacock, D.P.S., 1984, 'Amphorae in Iron Age Britain: a re-assessment', in Macready and Thompson 1984, 37–42.

Peacock, D.P.S., 1987, 'Iron Age and Roman quern production at Lodsworth, West Sussex', *Antiq. J.* 57, 61–85.

Peacock, D.P.S. and Williams, D.F. 1986, *Amphorae and the Roman Economy*, London, Longman.

Plog, F., 1977, 'Modeling economic exchange', in Earle, T.K. and Ericson, J.E. (eds), *Exchange Systems in Prehistory*, London, Academic Press, 127–40.

Poole, C., 1984, 'Briquetage containers', in Cunliffe 1984a, 426–30.

Poole, C., 1987, 'Salt working', in Cunliffe 1987, 178–80.

Poole, C., 1991a, 'Briquetage containers', in Cunliffe and Poole 1991, 404–7.

Poole, C., 1991b, 'The briquetage', in Sharples 1991b, 206–7.

Qualmann K.E., Rees H., Scobie G.D. and Whinney, R., in press, *The Oram's Arbour Iron Age Enclosure at Winchester*, Winchester, Winchester Mus. Service Archaeol. Rep. 3.

Raftery, B., 1984, *La Tène in Ireland; Problems of Origin and Chronology*, Marburg, Veröff. Vorgesch. Seminars Marburg Sonderbd 2.

Ralston, I.B.M., 1992, *Les Enceintes Fortifiées du Limousin: les Habitats Protohistoriques de la France non-Méditerranéenne*, Paris, Doc. Archéol. Franç. 36.

Reece, R., (ed.), 1977, *Burial in the Roman world*, London, Counc. Brit. Archaeol. Res. Rep. 22.

Rees, H., in press a, 'Briquetage', in Fasham and Keevill, in press.

Rees, H., in press b, 'Later Bronze Age and Early Iron Age settlement in the Lower Test Valley; evidence from excavations and finds 1981–9', *Proc. Hampshire Fld Club Archaeol. Soc.* 49, 1993.

Rees, H., forthcoming, 'Objects of fired clay', in Green *et al.*, forthcoming.

Reynolds, P.J., 1979, *Iron Age Farm: the Butser experiment*, London, Brit. Mus. Press.

Reynolds, P.J., 1980, 'The working agroscape of the Iron Age', *Landscape Hist.* 2, 1-18.

Robinson, P.H., 1977, 'A local Iron Age coinage in silver and perhaps gold in Wiltshire', *Brit. Numis. J.* 47, 5–20.

Rodwell, W. (ed.), 1980, *Temples, Churches and Religion: RecentRresearch in Roman Britain*, Oxford, Brit. Archaeol. Rep. Brit. Ser. 77.

Roymans, N., 1990, *Tribal Societies in Northern Gaul: an Anthropological Perspective*, Amsterdam, Cingvla 12.

Salter, C.J. and Ehrenreich, R.M., 1984, 'Iron Age iron metallurgy in central southern Britain', in Cunliffe and Miles 1984, 146–61.

Salter, C.J. and Northover, J.P., 1992, 'Reconstructing metallurgical processes at Hengistbury Head, Dorset, an Iron Age and Roman trading port', in Vandiver, P., Druzik, J., Williams, G. and Freestone, I.G., (eds), *Materials Issues in Art and Archaeology* 3, Pittsburgh, Materials. Res. Soc. Proc. 267.

Savory, H.N., 1976, *A Guide Catalogue to the Iron Age Collections*, Cardiff, Nat. Mus. Wales.

Schiffer, M.B., 1987, *Formation Processes of the Archaeological Record*, Albuquerque, Univ. New Mexico Press.

Sealey, P.R., 1985, *Amphoras from the 1970 Excavations at Colchester Sheepen*, Oxford, Brit. Archaeol. Rep. Brit. Ser. 142.

Sellwood, L.C., 1984, 'Objects of iron', in Cunliffe 1984a, 346–71.

Serjeantson, D., 1991, '"Rid grasse of bones": a taphonomic study of the bones from midden deposits at the Neolithic and Bronze Age site of Runnymede, Surrey, England', *Int. J. Osteoarchaeol.* 1, 73–89.

Sharples, N., 1991a, *Maiden Castle*, London, English Heritage/Batsford.

Sharples, N., 1991b, *Maiden Castle: Excavation and Field Survey 1985–6*, London, English Heritage Archaeol. Rep. 19.

Skibo, J., 1992, *Pottery Function: a Use-Alteration Perspective*, New York, Plenum Press.

Smith, K., 1977, 'The excavation of Winklebury Camp, Basingstoke, Hampshire', *Proc. Prehist. Soc.* 43, 31–129.

Smith, S., 1984, 'An Iron Age site at Maddison Street, Southampton', *Proc. Hampshire Fld Club Archaeol. Soc.* 40, 35–47.

Sørensen, M.L.S. and Thomas, R. (eds), 1989, *The Bronze Age–Iron Age Transition in Europe*, Oxford, Brit. Archaeol. Rep. Int. Ser. 484.

Spratling, M.G., 1979, 'The debris of metal working', in Wainwright 1979, 125–49.

Stead, I.M., 1991, 'The Snettisham treasure: excavations in 1990', *Antiquity* 65, 447–65.

Stead, I.M. and Rigby, V., 1989, *Verulamium; the King Harry Lane Site*, London, English Heritage Archaeol. Rep. 12.

Stopford, J., 1987, 'Danebury: an alternative view', *Scott. Archaeol. Rev.* 4, 70–5.

Strang, A., 1991, 'Towards a functional classification of round-houses', *Bull. Board Celtic Stud.*, 37, 159–66.

Talon, M., 1987, 'Les formes céramiques du Bronze Final et Premier Age du Fer de l'habitat de Choisy-au-Bac (Oise), in Blanchet, J.-C. (ed.), *Les Relations Entre le Continent et les Iles Britanniques à l'Age du Bronze (Actes du colloque de Lille)*, Amiens, Rev. Archéol. Picardie. Supp., 255–73.

Taylor, J.J., 1984, 'The Potterne gold bracelet and its affinities', *Wiltshire Archaeol. Natur. Hist. Mag.* 78, 35–40.

Tchernia, A., 1983, 'Italian wine in Gaul at the end of the Republic', in Garnsey, P.D.A., Hopkins, K. and Whittaker, C.R. (eds), *Trade in the Ancient Economy*, London, Chatto and Windus, 87–104.

Tchernia, A., 1986, *Le Vin de l'Italie Romaine: Essai d'Histoire Économique d'Après les Amphores*, Rome, École Franç. Rome.

Therkorn, L., 1987, 'The inter-relationships of materials and meanings: some suggestions on housing concerns in the Iron Age of Noord-Holland', in Hodder, I. (ed.), *The Archaeology of Contextual Meanings*, Cambridge, Cambridge Univ. Press, 102–10.

Thompson, M. W., 1958 'Recent building at Balksbury Camp, Andover', *Proc. Hampshire Fld Club Archaeol. Soc.* 21, 53.

Thomas, R., 1989, 'The Bronze–Iron transition in southern England', in Sørensen and Thomas 1989, 263–86.

Timby, J., 1985, 'The pottery', in Fulford, M.G., *Guide to the Silchester Excavations: the Forum and Basilica 1982–4*, Reading, Univ. Reading, Dept. Archaeol.

Trow, S.D., 1990, 'By the northern shores of the ocean: some observations on acculturation process at the edge of the Roman world', in Blagg and Millett 1990, 103–18.

Turnbull, A., 1983, 'Bronze Age and Halstatt finds from Rangebourne, Potterne', *Wiltshire Archaeol. Natur. Hist. Mag.* 77, 1982, 45–8.

Tylecote, R.F., 1986, *The Prehistory of Metallurgy in the British Isles*, London, Inst. Metals.

Van Arsdell, R.D., 1989, *Celtic Coinage in Britain*, London, Spink.

Van Arsdell, R.D., 1991, 'The coins', in Cunliffe and Poole 1991, 320–8.

Vidal, M., 1976, 'Le seau de bois orné de Vielle Toulouse (Haute Garonne): étude comparative des seaux de la Tène III', *Gallia* 34, 167–200.

Wainwright, G.J., 1968, 'The excavation of a Durotrigian farmstead near Tollard Royal in Cranborne Chase, southern England', *Proc. Prehist. Soc.* 34, 102–47.

Wainwright, G.J., 1969, 'The excavation of Balksbury Camp, Andover, Hants,' *Proc. Hampshire Fld Club Archaeol. Soc.* 26, 21–55.

Wainwright, G.J., 1979, *Gussage All Saints: an Iron Age Settlement in Dorset*, London, Dept Environ. Archaeol. Rep. 10.

Wainwright, G.J. and Davies, S.M., in press, *Balksbury Camp, Hampshire: Excavations 1973 and 1981*, London, English Heritage Archaeol. Rep.

Wait, G.A., 1985, *Ritual and Religion in Iron Age Britain*, Oxford, Brit. Archaeol. Rep. Brit. Ser. 149.

Wandibba, S., 1981, 'Petrological analysis', in Davies 1981, 92–3.

Wessex Archaeology 1989, *Cleveland Farm, Ashton Keynes; First Interim Report, June 1989*, Salisbury, Wessex Archaeology.

Wessex Archaeology 1992, *Rixon Gate Farm, Wiltshire: Archaeological Excavation, Summary Report*, Salisbury, Unpublished Wessex Archaeology Client Report W515.

Whimster, R.P., 1981, *Burial Practices in Iron Age Britain: a Discussion and Gazetteer of the Evidence c. 700 BC –AD 43*, Oxford, Brit. Archaeol. Rep. Brit. Ser. 90.

Williams, D.F., 1981, 'The Roman amphorae trade with Late Iron Age Britain', in Howard and Morris 1981, 123–32.

Williams, D.F., 1986, 'Report on the amphorae', in Foster 1986, 124–32.

Williams, D.F., 1987a, 'Amphorae', in Cunliffe 1987, 271–7.

Williams, D.F., 1987b, 'The amphorae', in Woodward 1987a, 79–81.

Williams, D.F., 1991, 'Amphorae', in Cox and Hearne 1991, 119–21.

Williams, D.F., and Peacock, D.P.S., 1983 'The importation of olive-oil into Roman Britain', in Blázquez Martínez, J. and Remesal Rodríguez, J. (eds), *Producción y Comercio del Aceite en la Antigüedad. II Congresso*, Madrid, Univ. Complutense, 263–80.

Wilson, B., 1992, 'Considerations for the identification of ritual deposits of animal bones in Iron Age pits', *Int. J. Osteoarchaeol.* 2, 341–9.

Wilson, C.M., 1981, 'Burials within settlements in southern Britain during the pre-Roman Iron Age', *Bull. Inst. Archaeol. Univ. London* 18, 127–69.

Woodward, A., 1993, 'Neolithic and Bronze Age pottery', in Woodward, P.J., Davies, S.M. and Graham, A.H., *Excavations at the Old Methodist Chapel and Greyhound Yard, Dorchester, 1981–4*, Dorchester, Dorset Natur. Hist. Archaeol. Soc. Monog. 12, 201–2.

Woodward, P.J., 1987a, 'The excavation of a Late Iron Age trading settlement and Romano-British BB1 pottery production site at Ower, Dorset', in *Romano-British Industries in Purbeck*, Dorchester, Dorset Natur. Hist. Archaeol. Soc. Monog. 6, 44–124.

Woodward, P.J., 1987b, 'The excavation of a Late Iron Age and Romano-British settlement at Rope Lake Hole, Corfe Castle, Dorset', in *Romano-British Industries in Purbeck*, Dorchester, Dorset Nat. Hist. Archaeol. Monog. 6, 125–180.

Woolf, G.D., 1993, 'Rethinking the oppida', *Oxford J. Archaeol.* 12, 223–34.